Birding
Minnesota

by
Jay Michael Strangis

FALCON

Falcon Press® Publishing Co., Inc.
Helena, Montana

AFALCONGUIDE

Falcon Press® is continually expanding its list of recreational guidebooks. All books include detailed descriptions, accurate maps, and all information necessary for enjoyable trips. You can order extra copies of this book and get information and prices for other Falcon guidebooks by writing Falcon Press, P.O. Box 1718, Helena, MT 59624 or calling toll-free 1-800-582-2665. Also, please ask for a free copy of our current catalog.

Printed in the United States of America

Falcon Press Publishing Co., Inc.
P.O. Box 1718, Helena, MT 59624

Illustrations copyright © by Vera Ming Wong 1995, all rights reserved. Bald Eagle illustration copyright © State of Minnesota Department of Transportation and Vera Ming Wong 1994.

Front cover photo: Pine Grosbeak by Stephen J. Krasemann/DRK Photo
Back cover photo: Common Loon by Daniel J. Cox/Natural Exposures

All black-and-white photos by the author unless otherwise noted.
♻ Text pages printed on recycled paper.

Library of Congress Cataloging-in-Publication Data
Strangis, Jay Michael, 1951-
    Birding Minnesota / by Jay Michael Strangis.
       p.   cm.
    Includes bibliographical references and index.
    ISBN 1-56044-425-8 (pbk.)
    1. Bird watching—Minnesota—Guidebooks. 2. Birds—Minnesota.
I. Title.
QL684.M6S77   1996
598'.07234776—dc20
                                                                96-13172
                                                                     CIP

CAUTION

Outdoor recreation activities are by their very nature potentially hazardous. All participants in such activities must assume the responsibility for their own actions and safety. The information contained in this guidebook cannot replace sound judgment and good decision-making skills, which help reduce risk exposure, nor does the scope of this book allow for disclosure of all the potential hazards and risks involved in such activities.

Learn as much as possible about the outdoor recreation activities you participate in, prepare for the unexpected, and be safe and cautious. The reward will be a safer and more enjoyable experience.

*"A child asked concerning a bobolink,
'What makes he sing so sweet, Mother?
Do he eat flowers?'"*

—Henry David Thoreau

© Vera Ming Wong 1995

Western Grebe with chick

Acknowledgments

Many people freely gave their time, energy, and knowledge in the preparation of this book. Without their assistance and support, its completion would never have been possible. First and foremost among these is Robert Janssen. A stalwart of the Minnesota Ornithologists Union and author of the book *Birds In Minnesota*, Bob's long-time dedication to the accurate listing of the state's birds is well known, and he provided the same interest and dedication in many hours of discussion and review through the course of this work. I can never thank him enough.

Thanks and credit also go to Mary Ann Knox, a great friend who accompanied me in the search for a number of sites and provided valuable research notes regarding many Twin Cities locales.

A core of Minnesota birders from around the state cheerfully provided their expertise in identifying local sites, and offered valuable birding tips as well as review of portions of the manuscript dealing with their home turf. These helpful people included Mike Hendrickson of Duluth, Warren Nelson of Aitkin, Dan Svedarsky of Crookston, Molly Hoffman of Grand Marais, Steve Wilson of Tower, Nelvina DeKam and Johanna Pals of Edgerton, Randy Frederickson of Willmar and last, but certainly not least, Fred Lesher of La Crosse, Wisconsin, an expert when it comes to birding in the extreme southeastern portion of Minnesota. My thanks to all for their interest in birds and for being representative of the true Minnesota spirit of warmth.

Other people who offered guidance, or provided ideas, input, or otherwise suggested a path when the way seemed blocked include Bruce Fall, Dr. Harrison "Bud" Tordoff, Dr. Robert Zink, Carroll Henderson, Kathy Heidl, Tony Hertzel, Alice Winsor, Tom Cousins, Carol Estes, and Jim Williams, as well as many other helpful people from the Minnesota Department of Natural Resources.

A special thanks to Dr. Dwain Warner for allowing me tremendous opportunities during my college years, and always a word of encouragement regarding my education, writing, and life in general—a true friend, mentor, and supporter for many years. Thanks also to Marie Ward.

For their unconditional encouragement and support, I'd like to thank my parents, Joe and Jackie Strangis, Aunt Rita and Uncle Carl Carlson, my brother Joel and sisters Mary, Michelle, and Teri. Thanks also to my friend and mentor Robert Charboneau.

Thanks to Lainie Johns and Anthea Strangis for their clerical help, and to Diana Dunn for her clerical help and encouragement.

Thanks to Renee Appel and Kristi Schmidt of the Duluth Convention and Visitors Bureau for their help and cooperation in my visits to Duluth and vicinity.

Also, credit must go to the Minnesota Historical Society for its valuable, highly organized, and accessible collection of public information, and to two books which provided both information and inspiration in the long road of research: *Streams And Rivers Of Minnesota* by Thomas F. Waters and *Minnesota Geographic Names* by Warren Upham.

Finally, thanks to Bill Schneider and Randall Green for the opportunity to work on this project, and to Eric Keszler for his editing skills. If I've forgotten to mention anyone, please pardon the oversight. Every effort has been made to eliminate errors in *Birding Minnesota*. If you find something in error or incomplete, please send your comments to Jay Michael Strangis, c/o Falcon Press, P.O. Box 1718, Helena, MT 59624.

Contents

Chapter 1. Planning a Minnesota birding trip

Chapter 2. The Minnesota landscape

Chapter 3. Minnesota's best birding areas

Twin Cities Region

Northern Boreal Region

Prairie Region

Southern Hardwood Region

Northern Deciduous Region

Chapter 4. Bonus birding—a guide to unique opportunities

Chapter 5. Minnesota checklist 221

Chapter 6. Minnesota's choice species 243

Preface

Portland, Oregon, seems an unlikely place to launch a Minnesota birding guide, but this project began there in 1993. I had traveled to that western city from my home in the Twin Cities to accept a natural history writing award. While in Portland, I made the acquaintance of publisher Bill Schneider of Falcon Press, who raised the discussion about this guide. Returning to Minnesota, I ran the idea of a popular, easy-to-read guide by some of those in the state closest to the subject, and I received unanimous encouragement. Only a few short months later, I had accepted the project and begun the long road of research and writing.

That research may have actually begun many, many years earlier while viewing the color plates of T.S. Roberts' *Birds of Minnesota*. As an eight-year-old, I sat awed by the amazing variety of birds that appeared on the pages of that venerable book. Their names, shapes, and colors provided a world of wonder I could only hope to see in the wild.

Most of my youth was spent stalking and watching wild critters in the marshes, fields, and forests close to my home in Robbinsdale, a burg that in those days still retained unbroken woodlots, creeks, and marshes. Brookdale, one of the first Twin Cities malls, had not yet been built, and a farm still operated on that property. The villages of New Hope and Crystal held farms, woodlots, and cornfields, and the city of Robbinsdale itself still entertained tractors, grain wagons, and freight trains at its active feed mill and grain elevator.

Each Easter I placed an order at the mill for a dozen wild, day-old Mallard ducklings, and I remember my excitement as I readied their backyard pen. I raised the birds to nearly flight-ready, then released them on the tiny, cattail-fringed Ryan Lake. Little wonder I feel such an affiliation with the many Mallards that now reside on Twin Cities lakes and rivers year-round. I treasure their morning flights and the promises that whisper from their wings.

I love Minnesota, and hope this book reflects my gratitude for the outdoor opportunities this beautiful state continues to provide. I vividly remember my summers with my grandparents in Detroit Lakes, and all the splendor of the rural roads where we picked chokecherries and I stored the sounds of goldfinches and meadow larks; the wonder of the shorelines of Lake of the Woods and the Rainy River in the Baudette area, where my aunt led us on fishing and berry-picking excursions and I learned about Cliff Swallows, Barn Swallows, and sighted my first Great Gray Owl; my first trip to the Boundary Waters Canoe Area with my brother, where the calls of loons were etched forever in my memory; the wildness of the Minnesota River valley, where I censused birds as a summer job and came closer than I ever had to so many of the species on the pages of T.S. Roberts' book.

Many birders, both trained and untrained and far more experienced than I, have touched my life over the years. A three-year college job at the James Ford Bell Museum of Natural History preparing study skins and working with the permanent bird collection greatly increased my fascination with the avian world. I was blessed with the acquaintances of many dedicated and enthusiastic birders, ecologists, and naturalists during those years. I hope this work represents them well. No one knows a specific area better than the birders that live in that place, and many local birders from around Minnesota have shared their knowledge and experience readily throughout the course of this work. Without their assistance, this book would not have been possible.

This book has been designed to offer a popular, easy-to-follow guide to the best birding in the state. If it saves the reader time, money, and energy, and sparks an interest in new birds and new places, then it has in part succeeded. Through historical essays, it also attempts to impart some of the cultural heritage of this great land of lakes, of the trials and accomplishments of its early inhabitants, of their passion for the forests, prairies, and waterways that many of us continue to feel today. These essays are dedicated to their hopes and dreams, and memory.

Jay Michael Strangis

Tundra Swans

Introduction

Minnesota presents one of the most formidable climates in the lower forty-eight states, yet it is a land rich in birds. An impressive 420 bird species crowd the state's checklist, including 41 of the United States' 50 warbler species, 39 different shorebirds, 37 species of ducks and geese, and 12 different owls. These birds, along with 291 other bird species, profit from Minnesota's diverse habitat types, as well as its varied and sometimes challenging weather.

Located on the 45th parallel, even the Twin Cities of Minneapolis and St. Paul rest farther north on the continent than most of Maine. Minnesota's winter temperatures have been recorded at more than 50 degrees below zero Fahrenheit, while summer extremes can reach an oppressive 100 degrees coupled with high humidity. International Falls, Minnesota, on the Canadian border holds the distinction of being the coldest spot, on average, in the continental United States.

As unwelcoming as such drastic climate swings may sound, these are extremes. For nature lovers, and apparently for birds, Minnesota remains one of the most welcoming spots on the continent, in any season. In fact, few places endear themselves to both resident and visitor as much as this land of lakes, prairies, and forests.

Birding through four seasons

Summer days in Minnesota average a comfortable 70 degrees. Even winter's reputation stands somewhat overblown. An average winter day may feature 20- to 30-degree temperatures and sunshine, creating a most pleasant time to be outdoors. Further lessening the state's icy image, winter holds a special enchantment for Minnesota birders. Owl species, not seen at other times of year, can be spotted during the "cold moon." Large flocks of waterfowl stage in open waters. Bald eagles congregate along unfrozen portions of the lower Mississippi River. Flocks of songbirds such as buntings, longspurs, and grosbeaks invade the state in large numbers. In all, Minnesota regularly enjoys approximately seventy bird species in the winter, including some outstanding and unusual visitors from the north seen in few places outside Canada.

Despite all this cold-weather activity, winter birding amounts to little more than a warm-up for the season to come. In Minnesota, spring arrives with a flood of bird color and song matched in intensity by few places. Arriving flocks of waterfowl follow the retreating ice on local lakes and ponds, shorebirds and wading birds track the mudflats and edges of temporary pools, warblers pepper the trees of mature woodlands, and resident songbirds sing their presence in territories covering every available piece of habitat.

Summer is the long-toothed brother of Minnesota's bright, green spring season. Lasting little more than three months (if measured from the last day of the possible snow season to the first day of the next possible snow season) the state's summers are as rich and intense as they are brief. Vegetation grows at a tremendous rate during this period, and the richness of the green landscape is matched only by the explosion of insect life. Mosquito swarms, black fly hatches, and the abundance of the larger deer flies and horse flies attest to summer's incredible productivity, and remind us why nesting birds return here to flourish among such abundant food supplies year after year.

The name Minnesota stems from the native Sioux (or more properly Dakota) language meaning "sky-tinted water," a most appropriate title. Anyone who has gazed upon the surface of one of the state's fifteen thousand lakes beneath a deep-blue summer sky becomes transfixed with the image; and the scene seems to repeat itself with each new lake around each new bend in the road.

For all of Minnesota's winter wonders, the rebirth of its spring, and the richness of its summer, fall brings a glory matched by few places. Autumn begins as early as July in most years, with the passage of flocks of southbound shorebirds. In seemingly short order, the state becomes a vacuum for winged migrants of central Canada and the Arctic, funneled by Lake Superior on the east and the great rivers—the Red, Minnesota, and Mississippi—further channeling the birds into and across the colorful, golden-hued landscape.

Early bird records

It seems unlikely that either Minnesota's beauty or its abundance of bird life were lost on its earliest inhabitants, the Dakota tribe. Prior to European settlement, the state's game-rich central lakes region was the scene of many territorial battles between the Dakota and their Ojibway enemies from the warbler-rich northeastern forests. Armed with the white man's firearms, the Ojibway pushed the Dakotas farther west, where they would share the prairies with Burrowing Owls, Upland Sandpipers, Whooping Cranes, Bobolinks, and other birds of the open grasslands.

Few useful records exist documenting Minnesota bird life prior to the 1800s. Early explorers of the region such as Sieur de la Verendrye, Jonathan Carver, Pierre Radisson, and Louis Hennepin reflect little in their writings on the great clouds of waterfowl, flocks of Passenger Pigeons, or impressive species such as the Whooping Crane or Trumpeter Swan, common residents at the time.

Not until the 1800s did the picture of Minnesota's bird life begin to come into focus. Several factors account for this absence of early information. First and foremost was the absence of qualified naturalists on early expeditions to the region, resulting in poor record-keeping at a time when the eastern and southeastern United States were enjoying an explosion of investigation, writing, and collecting by the greatest naturalists of the day.

Second, the emphasis placed on early investigation of trade and travel routes held most exploring parties to the courses of major rivers or the Lake Superior shoreline. In addition, Minnesota's harsh winter climate, dense forests, great bogs, and wetlands made the state's interior difficult to penetrate. Explorer Zebulon Pike's party reached the headwaters of the Mississippi and wintered there, but never reached Lake Itasca. A poor writer, Pike left little in his accounts to benefit students of the state's early bird life.

Finally, with the passage opened by Lewis and Clark in the early 1800s, the best naturalists and collectors of the day flocked to the West, leaving the upper

Midwest in a zoological vacuum. Despite these shortcomings, by the early 1800s a picture of Minnesota's bird life did start to emerge.

Major Stephen H. Long, who in 1823 traced the course of the Minnesota River and followed the Red River north, enjoyed a complement of able observers on his expedition including the talented entomologist and naturalist Thomas Say. While Long proved himself a poor journal keeper, he did mention meeting a party of natives (Dakota) and dining on a large swan killed by their hosts. Based on the number of people fed, it is likely the bird was a Trumpeter Swan.

Another member of the party proved to be a talented writer; a young army officer, James E. Colhoun, described sighting a common and colorful Minnesota bird in a most unusual place. The party encountered some fifty Native American men, most on foot but a few on horseback, who surrounded them, shooting off guns and making a great commotion. "One of them had a live Sparrow Hawk on his head by way of ornament," Colhoun noted.

By the mid-1800s, reliable accounts of Minnesota bird life began to appear. Naturalists of ranking who collected and documented bird life in the state included such notables as G.B. Sennet, W.W. Cooke, E.A. Mearns, G.A. Boardman, E. Coues, and J. Krider. Unfortunately, some of the species these pioneer birders witnessed in the state are absent today. The once-abundant Passenger Pigeon was extirpated by 1895 and extinct shortly thereafter. Also extirpated were the Whooping Crane, Trumpeter Swan, Swallow-tailed Kite, and Long-billed Curlew. (A captive breeding program has returned several hundred Trumpeter Swans to the state to this date. In 1993, twelve pairs produced fifty-four cygnets.)

The same factors that caused the demise of some species within the state by the late 1800s—settlement and its accompanying logging and agricultural practices—enhanced habitat for other birds. The Greater Prairie-Chicken, for example, once present only in the southwestern corner of the state, followed the ax and plow northward in a range expansion that included all of Minnesota except the north-central and northeast.

Fortunately for Minnesota birders, the late 1800s saw the arrival of a young man who would devote his life to collecting, documenting, and preserving information about the state's avian species with a vision and vigor yet unmatched. Thomas Sadler Roberts' first natural history journal notes were made in 1874, when the young ornithologist was sixteen years old. Thus began a lifetime spent studying birds in the state, culminating in the publishing of his classic *Birds of Minnesota* and the establishment of the University of Minnesota's scientific bird collection, which today includes many of the important specimens Roberts gathered himself or gleaned from other talented amateur ornithologists around the state.

What drew Roberts' dedication, and continues to enthrall the twelve thousand-plus Audubon chapter members and other bird lovers across the state today, is Minnesota's exceptional habitat diversity and the numbers of bird species.

A diverse birding landscape

Minnesota's 84,000 square miles (the seventh largest state) encompass some of the greatest habitat transitions on the continent. East to west, the state marks the end of the great Eastern forests and the beginning of the Western prairies. Hardwood forests dominate the southeastern part of the state, but traveling north, one can watch the forests' transformation to northern conifer, and finally a boreal environment.

It's not surprising that Minnesotans are a people who love water, waterfowl, and fishing; the state boasts some 3 million acres of surface water, not to mention the vast adjoining waters of Lake Superior, Lake of the Woods, and Rainy Lake. Its rivers and streams course almost 14,000 miles through the state, and bog areas—ancient lake beds now filled with spongy, decayed plant material and rich in bird life—cover hundreds of thousands of northern acres.

With a human population of about 4.5 million (more than half centered in the Twin Cities' seven-county area), Minnesota is largely a land of rural communities. In the agricultural regions, small towns seldom lie farther than 10 miles apart. Even so, the state remains sparsely populated for its size. The Twin Cities metropolitan area, though large for the upper Midwest, stands as one of the most beautiful, open-space urban areas in the country.

Minneapolis-St. Paul and their surrounding suburbs boast one of the largest urban park systems in the United States. Park reserves and regional parks alone account for almost fifty-thousand acres of preserved habitat in the seven-county metropolitan area, in addition to the many municipal and county parklands. As most visitors arriving in the Twin Cities note, the metropolitan area is dotted with scores of beautiful lakes. All this undisturbed land and sheer volume of surface water make for a wealth of birding opportunities within minutes of the busiest downtown streets. And Minnesotans do love birds. In 1991, more than 37,000 tons of bird seed were sold in Minnesota and $16 million was spent on nest boxes and feeders.

Also attesting to Minnesota's wild character are its fifty-seven state forests totaling more than 7.5 million acres, and some sixty state parks which welcome visitors to areas ranging from hundreds to tens of thousands of acres. Minnesota's state bird, the Common Loon, has long been considered a voice of the wilderness. The state enjoys a healthy breeding population of these primitive, fascinating birds in many northern lakes, but especially within the 2 million acres of the Superior National Forest and Boundary Waters Canoe Area.

Perhaps more symbolic of the state's wild character, the gray wolf, or timber wolf, exists in numbers enjoyed by no other state except Alaska. Some 1,500 wolves inhabit the northern third of Minnesota, and wolf numbers have been estimated as high as 1,700 in recent years. Accompanying the wolf are healthy populations of black bear, moose, and white-tailed deer, as well as lynx, bobcat, coyote, otter, fisher, pine marten, and even mountain lion—a rare but documented resident.

Endearing names

In addition to its remarkable wild creatures, Minnesota is a land of notable features and names. The Mississippi River bears the Algonquin name given by the Ojibways meaning "Great River," a farsighted tribute to the largest river in North America. Lake Superior, the largest of the Great Lakes and largest freshwater lake in the world, was called "Kitchigumi" by the Ojibways, or "Grand Lac" as translated by the explorer Champlain. Marquette mapped the lake, christening it "Superior" in 1673. The St. Croix River ("River of the Holy Cross") was named for the cross planted at its mouth to mark the grave of an early French explorer. The Mesabi Iron Range takes its name from the Ojibway word "Missaby," or "Giant," referring to the semi-mountainous tracts of land in that region of northeastern Minnesota. Today, an Olympic cross-country ski training facility near Biwabik claims the name "Giant's Ridge." The Red River and Red Lake were named for their distinctive vermillion-colored water, stained by iron deposits and the tea color produced by percolation through peat bogs.

Minnesota also enjoys complimentary nicknames such as "the North Star state," or "L' Etoile du Nord," as applied to the state seal by Governor Sibley in 1858. Equally as appropriate would have been "Le Pays D' Aurora Borealis," or similar mention of the Northern Lights, a common and beautiful spectacle in this wonderful north country. The Pan American Exposition of 1901 in Buffalo, New York, dubbed Minnesota the "Bread and Butter State" for the state's impressive agricultural products. Perhaps most apt and familiar to the state's residents, "Land of Lakes" has become a byword.

Worth discovery

Equally as endearing as these place names, a short list of regular Minnesota species provides some impressive reading: Red-throated Loon, Red-necked Grebe, American White Pelican, American Bittern, Harlequin Duck, Oldsquaw, White-winged Scoter, Northern Goshawk, Red-shouldered Hawk, Peregrine Falcon, Gyrfalcon, Greater Prairie-Chicken, Yellow Rail, Upland Sandpiper, Marbled Godwit, Parasitic Jaeger, Thayer's Gull, Caspian Tern, Northern Hawk Owl, Burrowing Owl, Great Gray Owl, Three-toed Woodpecker, Alder Flycatcher, Black-billed Magpie, Boreal Chickadee, Sedge Wren, Sprague's Pipit, Northern Shrike, Bay-breasted Warbler, Connecticut Warbler, Mourning Warbler, Blue Grosbeak, Le Conte's Sparrow, Snow Bunting, Lapland Longspur, Pine Grosbeak, Red Crossbill, and White-winged Crossbill.

The discovery of new bird species—those not found among Minnesota's 305 regular species, 37 casual species, or 78 accidental species—remains distinctly possible. New species have been added at a rate of slightly more than one per year for the last fifty years. The extreme southwest, west, and southeastern portions of Minnesota and the vast waters and shoreline of Lake Superior probably provide the most likely areas of invasion by new species, although new records may be found in any part of the state.

No matter where you bird watch in Minnesota, if you spot a species you feel might be rare or unusual, please report it. Records concerning Minnesota birds result from information gathered by recreational birders, as well as ornithologists. Those birders interested in contributing to our knowledge of Minnesota bird life should consult the addresses provided in this book (see Chapter 1). The more detailed the bird information you provide, the more it will stand the test of time.

Every birder finds his or her own adventure in the places, sights, and sounds of a trip outdoors, whether it be in the backyard, a local park, or relative wilderness. Few places can match the unique beauty that is Minnesota; from the sky-tinted waters to the golden-hued prairies, the stately hardwood forests to the boreal wilderness, this is a strong land that leaves strong impressions—enjoy them all.

These are Blue Jays, but Minnesota does have two species of jay. The Blue Jay is a permanent resident and migrant statewide, especially common in areas of hardwood forest. The Gray Jay is primarily a permanent resident of the northern boreal region.

How to use this guide

This book will guide you to some of the best places to see and hear birds in Minnesota. The book does not present detailed life histories of birds, nor is it about how to identify birds; references to books that cover life histories and other pertinent related information can be found in the back of this book. Think of *Birding Minnesota* as your tour guide to the state's birding hotspots, with an interesting variety of geological, cultural, and ecological information guaranteed to make your birding (and reading) more enjoyable.

No matter which season you visit Minnesota, or in which corner of the state you travel, this book can guide you to a likely birding spot, a bit of roadside history, or a scenic vista. This format adds variety to the serious birder's itinerary, and the more casual birder can choose from any number of birding opportunities while on a vacation or business trip. *For best birding results, refer to the Official Minnesota Highway Map when using this guidebook.* To obtain a copy of the map contact: Minnesota Office of Tourism, 100 Metro Square, 121 E. 7th Place, St. Paul, MN 55101. If you are in the Twin Cities, call 296-5029. Outside the metro area call (800) 657-3700.

Chapter 1 of *Birding Minnesota* covers the essentials for "Planning a Minnesota Birding Trip." Information includes when to go birding, where to stay, where to obtain maps, select contacts for special birding information, pests and hazards likely to be encountered in the field, essential gear, dressing for the weather, and birding ethics.

Chapter 2 orients the reader to "The Minnesota Landscape." Minnesota can be fairly clearly divided by its major ecological biomes, or habitat types. The four most significant biomes include prairie, northern deciduous, northern conifer, and southeastern hardwood.

This chapter details the vegetation you can expect to find in each region and explains their rough boundaries. It also traces a brief history of the geologic, glacial, and human events that shaped the landscapes.

Also included in Chapter 2 are discussions of the birds of the major Minnesota habitats. If you have a particular species or group of birds you hope to encounter, this section will help you narrow your search.

No Minnesota bird book would be complete without a discussion of climate, and a brief walk through the seasons presented here should prepare you for what the state's four contrasting seasons have to offer.

The final section of this chapter explains timing and migration routes followed by birds as they funnel through Minnesota on their way northward in the spring and southward in the fall. Unlike the southern United States, where flocks of interesting birds take up winter residence and become accessible to birders, Minnesota's prime seasons for winged visitors are the migration periods of spring and fall when millions of birds pass through the state. Less spectacular, but equally as interesting, are the migrations, termed *invasions*, that occur in winter.

The body of the book, **Chapter 3**, describes in detail "Minnesota's Best Birding Areas." More than fifty major birding areas and maps, each with numerous specific sites listed, are described here. The sites have been grouped into five regions, beginning with the Twin Cities metropolitan area. The other regions roughly match the major biomes, or habitat zones.

Area descriptions typically focus on features and birds commmon in summer, but sites that offer interesting birding during other seasons are also indicated. Birds commonly seen only during migration are listed accordingly. Birds at a given site may more typically be heard than seen, but for brevity's sake this book relies upon the terms "look for," "watch for," and "seen" when listing a site's bird species. Despite these term biases, birders can benefit themselves, and count more species, by learning to distinguish the songs and calls of particular species.

The area description format provides quick reference to specific sites without reading the entire text. **Boldface type** calls out site names.

-The first section describes the different **Habitats** found in the area.

-A short list of **Key birds** identifies species of particular interest that a birder can *expect* to find in this area.

-**Best times to bird** is your guide to planning a trip to see birds in the area.

-**Don't miss** is a short list of the best spots in the area.

-**General information** presents interesting (historical, geological, cultural, ecological) information about the birding area.

-A detailed **Birding information** section provides directions to the site and a list of its characteristic birds. Birds of special interest are highlighted here, as are other wildlife species of note, landmarks to aid in route-finding, and local hazards such as bad roads, biting insects, or noxious plants.

-A detailed **Birding map** indicates specific sites and access roads. These maps are drawn to scale and often show features of interest to birders that are not found on other maps. They are best used in conjunction with the Minnesota State Highway Map and topographical maps available from the U.S. Geological Survey.

-A list of **Additional help** for quick reference to facts about the area includes where to find gas, food, lodging, and camping, and where to obtain additional information.

Chapter 4, "Bonus Birding," reveals special situations, locations where you will find an unusual abundance of birds, or especially interesting species through each month of the year. If you are a visitor to the state, or somewhat new to Minnesota birding, use this *"calendar"* to guide you to some of the most remarkable birding spectacles the state has to offer at any given time of year.

Chapter 5 gives you a checklist of Minnesota birds, with a graphic representation of each bird's seasonal occurrence and relative abundance in the state.

Chapter 6 provides range, habitat, and key site information for more than 100 "special" Minnesota birds. These birds represent common Minnesota species important to out-of-state birders. The descriptions also include an advisory on the chances of encountering each species.

The book concludes with a list of suggested reading for interested birders, including books important to the author in the preparation of this work.

Finally, an index of bird species, site names, and maps, with references to appropriate pages, concludes the guide.

Canada Geese

CHAPTER 1

Planning a Minnesota birding trip

When to go birding

The best time to go birding in Minnesota, of course, depends on the birds. Unlike other pastimes, the best birding seldom waits until next week, or month, when we can find a convenient time to head afield. Except for the short summer breeding season, birds in Minnesota are primarily transitory; when they aren't in a northward or southward migration, they are far away on their wintering grounds. The object, then, is to time a birding trip to anticipate the presence, or movement, of birds.

Of Minnesota's 240 species of breeding birds, most are migrants. Their spring arrival times range from that of the Bald Eagle, which shows up in March and is nesting by the end of April, to the wood warblers, some of which don't arrive in the state until May, when their favorite insect foods are available. Most shorebirds nest and leave early, with their spring migration beginning in April and the fall migration peaking in August.

Weather not only plays a role in bird migration, it also influences their daily movements and the times birders will want to be afield. No birder enjoys extreme weather—either wet, cold, or hot; birds also are less active during

Many creeks from the Twin Cities southward stay open throughout the winter, attracting waterfowl and eagles.

such conditions. Minnesotans tend to be weather-watchers, placing a high priority on the 10 p.m. newscast and its weather report. Minnesota radio and television stations spend a lot of money on weather forecasting equipment and staff meteorologists; thus forecasts are fairly accurate, and can be relied upon in planning a birding trip. However, in some seasons the weather is less predictable than others, even for the computer-equipped weather guru.

Fortunately, most of Minnesota's best birding occurs during pleasant weather. The spring season probably offers the greatest variety of birding opportunities, although weather can be fickle from day to day. Around the first week in April, spring migrants begin passing through the state and resident birds have returned to their breeding territories. Males of the various species wear breeding plumage in spring, brilliantly colored and more easily identifiable. Songbirds are most vocal in spring, even those pausing in migration, which also makes them easier to identify. It's hard to rely on the accuracy of more than a two- or three-day weather forecast in spring, however, so caution is advised.

Few experiences can match a summer morning's chorus of birds in Minnesota. Summerlike weather begins about the 15th of May. Early summer (June) is the best time to hear and see birds on their breeding territories, and although the weather is generally good, May and June are wet months in Minnesota; daily weather forecasts are important. Early-summer weather seems to run in patterns—one or two days of rain followed by one to three days of sun, for example—but seven-day forecasts prove to be fairly accurate at this time of year.

Once the long, hot, dog days of summer have begun, song frequency drops off and Minnesota's breeding birds seem to retire. Some birds, however, become easier to find. Insect-eating birds such as swallows, Common Nighthawks, and Chimney Swifts enjoy peak numbers of prey at this time of year, and are extremely active and visible. Gulls have left their nests, and colonial birds such as pelicans, cormorants, herons, and egrets spend more time away from their isolated rookeries. Shorebirds begin appearing on mudflats and sod farms by late July, followed by large flocks in August. This is a time of rather consistent weather, although afternoon thunderstorms—some severe—can be expected to develop on any day.

Many birders would say that fall is their favorite time of year, not only because the weather can be clear and comfortable for days at a time, but because this is when birds form larger flocks, travel at a somewhat leisurely pace, and seem to move across wider fronts, which increases the chance of seeing rare or uncommon birds close to home. The timing of fall migration is species-specific, but generally begins about the first week of September for passerines, and extends through the end of November for waterfowl and gulls. (Of course, there are exceptions.) Seven-day weather forecasts are relatively accurate at this time of year.

Although it's hard to claim that everyone looks forward to a Minnesota winter, there are some special birding opportunities at this time of year. Many birds of the Canadian forest and tundra invade the state when conditions farther north limit their food sources. Winter weather seems to be fairly predictable out to about seven days, but short-range predictions are sometimes more difficult. For example, most forecasts can tell us of an impending winter storm, but predicting just when it will arrive has always seemed problematic. Heed severe weather warnings. It takes no planning at all to stay inside and enjoy watching a bird feeder.

To improve your chances of seeing a particular species, become familiar with that bird's distribution, breeding season, peak migration times, and winter range. To date, 420 species have been reported in Minnesota, but not all of these birds are found in large numbers, and some occur only rarely or are difficult to find.

What to wear

Asking someone what to bring on a Minnesota birding trip is a bit like asking someone what to eat: clothes and food come immediately to mind. Minnesota weather is so changeable during spring and fall, both winter and light summer clothing are advisable. You may need a stocking cap one day, and a T-shirt a couple of days later.

The best rule of thumb is to dress for a variety of conditions, but most importantly, bring adequate cold-weather clothing. Even in midsummer it can become cold and blustery, especially around water in the northern half of the state. Normally in summer, a pair of long pants, a sweater, and a good windproof shell should be packed along with your normal summer clothing. Fall and spring should be treated like winter—if you don't want to be caught out in the cold, so to speak. And always bring good rainwear in spring, summer, and fall.

Winter presents its own unique challenges. Many winter days can be quite pleasant, hovering around the freezing point and requiring nothing more than simple long underwear, pants, sweater, and warm jacket. But be prepared for extremes. In case of more severe cold you'll need the aforementioned, plus wool pants (or perhaps an insulated, windproof bib overall), winter parka with hood, mittens or gloves, hat, and scarf (to protect your face from wind chill). Remember that in cold weather, the wind is the number one cause of heat loss, so wear a warm underlayer covered by a nylon-shelled jacket, parka, or windbreaker to block the wind.

Tennis shoes are not adequate in winter; they didn't used to be in spring or fall either, because they won't keep your feet dry. However, Gore-Tex, or "seal skin," waterproof socks are a great investment. You can stand in a puddle of water, or walk through wet grass, completely soak your old tennis shoes, yet keep your feet dry and comfortable. They're great for those spring or fall days when you're getting in and out of a car a lot and don't want to wear a pair of heavy boots.

Essentials for a successful birding trip:

The following is a checklist of essential items for a Minnesota birding trip:

___ Official Minnesota State Highway Map

___ Other maps

___ This book

___ Binoculars

___ Spotting scope

___ Field identification guides for birds

___ *Birds In Minnesota* bird distribution guide, by Robert Janssen

___ Bird sound tapes

___ Sunglasses

___ Insect repellent and sunscreen

___ Toilet paper

___ Drinking water (especially for southwestern Minnesota trips)

___ Ice cooler and soft drinks or juice

___ Food

___ Travel money

___ Flashlight

___ Pocket knife

___ An open mind

Optional gear:

___ Camping equipment

___ Field journal

___ Camera and film

___ Tape recorder

Good binoculars are essential to good birding, and you usually get what you pay for. These 10 x 50 glasses from Zeiss represent some of the best quality optics made today.

Where to stay

Most of the birding sites in this book are within range of developed car campgrounds (for tents and recreational vehicles) or sizeable towns with the usual array of cabins, motels, hotels, and lodges. More adventurous birders will find that primitive camping is excellent in Minnesota. Camping allows birders to extend their field days, waking to the chorus of bird songs and drifting to sleep to the distant night calls of owls or migrating flocks. Be sure to plan ahead. The busier state parks require camping reservations. Contact: Minnesota State Parks Overnight Reservation Service, (800) 765-CAMP.

During the open-water seasons, a first choice might be a resort that offers a lakeside cabin, and there are literally thousands available in the state. Minnesota also offers hundreds of bed-and-breakfast establishments; most offer historical charm, a premier location, or both. Brochures listing hotels, motels, resorts, campgrounds, and bed-and-breakfasts are available from the Minnesota Travel Information Center, 100 Metro Square, 121 E. 7th Place, St. Paul, MN 55101; (612) 296-5029 or (800) 657-3700.

Field hazards

Minnesota is a relatively safe place for birding. That said, there are a number of hazards to note. The most immediately obvious is biting insects; mosquitos, black flies, deer flies, and horse flies all share a taste for humans.

Repellents work well for mosquitos and black flies, although the latter tend to bite in crevices. Fortunately, the season for black flies is brief: about two weeks in spring and two weeks later in the summer. Where they are present, wear a long-sleeved shirt, closed at the cuff and collar to prevent them from entering under clothing. They have a particular taste for ears, but smearing the ears with a bit of petroleum jelly is effective against bites.

Hats are particularly helpful to ward off horse flies and deer flies. They tend to become obsessed with the highest point on your body, and a hat will keep them up and away from your skin in most cases.

Poison ivy is a common problem during summer and fall. Learn to identify and avoid this noxious plant. If you do come in contact with the oily leaf, wash the exposed area thoroughly with strong soap and water. The longer the oil stays on the skin, the more irritated the skin becomes.

A few rattlesnakes can be found in southern Minnesota, particularly the bluff country of the southeast. If you do see a snake, consider yourself lucky. Give the snake a wide berth, and leave it alone. If you should be bitten, proceed calmly to the nearest hospital. Most local hospitals in the few counties with snakes stock antivenom.

Wildlife is seldom a problem in Minnesota, but two animals large enough to warrant respect are black bears and moose. Always give these animals wide berth. Black bears almost never attack humans. They are usually shy and retiring, but are most dangerous in places where they have become accustomed to humans. Moose can be unpredictable. Never approach a moose too closely, especially a cow with calf.

Bad roads are a problem that always seems to be ill-timed. In Minnesota, frost penetrates and freezes the ground as deep as 40 inches in a normal winter. In spring, the frozen ground thaws from the top down, forcing meltwater to sit within the soil, on top of the frozen underlayer. During this brief period (normally from about early April to mid-May), unimproved dirt roads are traps for automobiles and should, for the most part, be avoided. Exceptions can be made for roads in areas with sandy or gravel soils, which drain and dry quickly.

Other hazards which may be faced in birding country include: logging trucks (use caution on forest roads; do not park on blind corners); lightning (never be the highest object in the surrounding landscape during a lightning storm; lie flat on the ground if you must. Do not seek shelter under a lone tree, and avoid granite outcroppings. The inside of an automobile *is* a relatively safe, ungrounded location); and tornados (in open country, seek the lowest place possible, even a roadside ditch).

Finally, Minnesota's winter weather can be deadly serious, and should be treated as such. A few items (listed below) placed in the trunk of a car may save your life in case you are stranded without a heater. *Always* stay with your vehicle.

Winter automobile survival essentials:

___ Wool blanket

___ Extra clothing

___ Boots

___ Shovel

___ 3-pound coffee can (to store the below listed items)

___ Candy

___ Candles

___ Metal cup or can to melt snow

___ Matches or lighter

___ Space blankets (foil)

___ Charcoal-activated heat packets (hand warmers)

Maps

Always keep an Official Minnesota Highway Map handy; *Birding Minnesota* is designed to accompany this map. It can be obtained, free of charge, by contacting: Minnesota Office of Tourism, 100 Metro Square, 121 7th Place E., St. Paul, MN 55101; (612) 296-5029 (Twin Cities area); (800) 657-3700 (U.S.); (800) 766-8687 (Canada).

Another good companion for *Birding Minnesota* is the Minnesota Atlas and Gazetteer, published by DeLorme Mapping (P.O. Box 298, Freeport, ME 04032; (207) 865-4171, which divides the state into seventy-seven detailed quadrangle maps and shows many local features.

An excellent resource for locating Twin Cities birding sites listed in this guide is the *Twin Cities Birding Map*, published by Little Transport Maps (Dept. BM, P.O. Box 8123, Minneapolis, MN 55408) and available at better nature bookstores in the Twin Cities. Public Recreation Information Maps (PRIM) are a comprehensive overview of the recreational facilities and opportunities found in Minnesota. They cover the entire state and are available from: DNR Information Center, 500 Layfayette Road, St. Paul, MN 55155-4040; (612) 296-6157 (Twin Cities area); (800) 652-9747 (outside Minnesota).

Other site-specific map information may be obtained in *A Birder's Guide To Minnesota*, by Kim Richard Eckert (Dept. BM, Williams Publications, Plymouth, MN), also available in better nature bookstores in the state.

Information about federal lands in Minnesota, including national wildlife refuges, can be obtained by contacting: U.S. Fish and Wildlife Service, Federal Building, #1 Federal Drive, Fort Snelling, MN 55111-4056; (612) 725-3507.

Detailed U.S. Geological Survey maps (7.5- and 15-minute series) covering the state of Minnesota can be obtained by writing: USGS, Denver Federal Center, Lakewood, CO 80225. Request an index and price list of maps covering Minnesota. These same maps can be obtained from some outdoor equipment stores.

Guided field trips

The Minnesota Ornithologists Union (MOU) can provide local contacts in the region you plan to visit, and the MOU provides guided group birding trips for its members. Professional bird guides can provide personalized service, and know all the shortcuts to the best birding available during the period you plan to be afield. In northern Minnesota contact: Mike Hendrickson, 124 1/2 Orange Street, Duluth, MN 55811; (218) 726-0840. In central Minnesota contact Randy Frederickson, 416 19th St. NW, Willmar, MN 56201; (612) 231-1291. In southern Minnesota contact Fred Lesher, 509 Winona Street, La Crosse, WI 54603; (608) 783-1149.

Birding organizations

The nonprofit American Birding Association (ABA) is dedicated to all aspects of birding, including identification, bird finding, and conservation, and publishes an informative bimonthly magazine and monthly newsletter. For further information, contact: American Birding Association, P.O. Box 6599, Colorado Springs, CO 80934; (800) 634-7736.

The Minnesota Ornithologists Union (MOU, listed above) provides many membership benefits including a quarterly journal (*The Loon*), a newsletter (*Minnesota Birding*), organized field trips, and associations with other birders interested in learning more about Minnesota's bird resources.

National Audubon Society

There are eleven Audubon chapters and nine birding clubs in Minnesota. For further information on local chapters, contact the state Audubon office: Minnesota Audubon Council, 26 East Exchange Street, Suite 207, St. Paul, MN 55101; (612) 225-1830.

Minnesota Audubon chapters:

> Agassiz Audubon Society (Warren)
> Albert Lea Audubon Society
> Audubon Chapter of Minneapolis
> Austin Audubon Society
> Central Minnesota Audubon Society (St. Cloud)
> Duluth Audubon Society
> Fargo-Moorhead Audubon Society
> Minnesota River Valley Audubon Chapter (Bloomington)
> Mississippi Headwaters Audubon Society (Bemidji)
> St. Paul Audubon Society
> Zumbro Valley Audubon Society (Rochester)

Minnesota birding clubs:

> Bee-Nay-She Bird Club (Aitkin/Crow Wing counties)
> Cottonwood County Bird Club
> Hiawatha Valley Bird Club (Winona)
> Jackson County Bird Club
> Lakes Area Bird Club (Detroit Lakes)
> Mankato Bird Club
> Minnesota Bird Net
> Rice County Bird Club
> Roseville Bird Club

Reporting rare bird information

Ornithology is one of the few sciences in which amateurs can and do make significant contributions to scientific knowledge. Birders are encouraged to report interesting, rare, accidental, or unusual birds by contacting: Minnesota Ornithologists Union, James Ford Bell Museum of Natural History, 10 S. Church St., Minneapolis, MN 55455.

Minnesota bird hotlines

To report or find out immediately about recent sightings of rare birds, call:
-Minnesota Rare Bird Alert Line: (612) 780-8890.
-Duluth Hot Line: (218) 525-5952.

Birds on the Internet

The Minnesota Ornithologists Union maintains a web site that is open to Internet users. Information provided includes recent sightings; a list of Minnesota's 417 bird species and their occurrence and distribution including maps for migrants, casuals, and accidentals; an annotated bibliography of suggested reading; and a 75-year index of the MOU's journal, *The Loon*. The MOU's Internet address is: biosci.cbs.umn.edu/~mou.

The Minnesota Bird Net, a birding club not officially sanctioned as a listing organization, but one that allows users to exchange bird sightings on the Internet, also has a web site. The Net provides perhaps the fastest posting of new rare-bird sightings, but caution should be exercised because not all users are expert birders. The Minnesota Bird Net's Internet address is: www.skypoint.com/members/dac/mnbird.html.

Yellow-rumped Warblers

CHAPTER 2

The Minnesota landscape

Folklore has it that a giant man and his trusted animal companion created most of the land features in Minnesota. Paul Bunyan and Babe the blue ox traversed the state, it is told, leaving in their wake the prairies, forests, lakes, and rivers we see today.

Bunyan and his crew of lumberjacks were said to have cleared the forest to create the prairie country, dug Lake Superior as a pond for pure drinking water, and carved the rivers to carry their logs. Babe's footprints filled with water, forming the 22,000 lakes and wetlands in Minnesota.

Two thriving northern Minnesota cities, Brainerd and Bemidji, claim home rights to Paul Bunyan and Babe, and huge icons to the giant pair can be viewed in each location. (See if you can find the giant bird icons in separate locations in the state, including an enormous prairie chicken, crow, Bald Eagle, and Black Duck.)

Far more exact than such legends, studies of Minnesota's geologic history reveal a fascinating story of change resulting in the habitats that support birds in the state today.

Land, lake, and river formation

Picture Minnesota as a land of lakes, for the sky truly is mirrored in their thousands of shapes. Picture the state also as a land of flat prairie intruded upon by odd, gentle highlands; of vast bogs where soil and water merge in their battle to claim the land's surface; of wide river valleys and of mountains that wanted to be. Picture Minnesota as a place where earth and climate have battled for millennia; where the might of ice and water claim the most recent victories.

More than 600 million years ago, geologic forces were at work in Minnesota, pushing up mountains, creating shifting seas, and sending rivers of water across the state. The Ice Age began about 2 million years ago, creating miles-thick glaciers that scoured their way southward, depositing silt, sand, gravel, and rock from lands farther north, covering all of the state except the extreme southwest and southeast.

A mere twenty-thousand years ago, an unstable, gradually warming climate caused the glaciers to begin to retreat to the north, then advance and retreat over and over again. The movement of ice dug trenches or left loose drifts of debris that collapsed, later filling with water to form lakes. Terminal moraines—enormous hills of earth and rock deposited along the lower margins of the ice sheets—formed gentle highlands many miles wide, like those seen in the Alexandria area, the highest ground in western Minnesota. Ground moraines—broad areas of rich glacial till—were left by rapidly retreating ice, creating most of the prime topsoil in the flat agricultural lands of south-central Minnesota.

Glacial meltwater carrying suspended debris formed outwash plains—broad areas of sand and light soil as seen in the Anoka area. In the extreme northeast and along the shores of Lake Superior, glacial ice scoured the bedrock, exposing some of the world's oldest rocks to today's visitors.

Although the glacial ice has long since departed, oddities appear on the landscape as if deposited yesterday. Farmers in some central and northern counties still battle the constant upheaval of large, rounded boulders pushed through the rich till to the surfaces of their fields each spring by the heaving action of frost. Large piles of these boulders, collected over the years, adorn the centers of many farm fields. In the Louisville Swamp between Shakopee and Jordan, huge house-sized boulders dot the landscape in odd fashion. Similar "stranded" rocks can be seen near Ortonville in extreme western Minnesota.

While the power and force of the glaciers literally carved the face of most of the state, the rivers that sprang from the melting ice further left their imprint, gouging deep channels through rock, as seen in areas of the St. Croix; and in some places floodwaters formed miles-wide river valleys, like those of the Minnesota and lower Mississippi rivers.

Remnants of the greatest lake

In the northwestern part of the state, the meltwater of its last glaciers formed a huge lake, at one time covering some 17,000 square miles in Minnesota and another 60,000 square miles in North Dakota and Canada. Glacial Lake Agassiz existed for more than five thousand years after the Ice Age, and during its life span covered more surface area than all of the Great Lakes combined. Dammed by ice to the north, Agassiz's southern shore (at today's Lake Traverse north of Browns Valley) eventually eroded enough to allow massive amounts of water to escape. The Glacial River Warren (now the Minnesota River, for all intents and purposes) swelled to become an incredible torrent, carving the miles-wide Minnesota River Valley and causing similar erosion where it met the Mississippi channel and points below.

Today the broad Minnesota Valley and the deep bluffs and expansive valleys of the Mississippi below the Twin Cities are testaments to Lake Agassiz's volume. As you drive south from the Twin Cities suburb of Bloomington on Interstate 35W, you descend a long hill that is the northern side of the ancient riverbed. Look 2 miles to the south, where the land rises again, and you will gain an appreciation for the River Warren's immensity.

As Lake Agassiz drained, its changing shorelines left strands—beach lines of sand and gravel—in long, low ridges across northwestern Minnesota. Two such ridges run north/south for hundreds of miles, transecting the region between the towns of Fergus Falls and Breckenridge and beyond. Low lake bed areas have retained their water and can be seen today in the huge surfaces of Lake of the Woods, Upper and Lower Red lakes, and Rainy Lake.

Eventually, Lake Agassiz found its own level, draining north with the contour of the land. Its remnant watersheds, the Red River, which divides Minnesota and North Dakota, and the Rainy River, which divides Minnesota and Ontario, today drain the former lake bed region, sending the water north to Hudson Bay.

For Minnesota visitors, the headwaters of one of the world's greatest rivers offer a fascinating stopping point. You can walk across the infant Mississippi at Itasca State Park, where the small stream is born out of the northern bogs, starting its journey of more than 2,300 miles to the Gulf of Mexico. The Mississippi, and its allied bogs and wild rice lakes, once served as an important flyway for waterfowl (particularly mallards and diving ducks) that nest in northern Minnesota and Canada. Today, the creation of large reservoirs and associated crop production in the Dakotas seems to have shifted the bulk of the flight patterns toward the Missouri, Red, and Minnesota river flyways. Nevertheless, the Mississippi still serves as an important "highway" for migrants of many types, funneling them toward the Twin Cities and then along the lower Mississippi toward Texas and northern Mexico.

Two more major Minnesota watersheds, the Minnesota and St. Croix rivers, join the Mississippi at the Twin Cities. The St. Croix flows some 130 miles, beginning in northwestern Wisconsin and forming the Minnesota/Wisconsin border until its confluence with the Mississippi near Hastings. One of the original eight rivers in the United States to be protected by the Wild and Scenic Rivers Act of 1968, the St. Croix truly does possess outstanding scenic beauty.

Slow-moving and turbid, the Minnesota River meanders from Minnesota's western border some 250 miles to its junction with the Mississippi near Twin Cities International Airport. This river witnessed more early travel than any other in the state, and became the passageway for the first settlers who took up life on the rich prairie soils. Its broad valley is a major corridor for migrating birds, particularly waterfowl, funneling them toward the lower Mississippi. From just southwest of the Twin Cities to the mouth of the Minnesota River, large pieces of acquired land make up the Minnesota Valley National Wildlife Refuge. The valley holds some of the best birding in the state.

Habitats

If you are new to Minnesota, you need only visualize three distinct biomes, or uniform patterns of vegetation, to roughly familiarize yourself with the state's character. Minnesota biomes include the prairie grassland, northern boreal forest, and eastern deciduous forest.

When settlers first arrived, rippling waves of big bluestem and Indian grass brushed the shoulders of oxen teams, blanketing the land to the horizon and beyond on the tallgrass prairie—an area covering about one-third of the state. In the northeast, towering white and Norway pines stood like massive pillars, their seemingly endless aisles carpeted with needles under cathedral-like crowns. Separating these two tracts, the final finger of the eastern deciduous forest reached into the state. In central Minnesota, the giant trunks of sugar maple, basswood, elm, and red oak stood shaded by their own all-enveloping canopy, marking the "big woods."

Such natural wonders, combined with the country's rich wetlands and waterways, truly marked Minnesota as an inviting land of promise; but the face of the state would soon be transformed by the same settlers who so admired it. Wetlands were drained and prairie grasses turned under the plow; the incredible, rich, black soils that supported the "big woods" were too valuable not to be farmed, and the hardwoods were cut and cleared; the great pine forests were tumbled, nearly in their entirety, and the logs sent downriver to waiting mills.

The destruction of these ecosystems was accompanied by the loss of animal species, either through exploitation of the animals themselves or through loss of habitat. By 1900, elk, bison, caribou, and grizzly bear had been extirpated from the state. Similarly, the Passenger Pigeon, Whooping Crane, Long-billed Curlew, and McCown's Longspur were gone.

Fire, an important presettlement force which maintained biome vegetation (especially the prairie), was suppressed, allowing invasion by woodland plant species formerly denied a foothold. Fire had also played an important role in the boreal forest, creating a diversity of successive forest types; but logging and the absence of fire left vast continuous stands of aspen in the forest's wake.

Minnesota's vegetation patterns certainly have a great deal to do with the distribution of birds within the state. Understanding the plant communities found within today's major biomes helps in the search for specific bird species. Although the vegetation pattern within a biome appears somewhat uniform, each actually contains many plant communities in varying stages of succession.

The state's prairie habitats occur roughly west of a line bisecting the state from the northwest corner to the southeast corner, excluding the region from the Twin Cities to Mankato along the Minnesota River, formerly occupied by the "big woods." Generally, prairie lands are dominated by only a few kinds of grasses and forbs and can be divided into the fertile tallgrass prairie; drier shortgrass prairie; and the grass-, sedge-, and cattail-dominant prairie wetland. Less than 1 percent of native prairie exists today, but efforts to restore prairie habitats or preserve "islands" of native prairie have been made by organizations like The Nature Conservancy and within the state's Scientific and Natural Areas program. A list of these areas—often good birding sites—can be obtained by contacting the Minnesota Department of Natural Resources at (612) 296-3344.

Minnesota's deciduous forest runs southeast to northwest, almost the length of the state, in a band ranging from 20 to 100 miles wide. This land is interspersed with upland prairie and prairie wetland. The northernmost portion of this belt contains aspen parkland—stands of aspen trees dotted with prairie and wet meadow openings, as can be seen from Roseau County all the way south to Mahnomen County. Oak woodlands, dominated by bur oak mixed with grasslands and brushlands (an area still referred to as "savannah"), begins in Mahnomen County in the northwest and runs southeast all the way down to the Iowa border, where white oak and black oak are also common. In fact, much of southeastern Minnesota was dominated by this habitat in presettlement times. Fires that swept off the prairies maintained the semi-open character of the oak woodlands before settlement. Today, remnants of this habitat type are on dry, sandy soils unsuitable for agriculture; the best examples can be seen along State Highway 10 between Anoka and St. Cloud.

The maple/basswood forest also begins as far north as eastern Mahnomen County and can be found as far south as Houston County in the extreme southeast. The largest continuous tract of "big woods" occurred in south-central Minnesota (both north and south of the Minnesota River) from Wright County south to Nicollet County, and included some 7,000 square miles of continuous woodland. Explorer Stephen H. Long wrote in 1823 during his travels up the Minnesota River by canoe, "Entered a considerable forest called by the French 'Bois Franc,' from the circumstance of its containing timber trees of a few varieties only."

Professor N.H. Winchell may have been the observer who best described the "big woods" when he wrote in 1875, "The existence of this great spur of timber, shooting so far south from the boundary line separating the southern prairies from the northern forests, and its successful resistance against the fires that formerly must have raged annually on both sides, is a phenomenon in the natural history of the state that challenges the scrutiny of all observers." Winchell added, "It furnishes shelter for thousands of birds that winter among us, but which otherwise would become exterminated, or driven from the state." Unfortunately, the Big Woods has largely been reduced to cropland, although some wonderful remnants, like Wolsfeld Woods near the town of Long Lake, remain.

The entire northeastern portion of Minnesota has been termed "northern boreal" for the purposes of this book, but within this region are several inter-esting forest types. Within the boreal forest, where soils are rich and fire fre-quency low, patches of northern hardwood forest can be found. Dominated by sugar maple, basswood, red oak, and yellow birch, with conifers such as white pine, balsam fir, and northern white cedar scattered within, the best examples of this forest type can be found between Hill City and Grand Rapids and along the Lake Superior Highlands between Duluth and Two Harbors.

Also within the boreal forest, on the poorest soils, are tracts of jack pine forest composed of jack pine, red pine, oak, and hazel. Following the cutting of the great pine forests, and subsequent fires, jack pine forest actually in-creased in this region. Examples of this forest type can be seen in the Lake Itasca area and scattered throughout the Boundary Waters Canoe Area (BWCA). Some of the largest continuous vegetation types within the boreal forest region are peatlands, best seen in the bogs around McGregor and in the "big bog" area near Red Lake in Beltrami and Lake of the Woods counties. These bogs stand as the only ecosystem in the state primarily unaltered by man. They exist as fens, spruce bogs, sphagnum bogs, and cedar and ash swamps, and they support a wonderful variety of nesting birds and native plants. The Great Lakes pine forest also occurs within the northern boreal forest region. These stands once included the massive red and white pines exploited by timber operations in the mid-1800s. Today most of the land they occupied is dominated by stands of aspen and birch, but virgin pine stands can be found in the BWCA and Voyageurs National Park.

The floodplain forest is an important plant community in Minnesota which defies restriction to any particular region. Floodplain forests generally are composed of such species as silver maple, elm, cottonwood, and willow and occupy wide sections along Minnesota's major rivers. The large trees and relative lack of disturbance in such areas make them ideal locations for nesting colonial birds such as cormorants, herons, and egrets, and prime locations for cavity-dwelling birds such as goldeneye, merganser, Wood Duck, and Prothonotary Warblers as well.

The convergence of three distinct biomes within one state truly makes Minnesota unique, and results in a fascinating assortment of associated bird species. Viewed on a larger scale, the biomes represent the easternmost extension of the Great Prairie grasslands, the westernmost extension of the eastern deciduous forest, and a southern extension of the boreal forest more common to Canada than most of the United States. That these three major North American biomes terminate in the state means that for some birds, Minnesota marks the end of their range. For example, it would not be unusual to see a Western Grebe or Marbled Godwit in western Minnesota, but they would be a rare sight east of the state. Bell's Vireo and the Red-bellied Woodpecker can be found in southern Minnesota, but wouldn't be found "up north." The Spruce Grouse and Great Gray Owl reside in northern Minnesota year-round, but a sighting in southern Minnesota would be landmark.

Understanding and identifying habitat becomes important for birders because birds are so closely tied to the dominant plant communities of an area, and further to very specific habitats. One can look at the brushy border of a wetland and expect to find a Common Yellowthroat. We know that White-breasted Nuthatches, Red-eyed Vireos, and Rose-breasted Grosbeaks are regular denizens among the upper limbs of the deciduous forest. And what Minnesota grassland wouldn't hide a Savannah Sparrow or carry a Marsh Hawk across its rippling contours?

Birds unique to Minnesota's varied environments

Prairie Region

Eared Grebe	Black Tern
Western Grebe	Short-eared Owl
American White Pelican	Willow Flycatcher
Ruddy Duck	Western Kingbird
Swainson's Hawk	Horned Lark
Prairie Falcon (rare)	Sedge Wren
Greater Prairie-Chicken (local)	Marsh Wren
Sharp-tailed Grouse	Sprague's Pipit (local)
Yellow Rail	Loggerhead Shrike
Virginia Rail	Blue Grosbeak (southwest)
Sandhill Crane	Dickcissel
Upland Sandpiper	Field Sparrow (south)
Marbled Godwit	Lark Bunting (rare)
Wilson's Phalarope	Grasshopper Sparrow
Franklin's Gull	Le Conte's Sparrow
Forster's Tern	Nelson's Sharp-tailed

Bobolink
Smith's Longspur (rare)
Chestnut-collared Longspur
Yellow-headed Blackbird
Western Meadowlark

Northern Boreal Region

Common Loon
Red-throated Loon (LS)
American Bittern
Black Duck
Harlequin Duck (LS)
Oldsquaw (LS)
Black Scoter (LS)
Surf Scoter (LS)
White-winged Scoter (LS)
Northern Goshawk
Spruce Grouse
Whimbrel (LS)
Red Knot (LS)
Parasitic Jaeger (LS)
Little Gull (LS)
Glaucous Gull (LS)
Northern Hawk-Owl
Great Gray Owl
Boreal Owl
Northern Saw-whet Owl
Three-toed Woodpecker
Black-backed Woodpecker
Olive-sided Flycatcher
Yellow-bellied Flycatcher
Alder Flycatcher
Gray Jay
Common Raven
Boreal Chickadee
Red-breasted Nuthatch
Winter Wren
Golden-crowned Kinglet
Ruby-crowned Kinglet
Solitary Vireo
Hermit Thrush
Tennessee Warbler
Nashville Warbler
Northern Parula Warbler
Magnolia Warbler

LS = Lake Superior

Cape May Warbler
Yellow-rumped Warbler
Black-throated Green Warbler
Blackburnian Warbler
Pine Warbler
Palm Warbler
Bay-breasted Warbler
Connecticut Warbler
Le Conte's Sparrow
Lincoln's Sparrow
White-throated Sparrow
Dark-eyed Junco
Rusty Blackbird
Pine Grosbeak
Purple Finch
Red Crossbill
White-winged Crossbill
Hoary Redpoll
Evening Grosbeak

Northern Deciduous Region

Common Loon
Cooper's Hawk
Red-shouldered Hawk
Broad-winged Hawk
Sharp-tailed Grouse
Wild Turkey
American Woodcock
Black-billed Cuckoo
Long-eared Owl
Pileated Woodpecker
Least Flycatcher
Brown Creeper
Veery
Wood Thrush
Yellow-throated Vireo
Philadelphia Vireo
Golden-winged Warbler
American Redstart
Northern Waterthrush
Mourning Warbler
Canada Warbler
Scarlet Tanager
Indigo Bunting
Eastern Towhee
Lark Sparrow

Southern Hardwood Region

Cooper's Hawk
Red-shouldered Hawk
Wild Turkey
Northern Bobwhite
Common Moorhen
Black-billed Cuckoo
Yellow-billed Cuckoo
Barred Owl
Eastern Screech Owl
Red-headed Woodpecker
Red-bellied Woodpecker
Yellow-bellied Sapsucker
Pileated Woodpecker
Acadian Flycatcher
Willow Flycatcher
Least Flycatcher
Tufted Titmouse
Blue-gray Gnatcatcher
Bell's Vireo
Blue-winged Warbler
Cerulean Warbler
Prothonotary Warbler
Kentucky Warbler (rare)
Hooded Warbler
Louisiana Waterthrush
Yellow-breasted Chat
Indigo Bunting
Eastern Towhee
Lark Sparrow
Orchard Oriole

Climate

Minnesota's climate is greatly influenced by air masses that originate far away. The Rocky Mountains and intervening expanse of prairie of North and South Dakota contribute to summer storm patterns. The Gulf of Mexico sends moisture up the Mississippi Valley in spring, causing heavy rains, and huge cold air masses slip off the polar cap sending the state into a super deep-freeze for days at a time during winter. Of course, these events have an effect on the movement and activities of birds, as well as humans.

Minnesotans suffered an especially severe bout of cold weather in January 1994 and 1996. Human fatalities due to exposure are not uncommon during such periods, and birds suffer similarly—particularly when the cold is accompanied by high winds that quickly rob body heat. Conifers, tree cavities, and deep, thick grasses provide critical cover, which protects many birds from the elements in such cold weather. Ironically, extremely hot summer days in Minnesota, coupled with high humidity, also cause hardship. In the Twin Cities, the all-time low temperature and record high temperature are separated by 149 degrees. A state of extremes, to be sure. The all-time low in the Twin Cities, 41 degrees below zero, occurred in the month of January, but December has posted minus 39 and February minus 40. The record high of 108 degrees occurred during the month of July.

If you're new to Minnesota, or a temporary visitor, don't let the record extreme temperatures scare you away. Both winter and summer offer beautiful weather—providing you prepare accordingly. Average highs and lows for January in the Twin Cities are 21 and 2 degrees, respectively. Average lows and highs for July, the hottest month, are 60 and 83 degrees. The two best birding months offer splendid temperatures. May's average highs and lows are 69 and 46; September's are 71 and 48.

Because Minnesota spans over 400 miles from north to south, the climate is somewhat different from one end to the other. International Falls, on the Canadian border, is listed as the coldest spot in the continental United States, although a little hamlet called Embarrass, up in the northeastern part of the state, often records colder temperatures. On the other hand, the extreme southeast—in Houston County and along the Mississippi River valley—enjoys the mildest winters and a climate more akin to locales farther south. This area's bird and plant species lists reflect this more "southern" environment, including the Acadian Flycatcher, Bell's Vireo, Blue-winged Warbler, Prothonotary Warbler, Louisiana Waterthrush, and Tufted Titmouse.

Located so far north, Minnesota's day length changes as dramatically as its temperature from summer to winter. December 21, the shortest day, offers just 8 hours, 46 minutes of daylight, with sunrise just before 8 a.m. and sunset about 4:30 p.m. The longest day, June 21, offers almost 15 1/2 hours of daylight.

Ice-out dates for Minnesota's lakes reflect the differences in latitude within the state and have a bearing on the expected arrival of waterfowl in spring. Lake Minnetonka, in the Twin Cities area, generally loses its ice by the end of the first week of April, while Fall Lake near Ely, in the northeast, doesn't thaw until May in many years. Similarly, fall colors peak in the north about three to four weeks earlier than in the southeast, and most bird migrations follow approximately the same timing lag from north to south.

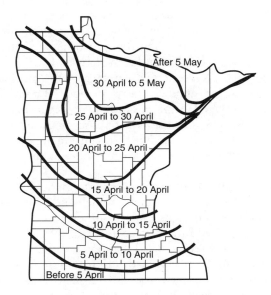

Dates on which lakes are no longer covered with ice. (Reprinted courtesy of Minnesota Agricultural Experiment Station.)

From season to season, Minnesota is a land of extreme change. Generally, as the calendar year progresses, the following weather events can be expected:

January: The coldest month

February: First thaws; earliest bird migrants return

March: Snowstorms likely, but lots of melting

April: Ice-out on lakes; rain season begins

May: Last frosts; woodlands bloom; trees begin to leaf out

June: Thunderstorms likely

July: Warmest and sunniest month; some severe weather

August: Another warm month; early bird migrants exiting

September: First frosts; peak of bird migration

October: Peak of fall color; crop harvest peaks

November: Cloudiest month; lakes freeze over

December: Expect snow cover; second coldest month

Migration

One of the most fascinating and mysterious aspects of bird behavior is their penchant and ability to migrate, the extensive, often incredible seasonal movements from breeding grounds to wintering grounds. Many of Minnesota's nesting birds winter in Mexico and Central America, braving great peril in their long annual journeys. In fact, eighty-six of the state's nesting bird species are considered neotropical, including most thrushes, flycatchers, swallows, vireos, warblers, tanagers, orioles, and some hawks.

Except for colonial birds like herons, egrets, pelicans, and cormorants, most Minnesota birds spend the summer season in isolated pairs, or individually, nesting and raising young. During migration, however, masses of a species may unite, creating spectacular sights for those of us along their path. An estimated fifty thousand common mergansers stage in migration on Lake Pepin each November, creating amazing open-water rafts as they feed on the lake's abundant shad.

Many theories have been put forth to explain this seasonal migration; two of the most widely held are the "northern home" and "southern home" theories. The first speculates that birds evolved in northern latitudes like Minnesota; that the Ice Age caused their displacement, and by migrating northward each year, birds are simply returning to their ancestral home.

The second theory suggests that birds originated in the tropics; that competition for food and nesting territories forced many species north into rich habitats like Minnesota each spring. Without question, migration affords Minnesota's nesting birds the tremendous advantage of plentiful food supplies, increased nesting space, and longer days for gathering food and raising young. Wintering in the south offers less extreme weather conditions. The fact that Minnesota is home to approximately 240 breeding bird species and just

81 breeding mammal species emphasizes the adaptive benefits that may be gained by long-distance movement.

Whatever the basis for bird migration, this unique behavior provides Minnesota birders with regular opportunities to observe species which would otherwise be absent in the state. Approximately sixty-five bird species are transients, *only* stopping in the state during periods of seasonal movement. Tundra Swans, which nest in the Arctic and winter on the Eastern Seaboard, offer a good example of this, and many of the shorebirds on the Minnesota list fall into this category. Other birds may nest only in one part of the state, but are seen at least once each year for a period of weeks in other parts of the state. Many of the wood warblers nest only north of a line that begins at about Duluth, but can be seen in all their glorious colors each spring as they stop over in southeastern Minnesota forests on their way north, and again in fall on their way southward.

Bird migration can take the form of a trickle of individuals working their way southward, or a mass movement in which large flocks, spurred by favorable weather conditions, undertake a long passage. These "trickles" of movement can be seen in many species that pass through the state in spring and fall. The first robin of spring, for instance, may truly be an individual migrating well ahead of its many counterparts. A few southbound shorebirds, probably those having suffered failed nesting attempts, begin to appear in the state as

Common Redpolls invade the state from the north in flocks ranging from a few birds to several hundred beginning in early October. In most winters they are common in northern and central portions of the state. BILL MARCHEL

early as July, although the larger concentrations won't arrive until almost two months later. Adult male Red-winged Blackbirds arrive on their Minnesota marshland nesting territories well ahead of the large flocks of juvenile and female redwings. Birders at Minnesota's famous Hawk Ridge near Duluth are quite familiar with days when only a few birds of a few species can be seen passing through. On the other hand, more than forty thousand Broad-winged Hawks have been reported in one spectacular day's watch at the Ridge.

Some migrants have made Minnesota the farthest stopping point in their southerly movement. Gyrfalcons, Snowy Owls, Lapland Longspurs, Snow Buntings, Red and White-winged Crossbills, Pine Grosbeaks, Tree Sparrows, and Common and Hoary Redpolls all regularly migrate into the state to remain all or part of the winter before heading north again.

Migration occurs about the same time each year for a given species, triggered by either lengthening or decreasing day length. Weather can also greatly influence the timing of migration and numbers of birds involved in a single flight. Clear, still nights provide ideal conditions for small birds that generally travel by night and rest and feed by day. The chirps and other contact calls of these small travelers can be heard from the darkness above on many a quiet fall night in Minnesota. Opposing high and low pressure systems, which create a trough of southerly airflow at their intersection, seem to favor mass migration of larger birds like hawks and waterfowl in the fall.

Most migrants through the state begin their travels under clear skies and high pressure, but apparently their speed enables them to actually overtake bad weather. Canada Geese have been known to land on Minnesota city streets during nights of particularly bad weather, and flocks of ducks have been found grounded and injured or killed in farmers' fields. Television towers, with their flashing lights and network of support cables, claim the lives of many migrating songbirds when cloud ceilings are low. The worst bird disaster recorded in Minnesota occurred in 1904 near Worthington, when it was estimated that more than a million Lapland Longspurs met their death during a night of heavy, wet snow. Caught by bad weather during a mass migration, the birds were literally forced into the ground and against buildings and power poles.

Fall freeze-up and spring ice-out has a great effect on the timing and location of water birds and eagles in Minnesota. In fall, river backwaters and small marshes and potholes freeze first, usually with the first windless nights that drop temperatures into the teens. These iced-over waters send remaining waterfowl, gulls, and wading birds onto rivers and larger lakes, and the concentration of these species begins to increase, as well as opportunistic Bald Eagles. When temperatures reach about 5 degrees or less on a windless night, the larger lakes freeze, forcing the remaining water birds onto major rivers or those lakes kept open by aerators or the warm water discharges of power plants, where some of the birds will remain for the winter. In spring, the first open water leads on frozen lakes will often hold a few migrating ducks.

Some migrant birds cross the state in haphazard fashion, but most—especially older, experienced birds—follow traditional flyways or corridors marked by major landforms and visit familiar stopovers each fall and spring. Hawk

Ridge receives predictably high numbers of migrants (and not just hawks) because birds moving out of the north tend to turn along the shoreline of Lake Superior rather than cross the open water—in effect, the birds are funneled toward the ridge. The major river valleys also funnel birds. The St. Croix channels birds from northern Wisconsin and Minnesota toward the lower Mississippi. The Red River valley moves birds to the Minnesota River, which in turn brings them across the state and into the lower Mississippi. And the Mississippi itself guides birds down through the center of the state, toward its lower waters and beyond.

Fortunately for those with an interest—perhaps a passion—for birds, the promise of seasons in Minnesota is also a promise of appointment: the birds will return. Landforms, plant life, and weather all have significant bearing on where and when birds move through the state. The following chapter will help you determine more precisely where, and when, to find them.

Map legend

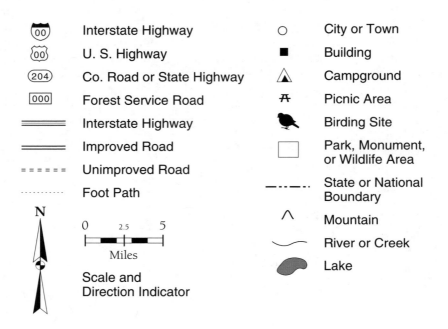

🛡00	Interstate Highway
🛡00	U. S. Highway
(204)	Co. Road or State Highway
[000]	Forest Service Road
≡≡≡	Interstate Highway
━━━	Improved Road
= = = = = =	Unimproved Road
··········	Foot Path

0   2.5   5
Miles

Scale and
Direction Indicator

○	City or Town
■	Building
▲	Campground
🜊	Picnic Area
🐦	Birding Site
▢	Park, Monument, or Wildlife Area
─ ·· ─ ··	State or National Boundary
∧	Mountain
～	River or Creek
◗	Lake

CHAPTER 3

Minnesota's best birding areas

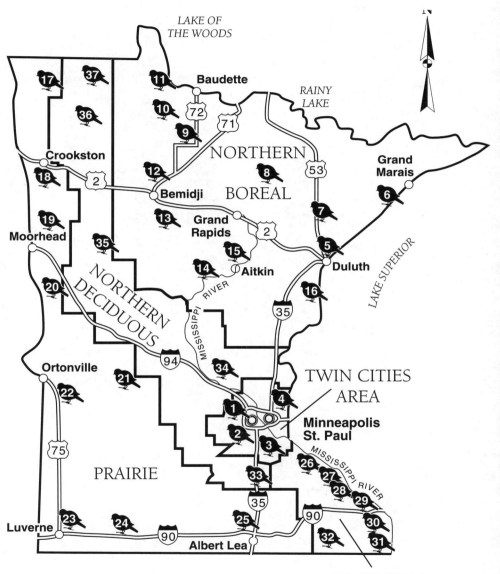

LAKE OF
THE WOODS

Baudette

RAINY
LAKE

NORTHERN

Crookston

Grand
Marais

BOREAL

Bemidji

Grand
Rapids

Moorhead

NORTHERN

DECIDUOUS

Aitkin

Duluth

LAKE SUPERIOR

MISSISSIPPI RIVER

Ortonville

TWIN CITIES
AREA

Minneapolis
St. Paul

PRAIRIE

MISSISSIPPI RIVER

Luverne

Albert Lea

SOUTHERN
HARDWOOD

Bald Eagle

Minnesota
Twin Cities Area

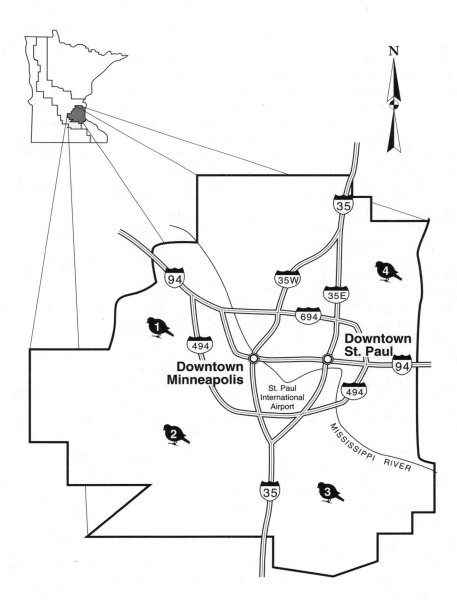

N

35
94
35W
35E
694
4
1
494
Downtown
St. Paul
Downtown
Minneapolis
St. Paul
International
Airport
94
494
2
MISSISSIPPI RIVER
35
3

Twin Cities Region

> *"While our way of life has changed, there is within us a feel for the land and what it used to be. . . ."*
>
> — Sigurd Olson
> Minnesota Conservationist

Few cities can claim the rich habitats or abundance of bird life seen in Minneapolis and St. Paul. With the exception of the regional parks, it would be generous to say that farsighted planning accounts entirely for this phenomenon. In truth, the nature of the Twin Cities lakes, marshes, and river floodplains has denied easy development of many parcels, preserving thousands of acres of "wild islands" that support not only birds, but also a wide variety of mammals such as deer, fox, raccoon, coyote, badger, beaver, mink, muskrat, skunk, and many more.

It is not just marginal land, however, that attracts birds to the metropolitan area. Some of the best birding areas were set aside for other purposes. Golf courses, wildflower gardens, parkways, and even Native American burial mounds contribute to the urban "wilderness" that makes the Twin Cities such a wonderful place to live or visit.

Examples of some of the country's best metropolitan area planning can be found in the Hennepin County Park Reserve System, where six large parks, from 1,000 to 5,300 acres in size, are managed to preserve 80 percent of the total acreage in its natural state. Large preserves or set-asides can also be found in the other seven metropolitan counties, in addition to three state parks and one national wildlife refuge.

1. Twin Cities Northwest

Habitats: Urban, agricultural, big woods, oak savannah, old field, lake, marsh, riparian

Key birds: Western Grebe, Trumpeter Swan, Cooper's Hawk, Whip-poor-will, Bobolink, Clay-colored and Lark Sparrows

Best times to bird: April-May; August-September

Don't miss: Eloise Butler Wildflower Gardens, Wolsfeld Woods

General information:

Hennepin County was named to honor Louis Hennepin (or Father Hennepin, as he has become known), a Franciscan missionary and one of the first European explorers to visit the area. In 1680, Hennepin named the broad St. Anthony waterfalls of the Mississippi River, on the north side of what is now downtown Minneapolis, in honor of his patron saint, St. Anthony of Padua.

Twin Cities Northwest

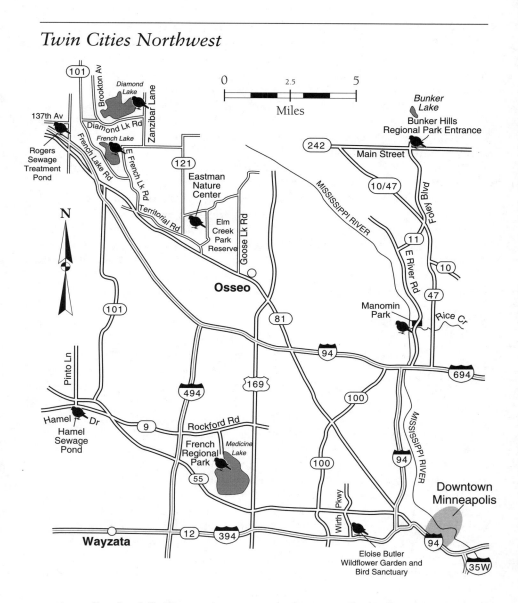

Actually, the falls Hennepin saw were about a mile farther downstream, but a slow, upstream erosion of the soft limestone riverbed moved the falls (at a rate of about 4 feet per year) to their present location, extending the beautiful, wooded river gorge that winds down to Fort Snelling and separates south Minneapolis from St. Paul. The University of Minnesota/Minneapolis campus straddles this part of the river. During settlement, the falls were diverted and modified to power lumber and flour mills, so that today they scarcely resemble the wild and beautiful vista Hennepin witnessed, although you can still see them where Hennepin Avenue crosses the river downtown.

The southern portion of the Twin Cities Northwest contains hills and pockets of lakes formed by glacial ice during the Pleistocene, or Ice Age, a little more than ten thousand years ago—truly some of the most picturesque land in Minnesota. Examples of these landforms can be seen north of State Highway 12, west of the village of Wayzata. Lake Rebecca Park Reserve, Baker Park Reserve, and the Wolsfeld Woods areas are prime examples of this glacial moraine. The rich, black topsoil of this area supported the maple/basswood forest of the "big woods" before settlers realized the soil's value and cleared most of the woodlands for agriculture.

The relatively flat Osseo, Brooklyn Park, and Champlin areas bear the influence of the ancient outwash of the Mississippi River, where potatoes have been grown; more recently sod farms and housing tracts have claimed the land. A distinct feature of this glacial outwash is the Anoka Sand Plain, a large area whose eastern edge surrounds the Mississippi River near the town of Anoka and extends toward the St. Croix River. The poor, dry soils of the sand plain offer scant support for vegetation, producing scrub grassland and stunted oak forests. Bunker Hills Regional Park provides a prime example of sand plain habitat, and the patterns of dunes can be seen surrounding Bunker Lake.

Birding information:

The northwestern portion of the Twin Cities offers the best birding during the spring, summer, and fall seasons. Always check the Twin Cities Birders' Hotline, (612) 827-3161, for recent sightings. Spring offers the highest number of species, including abundant waterfowl about the time when the ice leaves local lakes (the first week of April in most years), and excellent warbler migrations in May. Summer features resident nesting birds, including Trumpeter Swans in western Hennepin County; good southward migrations of shorebirds begin as early as late July and continue into September. Early fall witnesses many southward migrants and spectacular colors, particularly in the sugar maple woods of southwestern Hennepin County.

Twin Cities residents love to feed winter birds, attracting common visitors such as Black-capped Chickadee, White-breasted Nuthatch, Blue Jay, Northern Cardinal, American Goldfinch, and Pine Siskin, and occasionally such interesting species as Evening Grosbeak, Purple Finch, Redpoll, House Finch, and the opportunistic Northern Shrikes, which prey on the smaller birds. The feeders maintained by metropolitan county parks are good places for birders to drop in.

Hennepin County claims more species than any of the seven metro area counties, with some 335 regulars, casuals, and accidentals; unusual birds such as Swallow-tailed Kite, Clark's Nutcracker, and Kirtland's Warbler have been sighted over the years.

One of the gems of the Minneapolis Park System, **Eloise Butler Wildflower Garden and Bird Sanctuary's** mature hardwoods attract a dependable crop of migrating warblers each early May. Trails are short and comfortable in the 20-acre park named for its former curator, and the array of native plants is spectacular, especially in spring. Be sure to check the exhibits at the cabin known as the Crone Shelter, and the bird feeders outside the cabin for a good selection of common woodland bird species. The park rests in the larger, semi-wooded Wirth Parkway, which includes beautiful stands of mature woodlands and good birding.

A few miles west and northwest is **Clifton E. French Regional Park,** a 362-acre parcel at the north end of Medicine Lake. Unusual species such as the Yellow-breasted Chat have been observed here. The park primarily serves swimmers, boaters, and picnickers, but hiking trails are available. A sizable inlet of the lake invades the park's boundaries and wooded areas seem to attract a number of interesting birds. Check the marshes for Great Egret, American and Least Bittern, and waterfowl, and the woodlands for any number of common resident forest species. Medicine Lake itself is large enough to attract unusual gulls and waterfowl.

By following County 9 west to Highway 55, then west again to Pinto Lane, you can make a quick stop at the **Hamel Sewage Pond,** just a short hike south of Hamel Drive. During spring and early autumn many shorebirds may be sighted, and the opportunity for a rare sighting is always possible.

Farther northeast, just across the Mississippi River in the city of Fridley, you'll find another small Twin Cities gem, **Manomin Park,** about a mile north of 694 on East River Road where Rice Creek crosses under the roadway. A stop here during spring, summer, or fall is highly recommended. Park at the historic Banfill Tavern lot just south of Rice Creek, or in a small lot on the first street north of the creek. Although the park occupies only 15 acres, the creek, quaint trails, and shoreline of the Mississippi River make it an attractive setting. The park rests within a miles-long belt of riverside residential woodlands, just below a Girl Scout camp (to the north). In addition to songbirds, resident Osprey can be observed fishing this shallow stretch of river and Bald Eagles can occasionally be seen. The woods host Great Horned, Barred, and Screech-Owls and Pileated Woodpeckers.

By traveling north on East River Road, then turning right on County 11 (Foley Boulevard), you can easily reach **Bunker Hills Regional Park,** an area of tallgrass prairie and oak savannah typical of the Anoka Sand Plain. Lark Sparrow and Dickcissel can be found here, as well as Whip-poor-will, Upland Sandpiper, and an occasional Sandhill Crane. Wet areas support American Woodcock, and the 61-acre lake hosts a variety of waterfowl species during migration. You may want to start your birding in the woodlands adjacent to the archery range.

Across the Mississippi River, just northwest of the city of Osseo, you'll find **Elm Creek Park Reserve,** the largest of the Hennepin County reserves, though perhaps not the most scenic of the group. Three streams, five lakes, and a number of wetlands enhance the park's bird populations, supporting a rookery of Great Blue Herons, Black-crowned Night Herons, and Great Egrets in the treetops near the intersection of Elm and Rush creeks. The area was intensively farmed at one time, and old fields make up much of the landscape, although the Taylor's Woods area contains a remnant maple/basswood forest. Bobolink and Clay-colored Sparrows nest here, and Acadian Flycatchers have been seen on occasion. Sandhill Cranes nest in the reserve, but their nesting areas are closed to visitors. Start with a visit to the Eastman Nature Center and proceed along any of the almost 15 miles of marked trails, especially those that offer a mix of upland and wetland habitats.

Just down the road from Elm Creek you'll find **French Lake** and **Diamond Lake,** two bodies of water that for some reason attract Western Grebes—the farthest east you'll find this species in the United States. The big grebes occur in no small numbers. During a nesting season survey in 1993, 232 Western Grebes were counted on French Lake. Both French and Diamond lakes have also been known to attract Red-necked Grebes and Eared Grebes in addition to some interesting waterfowl during migration periods.

A few miles northwest of the park reserve is the **Rogers Sewage Pond,** on 137th Avenue, a spot worth checking for migrant shorebirds during April and between mid-July and the end of September.

A few miles west of Rogers, you'll find **Crow Hassen Park Reserve,** a 2,600-acre preserve bordering the Crow River. One-fourth of the park has been restored to prairie habitat, featuring many of the native grasses, forbs, and wildflowers that brushed the sides of settlers' carts. Crow Hassen hosts some of the region's reintroduced Trumpeter Swans; its marshes, old fields, brushland, and riparian habitats offer a good variety of bird species and extensive viewing trails. Cooper's Hawks are regularly seen here, and the prairies should produce sightings of Grasshopper and Savannah Sparrows.

Farther south, **Lake Rebecca Park Reserve** also rests along the slow-moving Crow River. This may be the most convenient area in the state to view Trumpeter Swans. Check the overlooks on the west side of the lake. The 290-acre lake and its adjoining marshes attract waterfowl, including Double-crested Cormorant, Ruddy Duck, and Green-winged Teal and a variety of wading birds. Osprey have nested here in recent years.

Both the **Lake Rebecca** area and **Baker Park Reserve,** to the east, offer good examples of glacial moraine, the hilly terrain dotted with lakes and marshes formed in the last Ice Age. If you visit Baker you may want to take time for a swim at the natural sand beach on Lake Independence after taking a hike around the tamarack bog in the park's southeast corner.

Trumpeter Swans can be seen in Baker, and the many wetlands support rails, bitterns, Marsh Wren, Common Yellowthroat, and a variety of flycatchers, hawks, and sparrows. While you're in the area, visit the **Loretto Sewage Pond** just south of the railroad tracks one-fifth mile east of town to check for shorebirds in spring and fall.

One of the best examples of remnant "big woods" in the state can be witnessed at **Wolsfeld Woods,** at the intersection of Brown Road and County 6. This 185-acre maple/basswood forest was part of farmland settled in 1855 by three brothers of the same name. Maples were spared for the sugar they produced and some of the virgin trees here are among the largest in the state. The site is designated as a Scientific and Natural Area, set aside to protect and perpetuate its exceptional features. Many of the forest plants flower in early spring before the dense forest canopy has grown closed. Summer offers a chance

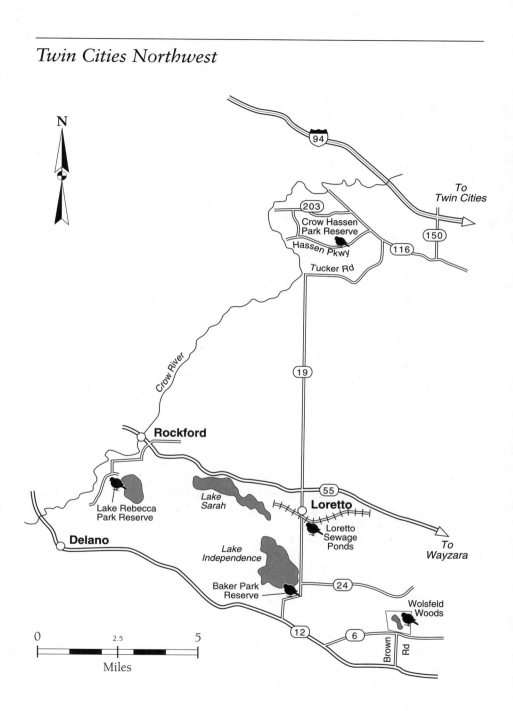

to see and hear resident nesting birds of this climax forest. Park in the north-east corner of the Trinity Lutheran Church parking lot to reach the entrance trail.

Additional help:

> **Minnesota Highway Map location:** J/16; Metro V-w/24-26
>
> **Hazards:** Mosquitos, poison ivy
>
> **Camping:** Baker Park Reserve, Bunker Hills Regional Park
>
> **Land ownership:** City of Minneapolis, Hennepin County, Anoka County
>
> **Additional information:** Hennepin Parks, 12615 County 9, Plymouth, MN 55441-1248; (612) 559-9000. (Parks may require a daily or seasonal vehicle pass for a nominal fee.)
>
> **Recommended length of stay:** 1 to 2 days

2. Twin Cities Southwest ───────────────

> **Habitats:** Urban, agricultural, big woods, prairie, old field, lake, marsh, river floodplain
>
> **Key birds:** Trumpeter Swan, Osprey, Broad-winged Hawk, Woodcock, Pileated Woodpecker, Willow Flycatcher, Wood Thrush, Blue-gray Gnatcatcher, Scarlet Tanager
>
> **Best times to bird:** April-May; August-September; December-January
>
> **Don't miss:** Carver Park Reserve, Black Dog Lake, Louisville Swamp

General information:

The southwestern portion of the Twin Cities includes some of the most beautiful landscapes the metropolitan area has to offer. Hundreds of years ago, the lands that surrounded Lake Minnetonka, Minnehaha Creek, the Minnesota River, and other lakes in this zone provided a rich lifestyle for the Native Americans who lived here. Wild game flourished in the woods and wetlands, and traces of ancient encampments and burial mounds testify that the area was well attended. Native residents benefited from abundant fish and wild crops such as rice, acorns, and maple sugar. The area was dominated by the "big woods," or what the Dakota called "Chahntonka."

With its mixture of prairie and deciduous forest, the area historically enjoyed a variety of bird species. Some, like the Passenger Pigeon, were incredibly abundant. Waterfowl flourished in the wetlands and prairie chickens enjoyed the mosaic of interspersed grasslands maintained by frequent wildfires. Even Ruffed Grouse, though absent today, could be found here. According to the journals of the late ornithologist Dr. Thomas Roberts, a variety of warblers and other songbirds were present in the late 1800s, and although these birds may not be present today in the abundance seen in Roberts' time, the area's species list is actually larger today than that recorded by Roberts in the early 1900s.

Twin Cities Southwest

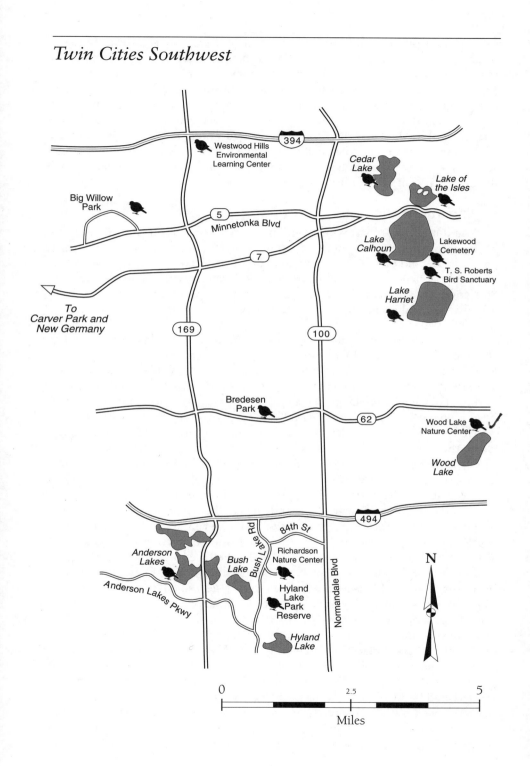

It is interesting to note that on modern bird surveys, significantly fewer birds are listed for the extreme southwest metro's Scott and Carver counties than for Hennepin. Of the 420 birds on the state list, Hennepin County enjoys 81 percent, while Scott and Carver boast about 66 percent. That these counties lie outside the metro area, and thus are less accessible to the multitude of metro-dwelling birders, may account for the lower count. They certainly are tougher to bird by road than the popular and populated Hennepin County. Also, many northern species, including some finches, owls, and others, don't show up here, seeming to have their southward movements "stopped" along the northern fringe of the Twin Cities.

Birding information:

You don't have to stray far from downtown Minneapolis to find interesting birds in Minnesota. Spring and fall migrations offer the best birding in city parks, lakes, and parkways, but winter can provide excellent opportunities to view gulls, finches, owls, and other species. Feeders, when located near suitable cover, attract many birds during winter. Open-water areas, such as those found around lake aerators, sewage treatment ponds, and power plants attract gulls and waterfowl.

If you want to start a morning's birding in the city, the lakes offer a good starting place. The city lakes offer great early-spring and late-fall birding, a time when anything from Harlequin Duck to California Gull can and has been spotted. Parkways skirt the lakes, restricting traffic to one-way in many cases. Parking adjacent to the lakes is not allowed on the parkways, but you should be able to park on nearby residential side streets with little difficulty.

Cedar Lake has woodlands along its north and east sides, and marshes along the northeast edge. Both areas offer interesting species from time to time, including warblers, owls, and rails. From I-394 take Penn Avenue south and follow 21st Street west to its end to reach the lake.

Lake of the Isles, Lake Calhoun, and **Lake Harriet** are busy places on any summer day, but during early spring and late fall they can offer excellent birding to those willing to show up at the crack of dawn. From I-94, take Lyndale Ave. south and follow Lake Street west to reach the connecting lake parkways. Walking trails around their perimeters make the lakes highly accessible. Lake of the Isles can be viewed from shore, but is best viewed by canoe. It's worth the effort. Two "wild" islands grace the small lake, which have provided treetop nesting to herons and egrets. Lakes Calhoun and Harriet are the largest of this troupe, and have been known to attract three species of loons, sea ducks, and unusual gulls just before freeze-up and just after ice-out. Calhoun's southern beach is a good place to watch gulls from November through freeze-up.

On the north side of Lake Harriet is the **T S. Roberts Bird Sanctuary**, named for the late "Father" of Minnesota birding. This small woodland may be the most visited by Minnesota birders over the years, and accordingly many rarities have been noted. Park in the lot on the north side of Roseway Road between King's Highway (Dupont) and the Lake Harriet Parkway and enter through the gate. To the north of Roberts Sanctuary is **Lakewood Cemetery,**

Twin Cities Southwest
Minneapolis Lakes Area

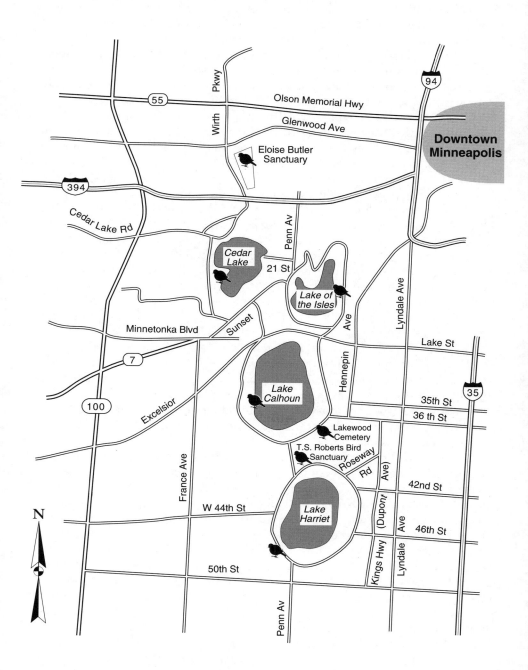

accessible from the entrance on the corner of Hennepin and 36th Street. Lakewood has proven a good spot for migrating warblers over the years. Check the trees on the north shore of the small lake on sunny mornings.

Wood Lake Nature Center is a rich 160-acre "island" of marshes, restored prairies, and woodlands which over the years has recorded well more than half the total bird species found in the state—despite its being sandwiched between a freeway and residential area. Three miles of trails course the area including floating boardwalks through marshy areas, observation decks, blinds, and an interpretive center. Wood Lake schedules many organized events for children, families, and schools. Check the bird list inside the nature center building. Another small, 200-acre park worth visiting lies at the end of Olinger Road just west of the Tracy Avenue exit off Crosstown Highway, 1 mile west of Highway 100. **Bredesen Park** is a wildlife preserve along the lowlands of Nine Mile Creek, which holds many marsh birds such as Least Bittern, Sora, Marsh Wren, herons, egrets, and a variety of waterfowl. The area is less developed than some city parks, but has two good walking trails.

Farther north, along Minnehaha Creek in Minnetonka, lies 97-acre **Big Willow Park**. Some of the park is taken up by softball fields, and these dominate your entrance. Don't be discouraged. Most of the acreage is undeveloped land, located north and west of the athletic fields, with a floating boardwalk that will get you across a marsh to more remote trails. The Minnehaha Creek corridor seems to move birds into and through this area, connecting it to Lake Minnetonka to the west and the Mississippi River to the east. Bald Eagles, Saw-whet and Long-eared Owls have been seen in this small park. Enter 1.5 miles west of Highway 169, on Minnetonka Boulevard.

Only a few miles northeast of Big Willow Park is **Westwood Hills Environmental Learning Center**, another small, 160-acre gem of marshes, restored prairie, woodlands, and a 60-acre lake. A planting of tamarack trees lines part of the lowlands, and an evergreen plantation provides cover for birds in winter. Floating boardwalks and 4 miles of trails are coupled with an exhibit building. Enter on the north side of Franklin Avenue, 0.3 mile west of Texas Avenue.

Lying just southwest of the intersections of Interstate 494 and Normandale Boulevard (Highway 100) is **Hyland Lake Park Reserve**. The 1,000-acre reserve is actually part of a complex of parklands totaling 2,500 acres, composed of Bush Lake Park, Tierney's Woods, Anderson Lakes Reserve, and Mount Normandale Lake Park. This is one of the most visited parks in Hennepin County, and one of the best staffed. Two of the prettiest patches of restored prairie in the Twin Cities can be found in the Hyland Lake Reserve; you can expect to find Eastern Meadowlarks and Bobolinks among the many birds here. **Anderson Lakes Reserve** contains some prime wetland habitat; it is known to support nesting rails, Ruddy Ducks, Pied-billed Grebes, and Black Terns and is also frequented by a variety of wading birds. Nearby woodlands support a number of owl species as well as woodland passerines. Be sure to stop first at **Richardson Nature Center** for information from their helpful volunteers. Better yet, call ahead: 941-7993. The trails around the nature center are

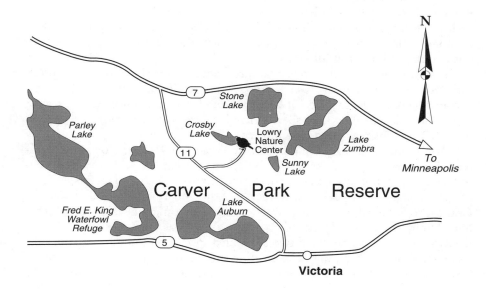

some of the "wildest" in the park, and the center offers impressive deer feeding sessions and bird banding sessions during winter.

If one area of the Twin Cities could be named an outstanding example of natural beauty, possessing abundant and diverse bird species in an accessible landscape, it would have to be **Carver Park Reserve,** 7 miles west of the village of Excelsior on Highway 7. The park entrance lies between Highway 7 and Highway 5 on County 11. The 3,500-acre park boasts a variety of forest, prairie, and wetland species including Trumpeter Swans (extirpated from the state in the late 1800s).

Minnesota's Trumpeter Swan recovery program began in Carver and a few other western-metro parks as a result of the farsighted efforts of Hennepin County Park Reserve District. The first birds were transported from Red Rock Lakes in Montana to Hennepin County between 1966 and 1969. By 1985, Hennepin County's flock had grown to 86 birds. The state joined in the effort, releasing more than 210 Trumpeter Swans between 1987 and 1994, most in northwestern Minnesota, and many have spread out and relocated into new nesting areas.

Weighing as much as thirty-eight pounds, with wingspans of 7 feet, Trumpeter Swans create an imposing sight. Released swans are marked with colored wing tags or neck collars, and information about Trumpeter Swan sightings is welcomed. Call (800) 766-6000, or 296-9662 in the metro area. Look for the swans on Carver Park's Sunny Lake.

Other interesting species you might expect to find in Carver Park Reserve include the Common Loon (nesting), Double-crested Cormorant, White Pelican, Ruddy Duck, Great Egret, Dickcissel, Eastern and Western Meadowlarks, Bobolink, Scarlet Tanager, Blue-gray Gnatcatcher, Eastern Bluebird, Forster's Tern, Yellow-headed Blackbird, and nesting Osprey. Specialties include nesting Wood Thrush and Blue-winged Warblers. The park's fine potholes and marshes attract a variety of ducks during migrations. Check out Autumn hiking trail for starters.

Be sure to first visit the **Lowry Nature Center** inside the park. The center's bird feeders themselves are worth the visit, especially in winter. Look for the entrance signs on the east side of County 11. A word of caution: Some areas of Carver are closed to protect specific nesting birds. Please observe signs and park instructions regarding closed areas.

Continuing west from Carver Park Reserve about 15 miles on State Highway 7, you reach an unlikely shorebird habitat near the town of **New Germany**. There is nothing of permanent significance which makes this such an attractive place for shorebirds. Rather, it is the impermanent levels of nearby **Crane Creek**, which frequently overflow into surrounding fields, that create ideal habitat for wading birds.

At least thirty of the thirty-two shorebird species on the state's regular list have been spotted here, and it seems that any heron or egret on the state list can be expected to occur at some time. Spring and late summer, during the

Twin Cities Southwest
New Germany/Crane Creek

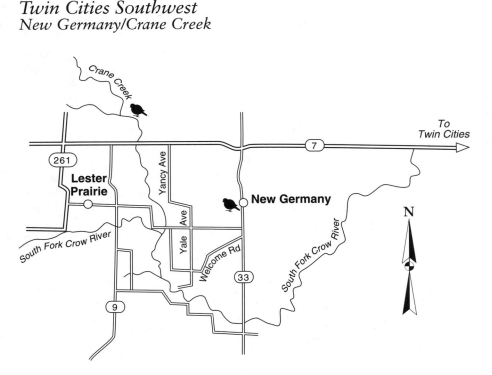

peak of shorebird movement, are the best times to visit the area, but good birding can be found anytime from spring through fall. Check any of the roads and temporary ponds along the creek area immediately west of New Germany.

Just below the bluffs on the east side of Twin Cities International Airport lies the confluence of the Mississippi and Minnesota rivers, and 3,200-acre **Fort Snelling State Park**. To reach the park take the Post Road exit off State Highway 5, between State Highway 55 and Interstate 494. The park contains beautiful forests and some expansive marshes. Walk the trails on the 0.5-mile-wide, 2-mile-long **Pike Island** for the best birding. The island is easy to reach and has good trails around its perimeter and a couple that bisect it. The long trail through the wetlands east of the Minnesota River that leads to Gun Club Lake can offer good birding, but it is often wet in the spring.

A beautiful and unique 2,300-acre park can be found adjacent to the Minnesota Zoo, just a few miles southeast of the airport. **Lebanon Hills Regional Park** offers enjoyable trails and excellent birding, particularly during spring and summer, with species like Pileated Woodpecker, Indigo Bunting, Scarlet Tanager, Eastern Towhee, and a variety of wading birds commonly present. To reach the park take Cliff Road east from I-35W to Pilot Knob road south, or take Pilot Knob Road south from I-35E. The park offers "one-way" canoe rentals and mapped portages that span six small lakes. Visitors can also rent horses from an adjacent ranch, though horse trails are more limited than general hiking trails.

Murphy-Hanrehan Park lies close to homes, shopping malls, and other development in Burnsville, but its 3,000 acres easily have been able to retain their wild flavor; this is one of the better parks managed by Hennepin County Park Reserves and certainly among the top birding parks. Many of the hawks and owls found in the northern deciduous forest region nest here as well as Wild Turkey, Olive-sided Flycatcher, Yellow-throated Vireo, and more. To reach the park from Interstate 35W, take County 42 west to Burnsville Parkway, then go south to the junction with County 75. Turn left into the park.

Murphy-Hanrehan is intentionally managed by the credo "less is more." The park offers little in the way of recreational facilities, but does have a network of more than 20 miles of hiking trails. Its wild character contributes to an interesting list of birds, which has included Yellow-crowned Night Herons, nesting Common Loons, and the park is the state's only nesting site for Hooded Warblers.

One of the nation's largest urban refuges, the **Minnesota Valley National Wildlife Refuge** comprises more than 17,000 acres in various units spanning a 34-mile stretch of the Minnesota River valley from the town of Jordan east to just below Twin Cities International Airport in Bloomington. Some of the best portions of the refuge lie as close as 10 miles from downtown Minneapolis.

This amazing mix of wild lands attracts 260 bird species each year, and accounts for about 120 nesting bird species. Stop first at the **refuge visitor center** by exiting off I-494 and turning south on 34th Avenue. Signs will direct you to the parking lot. The center features informative exhibits and a panoramic overlook.

Twin Cities Southwest

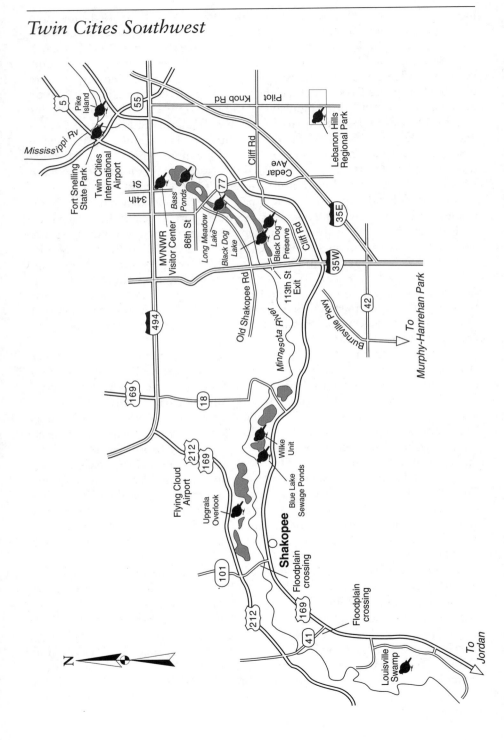

Just south of the visitor center is an area called the **Bass Ponds**, a series of ponds developed in the 1920s by the Izaak Walton League to raise fish for stocking in local lakes. Today the ponds are managed by the refuge and used for educational purposes, rather than fish. Dikes separate the level-controllable ponds; low water levels encourage the growth of plants favored by waterfowl, and exposed mud attracts migrating shorebirds. Adjacent **Long Meadow Lake** incorporates a rich marshland worth investigating. Follow 86th Street east from 24th Avenue to reach the ponds. You can follow foot trails west to reach the Old Cedar Avenue bridge, or drive south from the first stoplight west of County 77 on Old Shakopee Road to reach the bridge, a popular spot for woodland warbler watching in spring and for marsh birds in spring and summer.

Few places receive as much attention from local birders as **Black Dog Lake**. Although the open water seems to attract the most unusual birds—especially gulls and Bald Eagles—during migration and winter, summer residents include an interesting variety of nesting species. Bell's Vireo and Willow Flycatcher can be heard and seen here. The **Black Dog Preserve** can be reached by taking the 113th Street exit off I-35W to visit the north side of the lake (and observation area), or by traveling farther south and taking County 13 to reach one of two marked parking areas which feature two miles of hiking trail. The prairie and raised bogs here host not only interesting birds, but also spectacular late-summer color.

Black Dog Lake retains some open water throughout the year and is a magnet for gulls, often producing rarities.

Follow County 13 west (it turns into 101) 0.5 mile past the junction of County 18 to reach the **Wilke Unit** of the refuge. Look for the "Wood Duck" sign on the west end of a grove of pines to spot the entrance. There's a lot to explore in this 1,600-acre portion of the refuge, including floodplain forest, a pine plantation, lakes, wetlands, and small patches of prairie. This is an extremely rich area for waterfowl and wading birds during both nesting and migratory periods. A large heron rookery dominates the tall floodplain trees at the western end. In winter, check the pines for finches and owls. Just west of the Wilke Unit are the **Blue Lake sewage treatment ponds.** Easily accessible from the highway, these ponds have yielded some excellent shorebird and waterfowl sightings over the years and are good places to view wintering waterfowl.

On the opposite side of the valley, on the south side of Highway 169/212, lies the **Upgrala overlook.** The highway makes a long decline here, and the overlook rests about halfway down the bluff. Be careful with turns because this stretch of highway is notorious for serious accidents. The overlook gives an impressive view of a wide expanse of the valley, particularly of Upper Grass Lake, former home of the once-exclusive and highly productive Upgrala Duck Club, from which the overlook took its name. Where the highway reaches the top of the bluff lies **Flying Cloud Airport**, a good place to look for grassland sparrows and Upland Sandpipers.

Two river crossings—Highway 169, which runs south to Shakopee, and County 41—can be of interest, depending on water levels in the river valley. More often than not these wide floodplain forests are flooded in spring, creating miles of flooded timber which attracts and holds incredible numbers of waterbirds including ducks, cormorants, egrets, and herons.

While many areas listed in this book can be scouted with a quick visit (or even from the car), the **Louisville Swamp** is not one of them, although it is probably the best Twin Cities site for an extended day hike. Lying just south of the County 41 river crossing, the swamp is one of the wildest areas in this part of the state, partly because flooding causes large portions to become landlocked, or nearly so, about three years out of five.

In addition to its floodplain forest and wetlands, the valley land offers nearly every kind of habitat found in central Minnesota including oak savannah, prairie, and upland stands of aspen. Among the area's unique plants are some of the state's largest cottonwood trees and a small native cactus. Woodcock nest here, and the remote nature of the Louisville Swamp makes it a prime locale for nesting hawks and owls. A network of more than 10 miles of trails courses the area. North and south access sites are marked from Highway 169 south of Shakopee; the north access and parking can be found at 145th Street, and an access frequented by bowhunters during the fall lies another 2.5 miles farther south. The swamp can also be accessed from the north by at least one riverside canoe landing. The riverside trail is highly recommended, as is the loop around the Carver Rapids Unit.

Additional help:

Minnesota Highway Map location: J/17; Metro V-W/26-28

Hazards: Mosquitos, poison ivy, stinging nettle

Camping: Carver Park Reserve, Lebanon Hills Regional Park

Land ownership: Hennepin County, Carver County, Scott County, Dakota County, Department of Interior, state of Minnesota

Additional information: Hennepin Parks (see previous map section); U.S. Fish and Wildlife Service, 3815 E. 80th St., Bloomington, MN 55425, (612) 854-5900; Minnesota Department of Natural Resources, 500 Layfayette Rd., Box 40, St. Paul, MN 55155, (612) 296-6157; Carver County Parks, 10775 County Rd. 33, Young America, MN 55397, (612) 448-6082

Recommended length of stay: 3 to 4 days

3. Twin Cities Southeast

Habitats: Urban, agricultural, big woods, brushland, old field, lake, marsh, river floodplain

Key birds: Double-crested Cormorant, Bald Eagle, Turkey Vulture, Red-shouldered Hawk, Great Egret, Black-crowned Night Heron, Whip-poor-will, Pileated Woodpecker, Red-bellied Woodpecker, Western Kingbird, Wood Thrush, Indigo Bunting, Dickcissel, Field Sparrow

Best times to bird: April-May; October-January

Don't miss: Grey Cloud Island, Schaar's Bluff, Afton State Park

General information:

Though Minnesota seems relatively young in terms of settlement, more than three hundred years have passed since explorers of the 1600s made the turn at the confluence of the St. Croix River near Hastings and paddled up the Mississippi through the lands that would become the state's capital city. Native American encampments dotted the high river bluffs in those bygone days where updrafts carried Swallow-tailed Kites, oak limbs bowed under the weight of Passenger Pigeons, and prairie chickens danced in the openings of the oak savannah. The St. Croix Delta, the land between the St. Croix and Mississippi rivers, was once considered the richest timbered land in the state, supporting stands of white pines in which individual trees measured up to 5 feet in diameter.

In 1841, at a prime landing site on the Mississippi River, Father Lucien Gaultier built a crude log chapel to serve travelers and riverside squatters, naming it in honor of St. Paul. The settlement, and later the city, adopted the name of the chapel. A short distance upstream, Fort Snelling stood as the end of the line for keelboats and other river vessels that couldn't negotiate the fast, rocky stretches of water below St. Anthony Falls in the area that would later be named Minneapolis. Riverboats were able to conduct easy trade with St. Paul, and the city owes much of its foundation to such commerce. Today, barge traffic is a common sight on the river below St. Paul, but the city's famous heron rookery on Pig's Eye Island has survived plans for barge "parking lots" which once threatened. The rookery is one of only a few in the state visited by Yellow-crowned Night Herons, and hosts what was once considered the largest nesting colony of Black-crowned Night Herons in the United States.

Most of the best birding in this area seems dominated by the two major rivers: the Mississippi as it flows east from Minneapolis through downtown St. Paul and south toward its junction with the St. Croix River near Hastings, and the St. Croix and its beautiful valley, which creates a natural flyway for migrant raptors and passerines. Twin Cities Southeast offers plenty of birding opportunities in proximity to home, work, or airport hotel.

In addition to St. Paul's parks, lakes, and the rivers themselves, Washington County offers some excellent paved country roads worthy of a leisurely birding drive. In fact, the county hosts 300 of Minnesota's 420 bird species, including 75 nesting species.

Twin Cities Southeast consists of those portions of the metropolitan area roughly south of Interstate 94 and west of the confluence of the Minnesota and Mississippi rivers. The area has been divided into three maps for the purposes of this section.

Birding information:

Though it lies only a few miles from downtown Minneapolis and St. Paul, and appears inundated by air and barge traffic, **Crosby Farm** park offers several hundred acres of river bluff and river bottom habitat that can be a hotspot for migrant passerines, especially in spring. The area is dominated by floodplain forest and some small wetlands, including Upper Pond and Crosby Lake. In spring and summer, be sure to keep an eye out for Prothonotary Warblers, which may nest here. Boardwalks traverse wet areas at Crosby Farm and an observation deck overlooks Upper Pond. You'll find the park on the south side of Mississippi Blvd., just after it crosses under Highway 5. Take the Edgecumbe exit from Highway 5.

Shepard Road runs along the river to downtown St. Paul, offering views of the waterway, which can turn up unusual waterfowl and gulls, especially in winter. This street turns into Warner Road on the east side of the city. Just before the end of Warner Road are Child's Road and Pig's Eye Lake Road, which offer more viewing opportunities.

From the Lafayette Freeway, exit on Plato and go west to reach Water Street and **Lilydale Regional Park,** an area that is being developed as parkland after years of various human uses have left it rather tattered. Pickerel Lake here is worth visiting for its chance shorebirds and the herons and egrets that make regular feeding forays.

Above St. Paul is **Indian Mounds Park**, resting atop Dayton's Bluff and offering a spectacular view of downtown St. Paul, the river floodplain, and a

Twin Cities Southeast

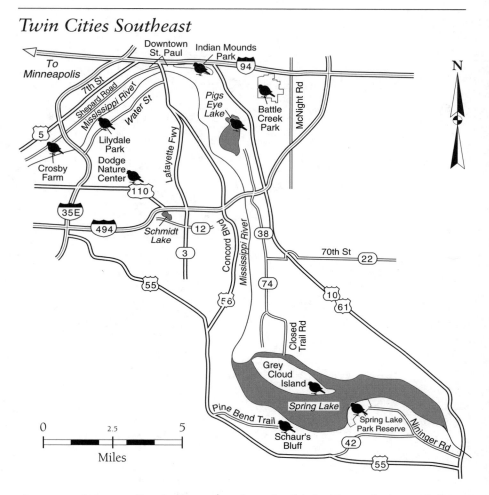

chance to view woodland migrants and nesting birds. To reach the park from I-94 (east of downtown St. Paul) take the Mounds Boulevard exit and follow Mounds Boulevard south back over the freeway. At the stoplight the road splits; take the right curve. About 0.5 mile farther look for the parking lot on the right between Plum and Cherry streets. A paved path begins here. Or take Mounds Boulevard about 1.5 miles farther to Earl Street and look for the shelter and picnic area. Six large Native American burial mounds situated near the highest point gave the park its name. The mounds are believed to have been created by a Hopewellian culture that emigrated from what is now Ohio and Indiana in about A.D. 400.

While you're in the downtown St. Paul neighborhood, you may want to visit the Minnesota Department of Natural Resources Headquarters at 500 Lafayette Road (612-296-6157), which has a great information center and nature store; the **Science Museum of Minnesota** at 10th and Wabasha Street (612-221-9488) also features a wonderful nature store and an Omni theater.

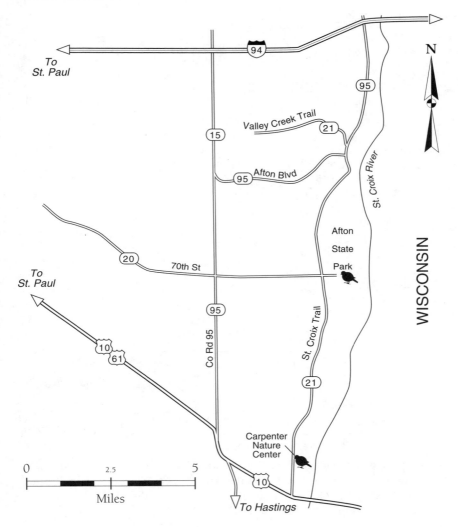

Battle Creek Park doesn't offer the most spectacular birding in the area, but it is easy to reach and offers good woodlands for spring warblers and some beautiful panoramas of the river valley. The park was named for the battle waged along this creek when Dakota chief Little Crow led his warriors against the Ojibway. Northern Saw-whet Owls have been heard here in April. To reach the park, head east from downtown St. Paul on I-94, take the McNight Road exit and go south.

One of Minnesota's most important rookeries, situated on an island in backwater **Pig's Eye Lake,** is as unlikely as it is interesting. Located just south of downtown St. Paul on the Mississippi River, the lake is best explored by boat, but is closed to visitors from April into July; a glimpse of the lake and mile-long Pig's Eye Island can be gained from Highway 10/61 on the east, or from Red Rock Road off Concord Boulevard on the west. This has become a good area to view Bald Eagles in late winter. An easier place to view feeding herons is Schmidt Lake, 0.5 mile west of Highway 3 on County 18.

Pig's Eye Lake and Island are named for Pierre Parrant, a liquor dealer with a deformed eye who settled near the lake in the mid-1850s. Prior to that time the lake had been known by the French name "Grand Marais," or "great marsh." The rookery, in the midst of the shipping district bustle, supports nesting Great Blue Heron, Great Egret, Double-Crested Cormorant, and Black-crowned Night Heron. Yellow-crowned Night Heron have nested here in the past, and continue to be a possibility.

A short distance north of Schmidt Lake is the **Dodge Nature Center,** one of the finest in the state. You can reach it by traveling east of Interstate 35E on Highway 110 and north on County 67, Charlton Street. Dodge is a good place to see a variety of nesting species including Black-billed Cuckoo and Bobolink. Though it occupies only about 300 acres, more than 200 species of birds have been recorded here.

About 5 miles south of Pig's Eye lies **Grey Cloud Island,** an area named for a Dakota woman who lived on the island and was married to a well-known white trader. The island can be reached by traveling south on County 75 from 70th Street. Perched at the edge of Spring Lake, a large pool created by a lock and dam, the island provides nesting habitat to Loggerhead Shrikes; good birding can be found during migration and in winter when waterfowl, gulls, and occasionally Bald Eagles are attracted to the open water.

Opposite the island, along the south shore, lies **Spring Lake Park Reserve,** another good place to stop and scan the open waters of the lake. Take County 42 west from Highway 61 in Hastings (or east from State Highway 55) and turn north on Idell Avenue to enter the park. Along the westerly edge of the park is the area known as **Schaar's Bluff,** steep bluffs whose updrafts attract soaring Turkey Vultures, Bald Eagles, and hawks. A good trail atop the bluff leads through oak forest with plenty of understory for nesting passerines.

Located only 19 miles from downtown St. Paul, **Afton State Park** offers a splendid example of the bluffs and steep ravines typical of the St. Croix and lower Mississippi rivers. To reach the park, travel east on I-94 from downtown St. Paul, then turn south on State Highway 95. When MN 95 turns west, proceed south on County 21 for 4 miles to the intersection with County 20.

Though much of the high ground was once farmed, efforts have been made to keep the 1,700-acre state park as pristine as possible, including offering twenty-four campsites that can only be reached on foot. Afton's wooded bluffs offer good birding in any season, but particularly during spring and fall migration, when passerines as well as many hawks and eagles follow the bluff line. An easy loop trail in the southeast corner of the park skirts prairie segments and the wooded bluffs. The swimming beach area and mouth of Trout Brook, about halfway up the park, offer good river views.

Several miles north of Afton State Park, Valley Creek Trail turns left, away from Highway 95, following the creek of the same name. This area has become commonly known as a good location to spot Louisiana Waterthrush by walking any of the small side roads away from County 21.

South of Afton State Park, on County 21 is a small but charming facility, the **Carpenter Nature Center**. It occupies little more than 300 acres, including a 60-acre apple orchard, but is worth a visit, especially during spring migration when the area's nesting birds have returned to their territories and migrating warblers, vireos, sparrows, and thrushes invade the woodlands along the St. Croix River. The nature center can also be reached from Highway 61 just north of Hastings by taking Highway 10 east 2 miles toward Prescott, Wisconsin, and traveling north 1.5 miles on County 21. The center is only open 8 a.m. to 5 p.m. weekdays and limited Sundays, and reservations are requested, but small groups of birders are welcome during those hours. Groups can call ahead: (612) 437-4359. The area has limited trails and two observation decks which overlook the bluff.

Additional help:

Minnesota Highway Map location: K/17; Metro Y-Z/27-28

Hazards: Mosquitos, poison ivy, stinging nettle

Camping: Afton State Park

Additional information: Dakota County Parks, 8500 127th St. E., Hastings, MN 55033, (612) 437-6608; Ramsey County Parks, 2015 Van Dyke St., Maplewood, MN 55109; Minnesota Department of Natural Resources

Recommended length of stay: 1 to 2 days

4. Twin Cities Northeast ─────────────

Habitats: Deciduous woodland, urban, agricultural, old field, lake, marsh, river floodplain, riparian

Key birds: Turkey Vulture, Broad-winged Hawk, Sandhill Crane, American Woodcock, Winter Wren, Mourning Warbler, Louisiana Waterthrush, Ovenbird, Indigo Bunting, Dickcissel

Best times to bird: April-May; September-October; January

Don't miss: Rice Creek Chain of Lakes Park, William O'Brien State Park, James Ford Bell Museum of Natural History, Carlos Avery Wildlife Management Area

General information:

The northeastern portion of the metropolitan area bears landforms and habitats as different from each other as the state's major biomes themselves. The eastern portion of this zone, close to the Mississippi River, is dominated by the Anoka Sand Plain—lands with loose sandy soils left on the surface by the outwash of glacial meltwater. Most of this area is relatively flat, and where the land has not been used to grow potatoes or other crops, the poor soils still support grassland and the mixed brush and scrubby northern pin and bur oak of the savannah. Before fire suppression allowed the forest to close, this was prime habitat for Loggerhead Shrikes; the birds can still be seen in semi-open areas.

Farther east, the low swamp country—now drained—supports the flat-surfaced sod farms. The large Carlos Avery Wildlife Management Area provides a glimpse of what the swamp and tamarack bog country here looked like before being drained and plowed. Sandhill Cranes continue to nest here, within minutes of the large metropolitan area. The closer one moves toward the St. Croix River the more the country begins to show the effects of the glacial moraine. Western Ramsey County and most of northern Washington County bear the rolling landscape and trademark lakes and potholes of the moraine. The well-maintained paved roads, beautiful scenery, and semi-rural landscape make northern Washington County an ideal place for a birding daytrip—or plan to stay overnight in one of the Stillwater area's fine bed-and-breakfast establishments.

Birding information:

Starting in either downtown Minneapolis or St. Paul, the **James Ford Bell Museum of Natural History** is a *must*-stop for any birder. The museum houses natural history dioramas, which capture the character of the state's birds and their habitats, and frequently offers special exhibits of artistic or historic value relating to Minnesota flora and fauna. The museum's Blue Heron Bookstore offers the Minnesota bird checklist in addition to its fine collection of books and gifts. Take 4th Street (a one-way) east from Interstate 35W about 1 mile to

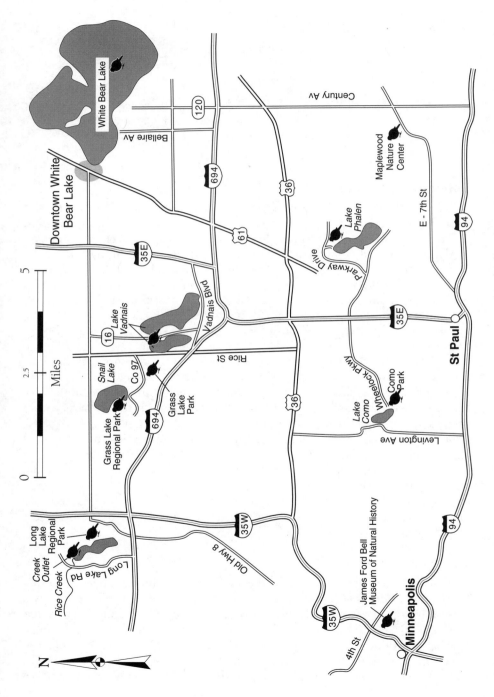

the corner of Church Street on the University of Minnesota campus. The museum is on the southwest corner of this intersection, at 10 South Church Street. Take a right on Church for public underground parking.

At the intersection of Lexington Ave. and Wheelock Parkway in St. Paul lies 370-acre **Como Park,** one of the oldest, best-planned city parks in the metro area. Of interest to birders are the mature woodlands scattered throughout, which seem to do their share of attracting migrating warblers and other birds each spring and fall. Trails in the southwest portion of the park provide good access to the area's wooded bird sanctuary. The Como grounds are also home to a conservatory, Japanese garden, zoo, and amusement park. A short drive to the east on Larpenteur Avenue lies **Lake Phalen,** the largest lake in St. Paul and another place where mature trees attract and hold migrating woodland passerines. The park itself offers about 270 acres of developed land including a golf course, picnic areas, and paved trails.

Maplewood Nature Center is tiny, but can also be a good place to view migrating warblers and other woodland birds. Take Century Avenue north from I-94, and turn left on East 7th Street to reach the center. Good trails course through the center's uplands and floating boardwalks bisect the marshes, making this an easy birding stop.

One of the largest lakes in the metro area, **White Bear Lake** has been known to attract some unusual migrants by virtue of its sheer size alone. October and November are the best months to scan the lake. Located on 5th Street east of

Open water in winter anywhere in Minnesota is a great attractant to waterfowl. This lead is created in Long Lake in New Brighton by the outflow of Rice Creek.

Twin Cities Northeast

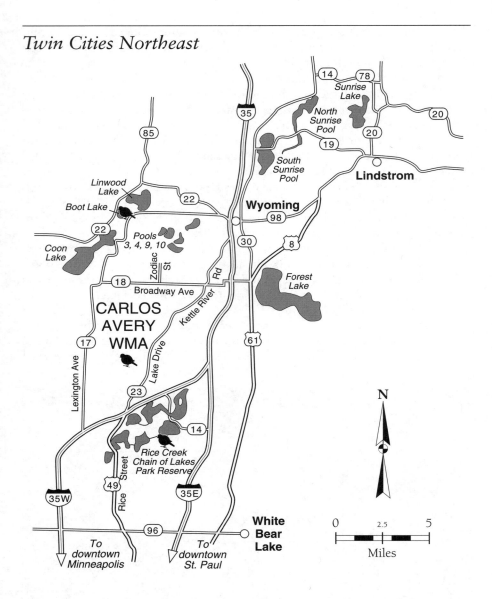

Highway 61 in downtown, the park offers a good view of the lake, although a better view of the big, open water is from the small beach area at the end of Bellaire Avenue. Migrating loons, including both Common and Pacific, have been known to stop here, as well as various diving ducks, scoters, and flocks of Tundra Swans.

Another good lake during migration lies farther west: **Lake Vadnais** is really two lakes surrounded by parkland. The eastern half lies close to Highway 49 (Rice Street) and County 16 bisects the two halves. Although Vadnais can offer some interesting birds such as scoters during migration, few are as strange

54

as the Neotropic Cormorant seen in 1992. Right next door is **Grass Lake Regional Park,** accessed by taking County 97 (Gramsie Road) west from Rice Street. The park borders the south shore of Snail Lake; a large marsh that can be scanned from a hilltop occupies the area south of Gramsie Road.

A dependable place to view Black-crowned Night Herons is **Long Lake Regional Park,** on the west side of Old Highway 8 in New Brighton. From I-35W, take the County 96 exit (immediately north of I-694), go west to Old Highway 8, and turn left; the park entrance is on your right. The herons like to roost in trees along the east shore of the lake, particularly in the bottleneck between the north and south portions.

A flock of several hundred mallards winters in the open water on the north end of Long Lake, where **Rice Creek** leaves the lake, crossing under Long Lake Road. Take the Long Lake Road exit off I-694 and go north about 1.5 miles to the bridge. American Black Ducks have been seen wintering among the mallards in the past, as well as scaup, and mergansers during migration. The best times to check the area are just after the lakes freeze in November, and again during the coldest days of winter. You'll be able to spot the nonlocal ducks by the wide berth they give the bridge area. There is no parking on Long Lake Road near the bridge, so park on a side street and walk to the bridge—be cautious of traffic.

A short distance up Interstate 35W from Long Lake is **Rice Creek Chain of Lakes Park Reserve,** stretching for 7 miles along Rice Creek and surrounding all or parts of seven lakes. Most of the uplands here are dominated by oak and basswood trees, but perhaps most significant are the many wetlands and marshes. The park supports a Great Blue Heron rookery, and Double-crested Cormorants, Black-crowned Night Herons, and Great Egrets are common. Watch for Osprey. The marshes are also inhabited by grebes, rails, terns, and gulls. The park entrance is located on County 14. Besides walking trails, birders have the option of scouting the course of the creek and lake shoreline by canoe.

Except perhaps for the Minnesota Valley National Wildlife Refuge, which continues to acquire land, the sprawling 23,000-acre **Carlos Avery Wildlife Management Area** is the largest chunk of public land in the metropolitan area. Take I-35 north to the Lexington Ave. exit and proceed north to County 18 (Broadway Avenue), then travel east to Zodiak Street and proceed north a short distance to headquarters for information on water levels and roads.

Once diked and alternately flooded and drained by a company harvesting marsh grass, the Carlos Avery WMA has been owned and managed by the state to benefit wildlife since the 1930s. A game farm here has housed everything from timber wolves to Trumpeter Swan cygnets over the years.

The Carlos Avery WMA is dominated by some six thousand acres of diked wetlands managed to produce aquatic plants, including wild rice, helping attract plenty of waterfowl in late summer and fall. Although most of the area is open to public hunting, the waterfowl season doesn't open until the first week of October. The area begins to teem with ducks throughout September and a dawn visit will reveal thousands of them making their morning flights. Keep an open ear for the distinctive call of Sandhill Cranes, which nest here.

Twin Cities Northeast

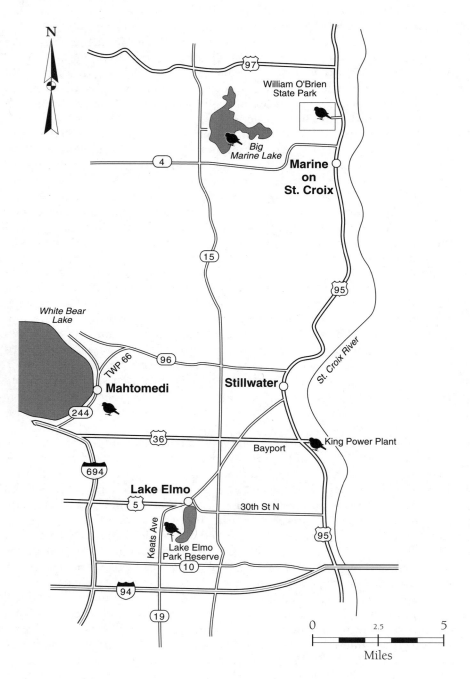

N

William O'Brien
State Park

97

Big
Marine Lake

4

Marine
on
St. Croix

15

95

White Bear
Lake

TWP 66

96

Stillwater

St. Croix River

Mahtomedi

244

36

King Power Plant

Bayport

694

Lake Elmo

5

30th St N

Keats Ave

Lake Elmo
Park Reserve

10

95

94

19

0   2.5   5

Miles

Because the area is not a park, the roads and trails are not developed, although some 57 miles of sandy roads wend through the area, offering adequate access, even when wet. Some of the better spots to visit include the Sunrise Pools, the area near Sunrise Lake, and the series of numbered pools north of the headquarters—good places to see shorebirds, herons, and egrets. Water-level control on some of the ponds provides excellent shorebird habitat during the spring and fall. Check with the headquarters for more information. Small roads, too numerous to detail here, access most locales and are all worth investigation.

Just south of Linwood Lake, on the west side of the management area, is the **Boot Lake Scientific and Natural Area,** accessible by traveling County 17. Many a census has been taken of this area; nesting Alder Flycatchers and Golden-winged Warblers have been noted, each at the southern edge of its nesting range. Other interesting nesting birds found here include Red-shouldered Hawk, Wild Turkey, Sandhill Crane, Red-breasted Nuthatch, Nashville Warbler, Pine Warbler, and Northern Waterthrush.

Other important area habitats for birders are the many sod farms—places which become popular stopovers during migration for sandpipers and plovers. Birders find the short greens of these grass fields easy to scan, making it possible to cover a lot of ground in a relatively short time.

Northern Washington County may arguably possess the most beautiful landscapes in the metropolitan area. From the pastoral, rolling farmland of its central portions to the beautiful forests and dramatic vistas of the St. Croix River valley, the area seldom disappoints its visitors. White Bear Lake makes a good starting point, particularly an auto tour through the thickly wooded areas near the village of **Mahtomedi** on the lake's east shore. The mature woodlands and pine plantings here attract and hold numbers of northern finches during late fall, winter, and early spring, as do the many backyard bird feeders in the area. A drive along tiny Township Road 66, which winds between County 244 and County 96, provides a chance to see any number of woodland birds or owls that often roost in the heavier pine cover.

Traveling from downtown St. Paul to northern Washington County, **Lake Elmo Park Reserve** makes a worthwhile stop. Go east from St. Paul on I-94 and take County 19 (Keats Avenue) north to reach the park entrance. Originally named Bass Lake, but renamed in 1879 for the popular novel *St. Elmo,* Lake Elmo lies at the center of this 2,000-acre reserve. Most of the land here was converted to agriculture many years ago, so it now exists as old fields. Remaining wetlands and woodlands provide important habitat for birds, and a substantial tract of old field has begun to be restored to native prairie vegetation. The best time to visit the reserve is during spring migration or during late September and October, when the area is visited by a surprising variety of waterfowl.

From Lake Elmo, drive east following 30th St. N. to Highway 95, then go north along the river to the **King Power Plant,** just south of Bayport and accessible from 10th Ave. N. In winter, the open water at the plant is a magnet for waterfowl and gulls. A pair of Peregrine Falcons nest on the power plant's smokestack. You can expect to find Common Goldeneye here most of the winter, and Barrow's Goldeneye have been reported.

Follow Highway 95 north about 12 miles to reach **William O'Brien State Park,** but consider stopping in Stillwater for lunch. This city holds the distinction of being the oldest in the state, and its main street features charming old buildings, interesting shops, and good restaurants—all with the river as a backdrop. Another good stop on the way up Highway 95 is the village of Marine-On-St. Croix, where the country store serves a scoop of real ice cream on a hot summer day. Two miles north is the entrance to the 1,300-acre William O'Brien park.

Although this beautiful park has been developed to accommodate high numbers of visitors, quiet areas can be found. During the busy summer season, the best time to bird the area is at the crack of dawn. Before May 30 and after September 1, the park is relatively quiet. The park's terrain is varied, from river floodplain to windswept hilltop, including the highest point in Washington County. Due west of the entrance are wetlands worth a visit, particularly in spring when vegetation is reduced and there is a greater chance of seeing rails. Past the wetlands, the land rises in wooded hillsides that offer good spring warbler watching. On the opposite side of Highway 95 is 60-acre Greenberg Island, dominated by floodplain forest and quiet backwaters. Great Blue Herons nest on the south end of the island, and chances of viewing Osprey or Bald Eagles are good.

Like White Bear Lake, **Big Marine Lake,** about 10 miles north of County 96 on County 15, seems to attract unusual water birds due to its sheer size, although there also must be something about this lake's location that contributes to its distinguished list of visitors in the fall. To reach the lake, take County 15 (Manning Trail North) north from County 96 (halfway between White Bear Lake and Stillwater). Big Marine Lake lies to the east just north of County 4.

Besides the normal groups of Mallards, Wood Ducks, and Canada Geese, the lake has been known to attract every duck and the three mergansers on the Minnesota list. However, even more interesting are some of the sea ducks and loons which have been spotted here over the years, including Oldsquaw, scoters, and Pacific Loon. Small private roads that lead to lakeside cabins dominate most of the lake, but the grounds of a retirement home about halfway up the lake's west side offers an elevated view of the lake. The two-story, early 1900s home is easy to spot from County 15, and birders who respect the property have been welcome to walk back for a view of the lake.

Additional help:

Minnesota Highway Map location: K/16; Metro X-Z/24-26

Hazards: Mosquitos, poison ivy, stinging nettles, wind chill

Camping: Lake Elmo Park Reserve, Rice Creek Chain of Lakes, William O'Brien State Park

Additional information: Ramsey County Parks, Washington County Parks, 1515 Keats Ave. N., Lake Elmo, MN 55042; (612) 731-3851; Minnesota Department of Natural Resources; James Ford Bell Museum of Natural History, 10 Church St., Minneapolis, MN 55455, (612) 624-4171

Recommended length of stay: 2 to 3 days

Minnesota
Northern Boreal Region

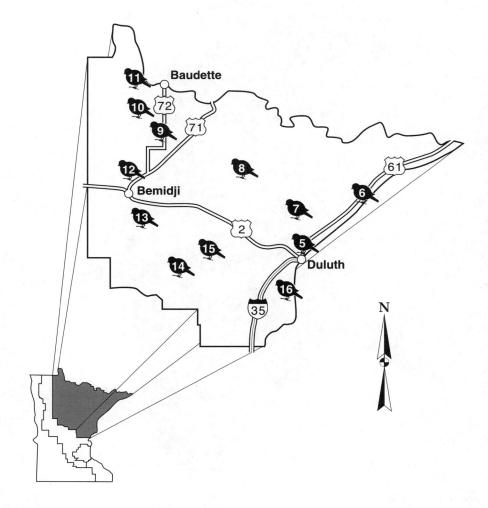

Great Gray Owl

Northern Boreal Region

Traveling north from the Twin Cities into Minnesota's northern boreal region, you enter what was once—and still remains—a primeval world. By night, the haunting calls of loons echo from lake to lake. By day, goshawks slip through the timber in search of grouse and snowshoe hares; Bald Eagles and Osprey claim the tallest, most remote nesting trees; ravens issue hoarse complaints across the forest canopy top, while beneath them colorful warblers, scolding chickadees, repetitive vireos, and nervous flycatchers claim most every piece of leafy habitat.

This is still a land surveyed from the silent perches of Great Gray Owls, where cold is legendary and a few of the most sought-after bird migrants appear from only one direction: out of the great, white north.

Except for the few surface scars from mining and the forest succession brought about by the once great logging boom, little has changed in Minnesota's extreme northeast since the first fur traders paddled and packed through its interior. Unlike other regions of the state, agriculture has had little impact on the landscape of the northern boreal region, where thin, rocky soils inhibit crops and biting insects and poor forage discourages livestock. Significant logging has increased in recent years, however, threatening birds that require mature, old-growth forests.

The boreal region remains a seemingly impenetrable land in certain places and seasons. Travel through the lake country of the Quetico-Superior Wilderness is mostly limited to waterways; except for the few roads, boats and canoes or snowmobiles are the primary mode of travel, depending upon the season. Farther west, vast bogs discourage travel anywhere save the few highways bisecting them.

At times, particularly during the fall freeze-up and spring thaw when lakes are impassable by any means, the boreal region can be a hauntingly silent place. During midwinter, the dense forest with its mantle of snow muffles all but the closest, most intimate sounds—the hoarse, high notes of the Boreal Chickadee; the soft, nasal call of the Red-breasted Nuthatch; or the bark-scratching movements of a Black-backed Woodpecker.

A dominant feature, Lake Superior bounds this region on the east. The largest body of fresh water in the world, its 1,300-foot-deep basin was created by volcanic activity that left a huge trough, later scoured to its present form during four different periods of glacial advance. The lake's Minnesota shoreline stretches 153 miles, from Duluth northeastward to Grand Portage along what is referred to as *The North Shore*. The native Ojibway called the big lake "Kitchigumi," or "great water," later immortalized in Longfellow's "Song of Hiawatha" as "Gitche Gumee, the Big Sea Water."

French traders found Lake Superior a dependable route into the "new wilderness," plying its shorelines in huge cargo canoes and ascending its rivers to the lake country beyond via grueling portage trails. "Lac Superieur," as the French christened it, was so named because it rested highest among the chain of Great Lakes' tributaries to the St. Lawrence River.

A major continental divide occurs in the boreal region along the 400-foot granite uprising known as "Giant's Ridge." Here, in the country west of Lake Superior, three watersheds are born, draining the country north through the Rainy River to Hudson Bay; east through the St. Louis River to the Atlantic Ocean; and south through the Mississippi River to the Gulf of Mexico.

Along the region's western side lies what many refer to as the "big bog": vast, flat peatlands left by the receding waters of ancient Glacial Lake Agassiz. A good view of these lands can be gained from State Highway 72, from the town of Shooks north to the town of Baudette. Much of this bogland is open, dominated by sedge grasses and low-growing shrubs, but interspersed are patches of swamp habitat, which supports some of the state's rarest plants. In addition to the alder brush, stands of black spruce and tamarack provide important nesting habitat for birds.

Bounding the region's north side, vast conifer forest and seemingly countless lakes stretch to the Canadian border and beyond. The area is well preserved within the massive Boundary Waters Canoe Area wilderness and Voyageur's National Park. Roads are few in this land of lakes, conifers, and ancient granite outcroppings; it is worth an extended visit.

Despite its dark, primeval-sounding title, the boreal region is picturesque, even colorful. It hosts more breeding birds than any other single region of the state, including the bulk of the state's nesting wood warblers. Its inland lakes are storied. Lake Superior's coastline matches any in the world for beauty. The region's forests offer spectacular viewing in fall, when patches of hardwood, dominated by maple, create beautiful mosaics of color which contrast the spruce, fir, and pine while tamaracks brighten the bogs with their rich, yellow needles.

Birds and more birds

The boreal region boasts a long and interesting list of Minnesota breeding birds; many unique migrants invade this region each year, including winter visitors such as Snowy Owl, Northern Hawk-Owl, Bohemian Waxwing, Gyrfalcon, Pine Grosbeak, Red Crossbill, White-winged Crossbill, and Common and Hoary Redpoll. Duluth and the North Shore in general seem to attract migrants seldom seen in other parts of the state. In addition to the many raptors funneled across Hawk Ridge on the city's northeast side, great numbers of passerines are counted here each fall.

Perhaps due to its immensity, Lake Superior accounts for a number of Minnesota's most interesting water birds and, on occasion, some of its rarest. Sea ducks such as Harlequin Duck, Oldsquaw, Black Scoter, Surf Scoter, and White-winged Scoter, and gulls such as Thayer's and Glaucous regularly occur both on and off Superior's shorelines. Pacific Loons have been spotted here, as well as two species of eider. You may be delighted by the sight of a Laughing, Iceland, or Great Black-backed Gull—but you wouldn't be the first. The lake also attracts several fascinating shorebirds during migration, including Whimbrel, Ruddy Turnstone, Red Knot, Sanderling, Buff-breasted Sandpiper, and others.

Like all the Minnesota regions, the boreal region hosts its own unique and interesting birds associated with its primary habitat types. The shy Black Duck breeds here in dependable numbers. Other boreal nesters include: Common Merganser, Sharp-shinned Hawk, Merlin, Ruffed and Spruce Grouse, Herring Gull, Boreal Owl, Black-backed Woodpecker, Yellow-bellied Flycatcher, Gray Jay, Winter Wren, Swainson's Thrush, Hermit Thrush, Solitary Vireo, Philadelphia Vireo, and twenty-four species of wood warblers, to name a few.

5. Duluth and vicinity

Habitats: Mixed conifer and deciduous forest, lakeshore, marsh, harbor backwater

Key birds: Common Loon, Broad-winged Hawk (fall), Sharp-shinned Hawk (fall), American Woodcock, Ring-billed Gull, Caspian Tern, Common Tern, Snowy Owl (winter), Northern Saw-whet Owl, Bohemian Waxwing (winter), Pine Grosbeak (winter)

Best times to bird: January; April-May; September-October

Don't miss: Hawk Ridge (fall), Minnesota Point/Park Point (spring, fall)

Bohemian Waxwings are locally common winter visitors to the north and east-central portions of the state, often in large flocks. They are similar to a Cedar Waxwing but larger and with darker underparts and have a strong white marking on wings. BILL MARCHEL

Duluth and vicinity

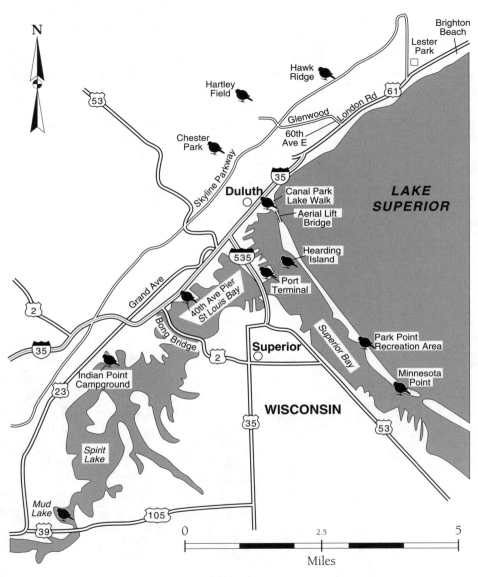

N

LAKE SUPERIOR

Brighton Beach
Lester Park
Hawk Ridge
Hartley Field
61
London Rd
Glenwood
60th Ave E
Chester Park
53
Skyline Parkway
35
Duluth
Canal Park Lake Walk
Aerial Lift Bridge
Hearding Island
535
Port Terminal
40th Ave Pier St Louis Bay
Grand Ave
Bong Bridge
2
35
Superior
Superior Bay
Park Point Recreation Area
Minnesota Point
Indian Point Campground
23
WISCONSIN
35
53
Spirit Lake
Mud Lake
105
39

0   2.5   5
Miles

General information:

Positioned at the head of Lake Superior, Duluth has always been an important stopover along the routes passing through the Minnesota territory. Explorers who first sought the North American interior were led here by the course of the St. Lawrence River. In seeking the headwaters of Lake Superior and Minnesota's St. Louis River—the headwater of the Great Lakes themselves—they found an important portage route across the short divide into the Mississippi drainage, today marked by Savanna Portage State Park, north of the town of McGregor.

The first travelers were funneled down Lake Superior to the narrow corner which is Duluth, much as migrating birds seem to be funneled here today. As the fruits of settlement increased, so grew Duluth, a hub of trade, providing transportation for timber, grain, ore, steel, and other commodities.

Although Duluth is a bustling international seaport, the western terminus of the St. Lawrence Seaway and the city's parks, backyards, harbor backwaters, sand bars, and mud flats attract long lists of interesting birds in spring and fall migration, and Lake Superior, whose sheer size resists freezing, attracts gulls and other rare water birds long into winter. And what birder hasn't heard of Duluth's famous Hawk Ridge?

Thanks to the very proactive Duluth Convention and Visitor's Bureau (and like-minded civic leaders), Duluth has become a wonderful tourist destination. The interstate transects the city with convenient exits and entrances, and planners did an excellent job with Canal Park and Lake Walk. Duluth can be conveniently reached by major highways from the north, south, and west, and is less than a three-hour drive up Interstate 35 from the Twin Cities. At almost any time of year Duluth offers plenty of accommodations; however, if you plan to stay overnight during the fall color season, you'll want to make room reservations a minimum of three months in advance.

Duluth can be a difficult city to navigate, especially for first-time visitors. The map presented here should help you identify the city's many birding sites and shows the major roads that connect them. Be sure to pick up the "Street Map of Duluth Minnesota/Superior Wisconsin," available from the Duluth Area Chamber of Commerce, 118 East Superior Street, Duluth, MN 55802; (218) 722-5501.

Birding information:

Hawk Ridge Nature Preserve may be Duluth's—and, for that matter, the state's— most famed birding site. Few places can rival the sheer numbers of fall migrants, especially raptors, which have been sighted over the years. A total of seventeen different raptor species have been identified from the ridge. Lake Superior's vast surface creates a natural barrier which funnels southbound migrants over the ridge, and wind currents coming up the North Shore's slopes no doubt provide ideal flying conditions. Viewing can be good from mid-August to late November, but the peak period runs from mid-September to late October. Cold, clear, high-pressure patterns with winds from the west/northwest bring the most migrants. Under any other conditions, viewing can be slow to static.

Flocks, or "kettles," of Broad-winged Hawks are common in the fall over the ridge; as many as 45,000 have been counted on a single September day. Other raptors appearing in notable numbers include Bald Eagles (usually later than hawks), Sharp-shinned Hawks, Turkey Vultures, Northern Goshawks (more than 5,000 in each of two fall seasons), Red-tailed Hawks, Rough-legged

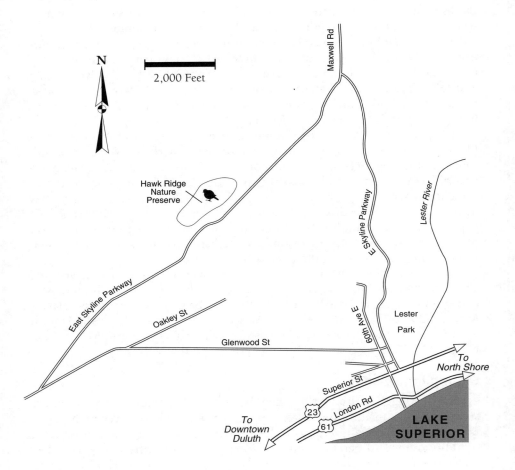

Hawks, and American Kestrels. Great numbers of nighthawks are common. Migrating owls also occur on the ridge, with hundreds banded each fall. And what would a premier migration stop be without passerines? Each year impressive numbers of traveling warblers, swallows, thrushes, waxwings, and other perching birds are counted from the ridge.

Birds not only fly over Hawk Ridge, they also stop to rest. In addition to passerines, you may find roosting Northern Saw-whet or Long-eared Owls, or even a Black-backed Woodpecker in the stand of pines about a mile down the

Duluth's Park Point stretches from Canal Park and the Aerial Lift Bridge toward the city of Superior, Wisconsin. Park Point is a natural way point for migrant water birds and passerines.

road to the northeast. Hawk Ridge is used not only as a recreational observation post, but also as a netting and banding station for further study of Minnesota birds.

To reach the ridge from the Twin Cities, take I-35 to Duluth and follow the North Shore signs. I-35 ends at London Road. Go east (right) on London Road to 60th Ave. East. Drive 2 blocks to the stop sign at Superior Street, cross Superior, and continue north 2 blocks to Glenwood Ave. Turn left and continue about 2 miles to East Skyline Parkway (the wide dirt road at the top of the hill on Glenwood). Follow the parkway northeast 1 mile to the second overlook.

From the North Shore, follow Highway 61 south to the Superior Street exit. Go west on Superior Street to the first stop sign (60th Ave. East) and turn right, then follow as above. A large, angular-shaped rock marks the overlook; it rests next to a stairway that descends the ridge. Across the road is a short, railroad-tie stairway which leads to the observation area paths. A sign marking the nature preserve should be in place during the fall birding season.

You may wish to access Skyline Parkway where it winds north from Superior Street near Lester Park, but use caution because this route is narrow, with one-lane bridges and blind curves. Don't miss the hard left turn at Maxwell Road.

Minnesota birders often refer to the 6-mile-long peninsula which protects St. Louis Bay and the busy Superior Harbor from the brute forces of Lake Superior as "Park Point," a deservedly popular birding spot. The tip of this peninsula is actually **Minnesota Point**, but the long bar incorporates the busy

Canal Park, a former warehouse area developed into shops and restaurants, and **Park Point Recreation Center,** a mile-long park featuring sports fields, trees, and beaches facing Lake Superior; the park begins at 43rd Street and runs southeast to the edge of Sky Harbor Airport.

The best time to visit the point is during spring and fall migration periods, and both are good. The month of May can be great, especially when foggy weather grounds spring migrants, particularly passerines. Fall probably outranks spring for both numbers of species and numbers of accidentals. You may see waterfowl rarities including scoters, Harlequin Ducks, Oldsquaw, or Red-throated or Pacific Loons. You can reach the peninsula by following the signs for **Canal Park** from Superior Street in downtown Duluth, or take the Lake Avenue exit off of I-35. Head toward the lake and you'll actually be on Canal Park Drive. In just a few blocks the road ends at the **Aerial Lift Bridge.** You'll probably want to park here to walk the breakwater wall, which extends from the bridge to scan the water for gulls, loons, and ducks (best in November); or take the **Lake Walk** (signs are well posted), which leads northwest along the shoreline back toward downtown Duluth. (In summer you'll see mostly Ring-billed Gulls and tourists here. Lake Walk is best for birds in fall and spring.)

Lake Avenue lies 1 block south of Canal Park Drive. This street will take you across the lift bridge and out onto the peninsula. Heading farther south along the peninsula, Lake Avenue turns into Minnesota Avenue. At 19th Street (watch for Bayside Market), turn right and drive in behind the apartment complex to view the harbor. You're in the right spot if you can see the back side of

The distinctive sand dunes of Park Point in Duluth, looking back toward the city shoreline. The entire peninsula here is worth birding in the fall.

Duluth Harbor's piers, docks, and islands attract gulls during the spring, summer, and fall; shorebirds during migration; and snowy owls in winter. Peregrine Falcons and Gyrfalcons are rare winter visitors.

nearby **Hearding Island** and its sand bars. A spotting scope is good for viewing the gulls, terns, and shorebirds which take their posts here regularly (best in spring). Watch for rarities.

Continue on Minnesota Avenue for good harbor views from empty lots and boulevards at 32nd, 33rd, 37th, and 38th streets and from the Duluth Rowing Club property at 40th street. **Park Point Recreation Area** starts at 43rd Street; you can view the bay anywhere from along here. Go to the end of the road and park to view **Lake Superior** from the sand dunes, or take the Park Point Nature Trail, which begins at the airport; the 2-mile hike to Minnesota Point, which overlooks the outlet of the St. Louis River, is worth the time in spring and fall when each day brings new migrants into the trees, along the beaches, and onto the lake itself. This area has some healthy poison ivy patches, so watch where you walk. During foggy weather in May, you may want to go to the west side of the ball field and check the shoreline trees that run all the way back to the park entrance; poor flying conditions can ground large numbers of passerines here.

Uphill from downtown Duluth and the lake, a couple of sweet little parks are worth a visit at any time of year, but particularly during fall and spring when passerines move through in abundance. To reach **Chester Park**, take Mesaba Ave. from Interstate 35 uphill to the four-corner stop sign. Veer right following the sign onto Skyline Parkway and continue to the second stop sign. Continue through the intersection (no turns) to stay on Skyline, and follow it across the bridge over the creek; look for the Chester Park sign posted at the entrance on your left. Chester Creek flows through the park.

One mile north lies **Hartley Field**, a sprawling park that incorporates a good stretch of Tischers Creek. From Chester Park, go east on Skyline Parkway to 19th Ave. East. Turn right and continue to the first stop sign, and turn left on 8th St. Continue to the stop lights, turn left on Woodland Avenue, and continue north to Arrowhead Road. Turn left and continue to Carver Avenue. Go right on Carver and take the first road to the left (Hartley Road). Park at the dead end and walk the hiking trail to the dam.

Working your way back down the waterfront, southwest of Canal Park you'll find the **Port Terminal** peninsula, a wide railroad yard and industrial area that offers more good views of St. Louis Bay. To reach the Port Terminal, take I-35 to I-535 East (marked "To Wisconsin"). At the foot of the High Bridge follow the signs for Port Terminal. Exit here and continue about 2 blocks. Watch for the UPS building and park across the street at the boat launch area.

The parking lot next to the UPS building offers a view of the bay to the southeast, and a short way farther, past the open gate that leads to the eastern corner of the peninsula, you'll find another view of the opposite side of **Hearding Island**. These areas are good in winter for spotting eagles and occasionally Gyrfalcons or Snowy Owls that roost on the bay ice. Watch for eruptions of Rock Doves to indicate a raptor or owl is nearby.

Check the bay side of the ready-mix cement plant around the corner to view Interstate Island. Caspian Terns can be seen here, as can a small colony of Common Terns, which nest here, and a large colony of Ring-billed Gulls. A variety of shorebirds may be seen during spring migration. In winter, look for Snowy Owls on building rooftops, grain elevators, and on the ice.

Continuing down the bay, just northeast of the Bong Bridge, is the **Erie Pier**, better known as **40th Ave. West**. To get there, take I-535 north and merge back onto I-35 south. Exit at 40th Ave. West and turn left at the stop sign. Go to the second stop sign and park near the large yellow gate. The gate may be open or locked at any time, so walking the block and a half to the levee pond is advised. The is the *best spot* in Duluth for viewing shorebirds in spring and fall. The perimeter road can be followed to scan the bay.

Just southwest of the pier lies **Indian Point Campground**, a respectable viewing spot for waterfowl and shorebirds, and outstanding for warblers during both spring and fall migration periods. To reach the point, get back on I-35 and go south to Highway 23 (Grand Avenue). Exit on the left and follow Highway 23 until you see the zoo on your right. A sign is posted for Indian Point. Turn left just south of the Willard Munger Motel to reach the point.

Another must-stop for spring viewing is the **Mud Lake** basin at the far end of the bay where the St. Louis River enters after its tumble from Jay Cooke State Park. Ducks, Tundra Swans, and eagles favor this area, as well as a number of wading birds. Take Grand Avenue (State Highway 23) south from Interstate 35 about 6 miles. Just before the road turns to the west is McKuen St. (State 105). Go left (east) on McKuen and either park under the railroad bridge and follow the railroad tracks north to Mud Lake (the train runs only during the fall color season) or continue on to the parking lot at WWJC Radio to scan the marshes located here. Finally, **Jay Cooke State Park**, just west of here, has a good mix of forests including old-growth northern hardwood, pine, and aspen-birch; the area offers numerous hiking trails with beautiful views of the St. Louis River.

Additional help:

Minnesota Highway Map location: M-10

Hazards: Poison ivy

Camping: Indian Point Campground, (612) 432-2228; Jay Cooke State Park, (218) 384-4610

Additional information: Duluth Convention and Visitor's Bureau, (800) 892-4997 or (218) 722-6024; Duluth Area Chamber of Commerce, 118 East Superior Street, Duluth, MN 55802, (218) 722-5501.

6. North Shore and vicinity

Habitats: Spruce, fir, pine, paper birch, aspen forest; tamarack, black spruce bog; northern hardwood (maple, basswood, yellow birch, red oak) forest; open water; coastal-like shoreline

Key birds: 20-25 nesting species of boreal warblers, Spruce Grouse, Great Gray Owl, Boreal Owl (April), Black-backed Woodpecker, Hermit Thrush, Veery, Swainson's Thrush, Solitary and Philadelphia Vireos, Pine Grosbeak, Evening Grosbeak

Best times to bird: April-May; August-December

Don't miss: Stony Point (fall), Lake County Road 2, Grand Marais Harbor (fall)

General information:

In the 1600s, French explorers poked and probed the country facing Lake Superior in search of the best route to the country's interior, the rich fur-bearing lands that lay farther west/northwest: a fabled Northwest Passage. The English had capitalized on the easiest route into the continent's western interior via Hudson Bay. Stymied by the North Shore's steep, short streams, the French finally settled on the easiest trail into the lake country: the Pigeon River and the 9-mile Grand Portage Trail.

The passage was later controlled by the English, then the United States following the Revolutionary War, but a vague "water communications" boundary established by the Treaty of Paris nearly delineated the territory's northern border much farther south at the St. Louis River. Fortunately, the Treaty of

1842 established the Pigeon River as the national boundary in the region, preserving the North Shore as one of the most precious natural possessions of the soon-to-be-created state of Minnesota.

Birding information:

Lake Superior's North Shore and the region surrounding it could be viewed as two separate life zones. The interior of the region, behind the steep ridge that guards the lake's northwest side, enjoys the shortest summers, endures the longest winters, and records the state's coldest temperatures. The town of Embarrass commonly posts the coldest winter temps of any Minnesota city. This truly is the heart of the boreal region, where spruce and fir dominate, and species such as Spruce Grouse, Black-backed Woodpecker, Three-toed Woodpecker, Gray Jay, Boreal Chickadee, Red Crossbills and White-winged Crossbills, and Evening Grosbeaks are counted as regulars.

On the lake side the climate changes, and the bird list follows—dramatically. Although it gathers a shifting ice pack, Lake Superior seldom, if ever, freezes solid. Its waters remain relatively cold in summer and warm in winter, compared with the climate of the land mass; its vast bulk extends its influence inland, causing cool summers and relatively mild winters with heavy snowfall. Rain and fog are common in spring and fall. The lake attracts late-migrant gulls, loons, and sea ducks in early winter and shorebirds in spring and fall; the shoreline forests around Grand Marais host Whip-poor-wills.

The "coastline" of Lake Superior offers opportunities to see big-water birds seldom seen in Minnesota, including loons, scoters, and eiders.

Over the hill from the North Shore, the boreal region's inland lakes create a picturesque background for birding. This is Esther Lake near Hovland.

Atop the ridge guarding the North Shore (referred to as the North Shore Highlands) run forests of sugar maple, basswood, yellow birch, and red oak, which are renowned for the glorious fall colors they infuse into this landscape and the Black-throated Blue Warblers which nest here. Farther inland, stands of towering red and white pine once dominated the forest landscape, but logging interests prevailed over efforts to preserve even a portion of these stands, except in the most remote regions of the lake country. Where the virgin pines do occur, they have become important nesting sites for Osprey and Bald Eagles.

Moving up the North Shore from Duluth (between Duluth and Two Harbors follow North Shore Scenic Drive, *County Road 61*; at Two Harbors return to *State Highway 61*), take the time to stop at the beaches and bays all the way up the lake. Be a little creative; a look will probably be rewarded. Check out any of the eight state parks along the North Shore, beginning with Gooseberry Falls north of Two Harbors and ending with Grand Portage near the Canadian border; they are some of the finest in Minnesota and feature inspiring panoramas, rushing rivers, and scenic hiking trails.

As you travel the boreal forests in search of birds, remember that you are really depending on songs rather than sights. There are many warblers in the dense forest here—sometimes referred to as "the bush"—but you're only going to *see* a small percentage of them. It's easy to spend an hour or more tracking a single, singing bird down in the dense foliage. Learn the region's birdsongs and your birding will be greatly enhanced.

A final note about the forested lake country: The edges of recently burned areas (consult local Minnesota Department of Natural Resource or U.S. Forest

Service stations) commonly attract Black-backed and Three-toed Woodpeckers and Olive-sided Flycatchers for first few years following a burn; areas of spruce-budworm infestation (look for green spruce trees with brown, dying tips) attract warblers in good numbers, especially Bay-breasted, Cape May, and Tennessee Warblers.

Traveling north from Duluth's Lester River on State Highway 61, follow the signs directing you to turn right onto North Shore Scenic Drive (County 61), which continues to Two Harbors. In the fall, stop at the Lakewood Pumping Station on the corner of Lakewood and County 61 (an on-and-off census site at this time of year). Volunteers here have witnessed thousands of a single species in the same day, including such staggering one-day totals as more than

North Shore and vicinity
Stony Point

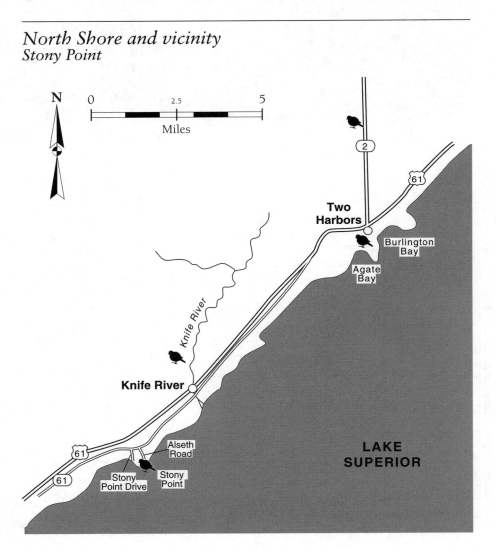

74

40,000 Common Nighthawks and more than 60,000 American Robins. A few miles farther, the mouth of the **French River** provides a good spot to view the lake for loons, waterfowl, and gulls.

Continuing northeast on County 61, **Stony Point** is a *must*-stop. Take Stony Point Drive from County 61, across from the Tom's Logging Camp (gift shop) sign, which takes you directly to the lake overlook. The point offers good birding in spring, but tremendous birding in fall, with a long list of regular and accidental birds. You may see any of three species of loons, scoters, a variety of gulls, hawks, owls, or various passerines. In winter, check the trees and brush for roosting Saw-whet and Boreal Owls and northern finches.

Another few miles up County 61, the town of **Knife River** occasionally hosts some interesting fall and winter migrants, especially gulls. In addition to the gravel beaches and harbor, check the trees in town (particularly mountain ash and conifers) for Bohemian Waxwings and finches. Visit the Knife River Marina (posted on Highway 61 in Knife River) to scan the offshore island for gulls, and the beaches for shorebirds. This can be a great spot for rarities.

The many mountain ash trees scattered among the residential streets of **Two Harbors** act as excellent Bohemian Waxwing magnets in late fall and winter. First Street, at the east edge of town, has become a popular right turn off Highway 61 for visiting birders looking for waxwings. You may also find oddities here, such as Varied Thrush and Townsend's Solitaire. Check also in the "two harbors," Agate Bay and Burlington Bay, for loons and gulls.

Two Harbors also marks the start of **Lake County Road 2**, a 46-mile tract of forest highway famed by Minnesota birders. This may be one of the most consistent places to see Spruce Grouse, particularly in winter, and certainly is the most easily traveled thoroughfare to feature this bird. Lake County 2 and the trails winding away from it penetrate boreal forest habitat that supports most of the interesting Minnesota species associated with it. Gravel forest roads in this region are mostly closed in winter and muddy in spring; use common sense when traveling them to avoid being stranded.

About 25 miles up County Road 2 from Highway 61, start looking for the County Road 15 sign. County 15 runs west, but you'll want to take the next right, east on **Forest Highway 11** (designed to eventually go to Silver Bay), which can connect you to **Stony River Road** and **Whyte Road**. These routes may be best in early June when any number of wood warblers may be heard singing on nesting territories and Alder, Olive-sided, and Yellow-bellied Fly-catchers will also be found. A couple of short diversions lead onto Forest Road 104, but this road is impassible in one stretch.

Whyte Road connects with Forest Road 102, which leads to County Road 1. Turn left on County 1 to go to Isabella. A few miles past Isabella, the left-hand loop of **Forest Road 103** is another good warbler transect, or continue on and turn right onto **Mitawan Road** (Forest Road 173/177), one of the best roads in the state for Boreal Owls, but often not plowed. Red pine stands here may produce Red Crossbills, and jack pine stands often harbor Black-backed Woodpeckers. Watch for moose, timber wolves, pine martens, and fishers that may be seen in the early morning hours.

North Shore and vicinity
Lake County Road 2

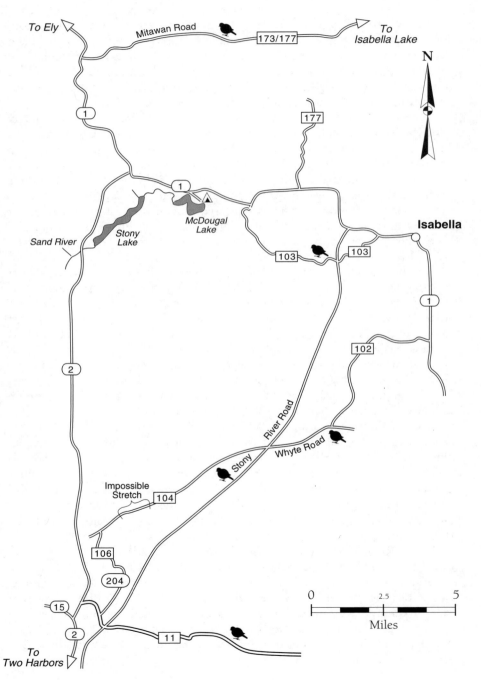

If you'd rather not face the vagaries of forest roads in winter or early spring, County Road 2 itself provides dependable year-round travel through much the same habitat. Keep an eye out for stands of large pines, which may produce such winter birds as Red Crossbills, White-winged Crossbills, Evening Grosbeaks, and Hoary and Common Redpoll. Between dawn and about 9 a.m., look for Spruce Grouse (from the Sand River north to the junction with County Road 1 may be the best place in the state for these), Great Gray Owls, or even Northern Hawk-Owls. Or stop and listen on a late March or April evening for Northern Saw-whet, Long-eared, Boreal, or Barred Owls.

County 2 leads to County 1, where a left turn will put you on course for the lake-country wilderness-gateway town of Ely. On the way, consider taking the Spruce Road. A sign for this road is posted on the right. Go 1 mile, park, and walk the road. Listen for the scratching of Black-backed and Three-toed Woodpeckers, and watch for Spruce Grouse, Boreal Chickadees, and Gray Jays. This is a good road year-round. In Ely, Fernberg Road (County 18) and Echo Trail (County 116)—well-marked when traveling east out of Ely on State Highway 169—offer a taste of the Boundary Waters Canoe Area, with no canoe paddle necessary. Echo Trail is particularly good for Spruce Grouse in winter, as well as the birds mentioned above and finches.

Back on the North Shore, it's approximately 33 miles north on Highway 61 from Two Harbors to the Palisade Head, a promontory 2.8 miles north of the town of Silver Bay, which offers a beautiful lake vista. Peregrine Falcons nest on the cliffs below the parking lot here. Follow the marked road off Highway 61.

Less than 2 miles up the highway from Palisade Head you'll find Tettegouche State Park, one of the most recent additions to the state park system and one of the finer. Tettegouche preserves thousands of acres of North Shore Highlands and a mile of Lake Superior shoreline including Shovel Point, which is worth the short hike from the northernmost side of the Baptism River rest area parking lot off Highway 61. This area marks the southernmost population of nesting Black-throated Blue Warblers. You can reach the back side of Tettegouche (and some of the best Black-throated Blue habitat anywhere) by turning north on County Road 4 in Beaver Bay. Continue up County 4 past the Lax Lake public boat access (on your right) for 0.5 mile to a small parking area (also on your right). From here, hike the trail east into the park. Many singing male Black-throated Blues have been recorded in the hills above.

A more-often visited birding spot exists near the unlikely hamlet of **Cramer**, 10 miles to the north. To get there, turn left onto County Road 1 from Highway 61 at the North Shore town of Schroeder. Follow County 1 (which turns into County 8 at the county line) to its intersection with County 7, then go north. Park anywhere here and walk the road to locate Chestnut-sided, Nashville, Blackburnian, Yellow-rumped, Magnolia, and Canada Warblers and American Redstart. Pay attention to the trees, where Philadelphia Vireo may be heard. County Road 7 provides good birding all the way up past Nine-Mile Lake to Crooked Lake and the Trestle Restaurant. Keep an ear out for Black-throated Blue Warblers, which have been located in the maple forests near Goldeneye Lake. **Crosby-Manitou State Park** lies south on County 7 and offers

North Shore and vicinity
Cramer/Oberg Mountain

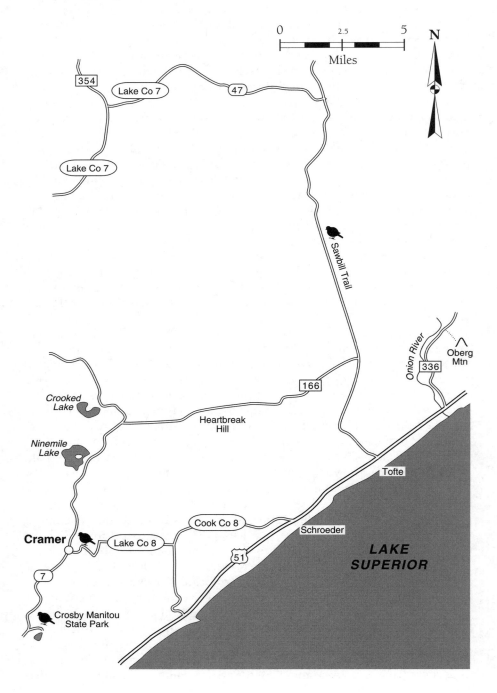

0   2.5   5

N

Miles

354

Lake Co 7

47

Lake Co 7

Sawbill Trail

Crooked
Lake

Onion River

Oberg
Mtn

336

166

Ninemile
Lake

Heartbreak
Hill

Tofte

Cook Co 8

Cramer

Lake Co 8

Schroeder

51

LAKE
SUPERIOR

7

Crosby Manitou
State Park

a good network of hiking trails; the Middle Trail to the West Manitou River Trail offers no less than five scenic overlooks and plenty of good birding.

If road conditions are good, you can cut back across to the **Sawbill Trail** along Forest Road 166, or catch the Sawbill from the town of Tofte and head north as far as the trail's namesake, Sawbill Lake, if you like. The lake was named for the "Saw-billed Ducks" seen here—mergansers, no doubt. The road is well maintained. It might be more productive, however, to visit **Oberg Mountain**, a dependable location for Scarlet Tanagers and Black-throated Blue Warblers. To get there, turn north from Highway 61 onto Forest Road 336, about 5 miles north of the hamlet of Tofte (about 1.5 miles beyond the Onion River), and follow this short, 2-mile road to the parking area on the left; cross the main road where a trail leads up the mountain. Keep your ears open as you near the top for the hoarse, robinlike song of the tanager or the ascending song of the Black-throated Blue Warbler.

As you move farther up the North Shore on Highway 61, the 2,800-acre **Cascade River State Park** offers lots of trails for the adventurous birder. This park also hosts the Jonvik Deer Yard, the largest deer wintering yard in Minnesota, where the south-facing slope gathers the meager warmth of the winter sun and protects the whitetails from the cold, prevailing winds.

Another 5 miles up Highway 61 lies the city of **Grand Marais** (260 miles from the Twin Cities), which for most Minnesotans is the "last stop" on the North Shore—next stop, Canada—even though it is a full 42 miles farther to Grand Portage and the border. Grand Marais has listed more bird rarities than might be expected for a tiny town, perhaps because it is so popular with visiting birders and because some particularly knowledgeable birders live here. What Fieldfare, Anna's Hummingbird, and Fork-tailed Flycatcher might be doing here is beyond explanation. More plausible are the regular occurrences of such rare Minnesota visitors as Harlequin Ducks, Oldsquaws, Northern Mockingbirds, and Thayer's, Iceland, and Glaucous Gulls (almost all recorded in fall).

The city of Grand Marais received its name from the French, meaning "great marsh," a reference to a 20-acre wetland which rested at the back of this protected bay. It was the bay's shelter, rather than its marsh, that attracted lake travelers to Grand Marais and caused them to settle; it's likely the reference was meant to distinguish "the bay with the marsh" from other safe ports along the sometimes perilous lake.

The Grand Marais harbor attracts many travelers, including birders, and should be the first stop on a visit to this area. Fall is definitely the best time to search the bay for its unusual winged visitors. Herring Gulls and Common Mergansers are regular bay residents, but you can expect to see much more between September and December in the harbor. In addition to species listed earlier, watch for Red-throated Loons; Black, Surf, and White-winged Scoters; Oldsquaws; Common and King Eiders; Whimbrels; and Glaucous, Iceland, Thayer's, Lesser and Great Black-backed, and Ivory Gulls. Check both sides of the harbor area, as well as the breakwater on the east side and beyond.

Like Two Harbors, the residential streets of Grand Marais, with their mountain ash trees and bird feeders, cannot be overlooked. With just a little luck

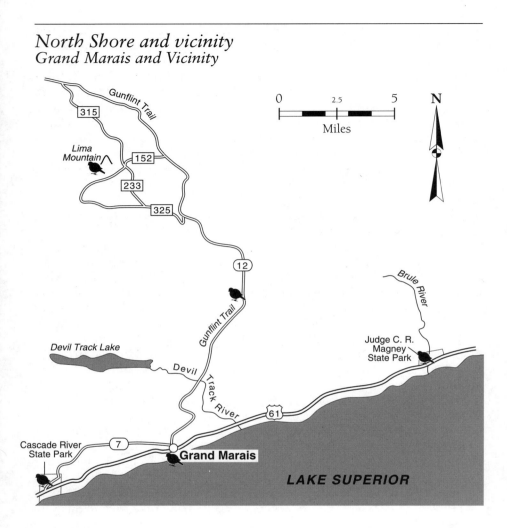

you should be able to find Bohemian Waxwings, Common Redpolls, Purple Finches, and Evening and Pine Grosbeaks. Rarities such as Varied Thrush, Townsend's Solitaire, Northern Mockingbird, and Mountain Bluebird are possibilities, too.

There are more birding spots along the Lake Superior shoreline and inland on the way northeast up Highway 61 to Grand Portage, but the best include Paradise Beach, about 14 miles up Highway 61 from Grand Marais—a great place to spot scoters and Oldsquaws, with a view of the lake and small islands. **Judge C.R. Magney State Park,** where the Brule River empties into the lake in front of Naniboujou Lodge, is another good place to scan the lake for scoters and Oldsquaws. The mouth of the river is private property with a cabin on the west side and Naniboujou Lodge on the east side. The lodge owners do not, however, discourage birders. The sandbars at the river's mouth attract shorebirds at the right times of year.

Most birders, however, choose to travel up the famed **Gunflint Trail** (County Road 12) from Grand Marais due north. Again, spruce-budworm infestation areas and burn edges are good; if you can recognize a bog, with its tamarack and black spruce, it is worth a stop, look, and listen. One particularly productive area over the years has been the roads to **Lima Mountain** (Forest Roads 325, 152, and 315), about 20 miles north of Grand Marais. While logging and fire have claimed some of the best habitat, this is still a good area for Spruce Grouse, Black-backed and Three-toed Woodpeckers, Yellow-bellied and Olive-sided Flycatchers, Boreal Chickadees, and any number of nesting warblers. Also, although not a confirmed nesting species here, Great Gray Owls are seen fairly often.

You can continue checking up the Gunflint for about another 30 miles, but the road terminates between Seagull and Saganaga lakes. Resorts here will rent you a boat if you'd like to experience the bird life on the many small islands and the beautiful character of this lake country. Seagull is the more protected of the two waters. Relatively little logging has occurred in this region and some of the islands feature virgin stands of pine. Watch for Bald Eagles and Osprey, Common Raven, Common Goldeneyes, Black Ducks (in the marsh areas), Ring-necked Ducks, mergansers, and, of course, Common Loons in addition to the forest birds you've seen thus far.

Additional help:

Minnesota Highway Map location: M-R—6-10

Hazards: Mosquitos, black flies, icy roads, muddy roads, logging trucks, snowstorms

Nearest food, lodging, gas: Two Harbors, Silver Bay, Lutsen, Grand Marais

Camping: State Parks at Cascade River and Gooseberry Falls; McDougal Lake; South Kawishiwi River; Grand Marais

Land ownership: USFS, state of Minnesota, private

Additional information: DNR information, (612) 296-6157 or (800) 766-6000; Minnesota Office of Tourism, (612) 296-5029; Camping Connection (private campgrounds), (612) 922-9000 or (800) 246-CAMP; Snowshoe Country Lodge, Isabella (accommodates birders with camping and private cabins, birding trails, rustic fireplaces, and a good sauna), (218) 365-2126

Recommended length of stay: 3 to 7 days

7. Sax-Zim and vicinity

Habitats: Tamarack and black spruce bog, aspen stands, sedge meadow, hay fields

Key birds: Sharp-tailed Grouse; Yellow Rail; Great Gray Owl; Yellow-bellied Flycatcher; Boreal Chickadee; Sedge Wren; Connecticut Warbler; Swamp, Clay-colored, White-throated, and Le Conte's Sparrows

Best times to bird: April-June; December-January

Don't miss: Meadowlands turnoff from Highway 53

General information:

It would be fascinating if the name of this birding locale had some deep significance—it certainly is important enough to Minnesota birders. But alas, these tiny hamlets are little more than former railway stations. Saxe (original spelling) was named for Solomon Saxe, an Eveleth landowner, and Zim was named for a man named Zimmerman, who ran a nearby logging camp. Stations like Sax, Zim, Kelsey, and others were railway loading points, established to carry logs to Duluth mills, but were abandoned when the timber supply became exhausted.

The Le Conte's Sparrow is an uncommon but welcome sight to Minnesota birders. These birds prefer marsh edges and brushy borders of wet meadows. Though uncommon, they can be found in all but the extreme northeast.
BILL MARCHEL

Sax-Zim Bog

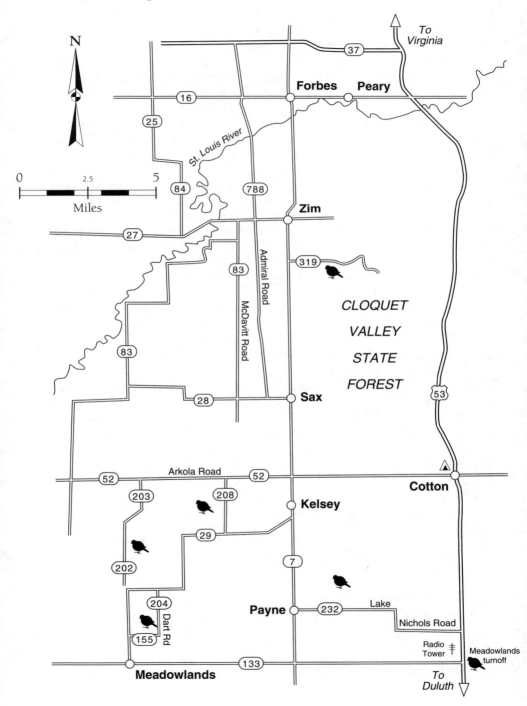

Birding information:

For the serious Minnesota birder, few places may be as familiar as the **Sax-Zim** forests and bogs, primarily because the birds regularly found here are just plain tough to find without traveling to points scattered much farther away. The Great Gray Owl, for example, occurs here year-round, as does the Ruffed Grouse, Sharp-tailed Grouse, and Boreal Chickadee. Spring brings Sandhill Cranes, while summer hosts Yellow-bellied Flycatchers and Connecticut Warblers. Most winters bring Pine Grosbeaks and White-winged Crossbills.

The bogs, aspen stands, and meadows of Sax-Zim lie about 35 miles northeast of Duluth, just west of U.S. Highway 53. From the Twin Cities, take I-35 to the Cloquet exit (135 miles), then follow Highway 33 north through Cloquet, to Highway 53 north. From Duluth follow Highway 53 north. Any of the roads through the Sax-Zim area can produce discoveries, but a few are reliable for their specialties. A good starting place is the **Highway 53 Meadowlands turnoff** at County Road 133 (there is a posted sign), or at the town of Cotton. The most likely place to spot Great Gray Owls, Boreal Chickadees, and Connecticut Warblers is the short stretch of **County Roads 202 and 203** just south of County Road 52. Just south of these is the Sharp-tailed Grouse lek off **Dart Road**; another lies just west of **County Road 208**. Also worth checking (east of County Road 7) are **County Road 319** and **County Road 232** (Lake Nichols Road) and the roads that crisscross the bog areas between them. County 319, 1.5 miles east of County 7, is a proven place to listen for Yellow Rails from early May to about mid-June.

In addition to the species mentioned, you may also find (in winter) Northern Goshawk, Snowy Owl, Northern Hawk-Owl, Black-backed Woodpecker, and Northern Shrike; (in spring and early summer) Upland Sandpiper, Black-billed Cuckoo, Black-billed Magpie, Olive-sided and Alder Flycatcher, Winter Wren, Mourning Warbler, and Le Conte's Sparrow.

One final note: The DNR Area Wildlife Office property, just north of the Sax-Zim bog on Highway 37, commonly has Pine Warblers singing in the pines around the buildings. Red Crossbills occasionally nest here also. The office is located 0.25 mile west of Highway 53.

Additional help:

Minnesota Highway Map location: N-8

Hazards: Mosquitos, black flies, icy roads, muddy roads, snowstorms

Nearest food, lodging, gas: Cotton, Eveleth (north on Highway 53)

Camping: Cotton

Land ownership: State of Minnesota, private

Additional information: Mike Hendrickson, Duluth (218) 726-0840; DNR Area Wildlife Office (just north of the bog on Highway 37), (218) 749-7748

Recommended length of stay: 1 day

8. Bear Lake and vicinity _____

Habitats: Tamarack and black spruce bog, cedar swamp, aspen forest

Key birds: Osprey; Bald Eagle; Northern Goshawk; Spruce Grouse; Black-backed Woodpecker; Olive-sided Flycatcher; Swainson's Thrush; Veery; Yellow-rumped, Chestnut-sided, and Mourning Warblers

Best times to bird: April-June; December-January

Don't miss: Small forest trails, Scenic State Park

General information:

North of the Minnesota cities of Hibbing and Grand Rapids, about 25 miles north of the small town of Nashwauk, lies a remote forested region whose bogs, streams, and rivers drain northward to the Rainy River, and eventually to Hudson Bay. First named as "forks" of the Rainy River, the watersheds of the Big Fork and Little Fork rivers empty almost 4,000 square miles of forested country, bordered on the south and east by an ancient granite mountain range called the Giant's Ridge.

The heart of this area was never as heavily populated by Native Americans as the lake country farther south and west, but the Sioux did live here until forced west by the Ojibway, and fur trappers found the region a paradise of valuable beaver pelts. One reason the area may have been somewhat overlooked was the lack of a major travel route—river or trail—bisecting it. Thus it remained more or less "the end of the road," much as it exists in the minds of many Minnesotans today.

Large timber firms turned their attention here during the late 1800s and early 1900s, harvesting some of the state's last large stands of red and white pine. A few hearty souls tried to farm the clearings left by the loggers, but soon found the soils too thin to support crops. Today, logging of second-growth timber, primarily aspen, continues to be the major economic activity in the area.

Birding information:

Bordered on the west by the Chippewa National Forest, and on the east by the Superior National Forest, the country around the tiny **Bear Lake Campground** features no outstanding natural feature, unless you consider thousands of square miles of remote country outstanding in itself. To reach Bear Lake, take U.S. Highway 169 northeast 21 miles from Grand Rapids (173 miles north of the Twin Cities), or southeast 19 miles from Hibbing (76 miles from Duluth), to the town of Nashwauk; then travel north on Highway 65 about 25 miles to County Road 52, go west about 1.3 miles, and turn left on County 552 to the campground. Although not well known among Minnesota birders, the area deserves attention; there are enough backcountry roads here to keep a birder busy for a lifetime. Literally scores of unmarked forest trails radiate from the campground itself, penetrating through and around the spruce bogs,

Bear Lake and vicinity

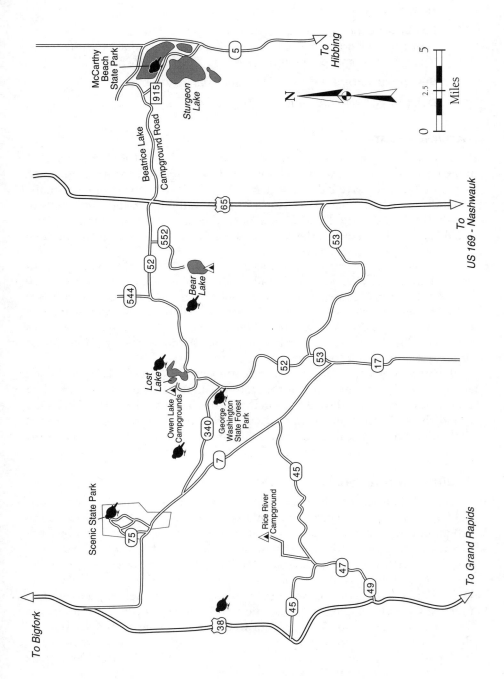

cedar swamps, and aspen islands. Because many of the tiny area lakes offer fishing access, many of the winding forest roads are "moderately maintained."

Nesting birds in this area include Common Loon; American Bittern; American Black Duck; Hooded Merganser; Turkey Vulture; Northern Goshawk; Cooper's, Sharp-shinned, and Broad-winged Hawk; Bald Eagle; Osprey; Spruce and Ruffed Grouse; Virginia Rail; American Woodcock; Spotted Sandpiper; Black-billed Cuckoo; Long-eared, Great Gray, and Northern Saw-whet Owl; Whip-poor-will; Pileated and Black-backed Woodpecker; Yellow-bellied Sapsucker; Yellow-bellied, Alder, Least, and Olive-sided Flycatchers; Gray Jay; Common Raven; Boreal Chickadee; Red-breasted Nuthatch; Winter, Marsh, and Sedge Wren; Wood and Swainson's Thrushes; Veery; Golden- and Ruby-crowned Kinglet; Red-eyed, Solitary, and Philadelphia Vireos; twenty-three warbler species including abundant Yellow-rumped, Chestnut-sided, and Mourning Warblers; Purple Finch; and Grasshopper, Le Conte's, Vesper, Clay-colored, White-throated, Lincoln's, and Swamp Sparrows.

A couple of key stopping—or starting—points are **Bear Lake Campground, Lost Lake Campground**, and **Owen Lake Campground**, all off County Road 52 (look for the signs). Bear Lake offers the most trails. A good-sized piece of country just north of Bear Lake is accessible from nearby **County Road 544**, abut 3.3 miles west of Highway 65. For the less adventurous, or if roads are in poor condition, **McCarthy Beach State Park** offers good hiking trails which course the edge of a glacial moraine. To reach the park head east on the Beatrice Lake Campground Road (off State Highway 65 just south of the County 52 intersection) to Forest Road 915. Farther west, **George Washington State Forest Park** (continue past the Bear Lake turnoff on County Road 52, then travel west about 0.125 mile on County Road 340) offers a good stopover, and **Scenic State Park** (continue on County 340 and turn right on County Road 7 for 2 miles) features virgin pine forests around Coon and Sandwick lakes and dependable habitat for Spruce Grouse and Three-toed Woodpeckers. **State Highway 38**, between here and Grand Rapids, is a beautiful roadway cut through classic Minnesota lake country, and a perfect place to spot a goshawk, Bald Eagle, or Osprey.

Additional help:

Minnesota Highway Map location: J-7

Hazards: Mosquitos, black flies, muddy roads

Nearest food, lodging, gas: Bigfork, Nashwauk

Camping: Bear Lake, Lost Lake, Owen Lake, Rice River Campground, McCarthy Beach State Park, Scenic State Park

Land ownership: State of Minnesota, private

Additional information: Scenic State Park manager, (218) 743-3362; McCarthy Beach Park manager, (218) 254-2411; Minnesota DNR, (612) 296-6157

Recommended length of stay: 2 days

9. Waskish and vicinity

Habitats: Lakeshore, open water, tamarack and black spruce bog, sedge marsh, aspen islands

Key birds: Hooded Merganser; Sharp-tailed Grouse; Yellow Rail; Snowy Owl (winter); Great Gray and Saw-whet Owls; Black-backed Woodpecker; Olive-sided and Yellow-bellied Flycatchers; Hermit Thrush; Connecticut, Mourning, and Nashville Warblers; Le Conte's and Nelson's Sharp-tailed Sparrows

Best times to bird: April-June; October-November; December-January

Don't miss: First view of Upper Red Lake from Highway 72 bridge

General information:

The tiny hamlet of Waskish (on State Highway 72 northwest of Grand Rapids and northeast of Bemidji) borders the east side of Upper Red Lake and is notable only because of the lack of landmarks on this stretch of highway. "Blink and you miss it," certainly applies here; but if you miss Waskish, you also miss Red Lake, and that would be unfortunate. There remains some question whether Red Lake was named for its iron-stained feeder creeks, Indian wars, or the magnificent crimson sunsets that reflect off its waters; most likely

Typical spruce bog habitat like that seen across the western side of the boreal region north and east of Waskish.

Waskish and vicinity

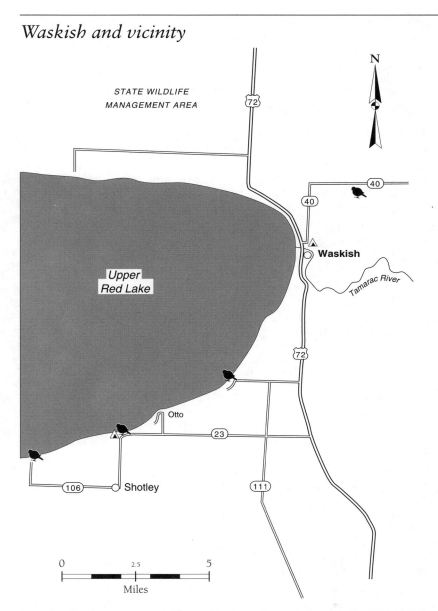

it is the final reason, and if you happen through Waskish around sunset and look to the west across this massive lake, you will see why.

Waskish itself is taken from the Ojibway "Wawashkeshi," or white-tailed deer, a common sight in this region. But there is more to see on the edges of the Red Lake Indian Reservation. Red Lake easily surpasses all other Minnesota lakes in size; it is the largest body of water lying entirely within the state. This shallow lake, like Lake of the Woods, is a remnant of the vast Glacial Lake Agassiz. The portions of the former lake bottom no longer covered with water make up what is commonly referred to as the "big bog," an area stretching north into Lake of the Woods County and east far into Koochiching County.

Birding information:

To reach Waskish (about 270 miles north of the Twin Cities) from Grand Rapids: follow U.S. Highway 2 for 13 miles west to Deer River, turn north on State Highway 46, and drive 47 miles north to Northome. Then turn left on U.S. Highway 71, drive south 3 miles to State Highway 1, and turn right. Head west 5 miles to Shooks, and turn right (north) on State Highway 72. From Bemidji: go northeast on U.S. Highway 71 for 25 miles to Blackduck, then turn left (north) on U.S. Highway 72. You don't need to travel far from **Waskish** to view **Upper Red Lake**; a quick scan of the lake from various vantage points is worthwhile, as this large lake attracts loons, scoters, and other sea ducks. Uncommon gulls such as Herring and Ring-billed frequent the lake. Wild rice paddies at the shoreline often attract migrating Tundra Swans and a variety of dabbling ducks, and the fish-rich waters attract pelicans and cormorants.

Check the lake shorelines at the ends of **County Road 111** and **County Road 23** (about 3 and 5 miles south of Waskish on Highway 72, respectively) as well as the boat access off **County Road 106** west of Shotley (Shotley is about 8 miles west of Highway 72 on County 23) for waterfowl, gulls, and shorebirds which may use the sand beaches and sandbars.

In addition, check the road on the north side of Waskish (not numbered, but the one road to the left about 4 miles north of Washkish on Highway 72) which runs west into the wildlife management area. Besides being a hotspot for Sharp-tailed Grouse, this road terminates at the lakeshore, offering another view of the broad waters of Upper Red Lake.

By turning east out of Waskish on **County Road 40** you can transect the extensive spruce and tamarack bogs and aspen islands of the "big bog" all the way to the town of Bigfork. If you aim to experience all that Minnesota has to offer, a view of the extensive and beautiful bogland is imperative; you can also view the bog by traveling north from Waskish on State Highway 72, a road that is dependable year-round (sans blizzards and November ice storms).

Additional help:

Minnesota Highway Map location: G-5

Hazards: Muddy roads, ice storms, blizzards

Nearest food, lodging, gas: Kelliher, Baudette

Camping: Waskish, Shotley (both low quality)

Land ownership: State of Minnesota, private, Red Lake Indian Band

Additional information: Minnesota DNR, (612) 296-6157

Recommended length of stay: 1 day

10. Beltrami Island Forest and vicinity ──────────

Habitats: Tamarack and black spruce bog, sedge marsh, aspen islands, balsam fir stands, jack pine stands, mixed deciduous forest

Key birds: Turkey Vulture, Spruce Grouse, Ruffed Grouse, Snowy Owl (winter), Great Gray Owl, Black-backed Woodpecker, Yellow-bellied Flycatcher, Gray Jay, Black-billed Magpie, Common Raven, Sedge Wren, Swamp Sparrow, Snow Bunting (winter)

Best times to bird: April-June; late October-November; December-January

Don't miss: County Road 1 turnoff from Highway 72 to explore area roads

General information:

There are no islands in the country north of Red Lake, primarily because there are no lakes. However, when Glacial Lake Agassiz covered this region of the state, it contained one island between Red Lake and Lake of the Woods. Today the island stands as a forested land mass raised slightly above the bogs and peatlands of these portions of Lake of the Woods and Roseau counties. Beltrami Island State Forest takes its name from the Italian explorer Giacomo Beltrami, who first entered the region west of here as a member of the Major Stephen Long expedition of 1823.

Beltrami continued to explore the region to the south, from Lower Red Lake to the upper Mississippi watershed, tracing the Red Lake River and searching out and following the Mississippi River to its entry into Leech Lake. He met and received the assistance of many regional Native Americans during his independent travels, and published a narrative of his discoveries in 1824. Beltrami Island, as this unique land mass was later named, rests 130 feet above the level of Red Lake. At one point in the life of Lake Agassiz, Beltrami Island encompassed more than 1,100 square miles.

Birding information:

As you travel the "forever straight" **State Highway 72** north from Waskish, you bisect some of the wildest land Minnesota has to offer, outside Voyageur's National Park and the Boundary Waters Canoe Area. Perhaps it is the lack of traffic and few highway openings in this bogland that make this road a magnet for wildlife. Beaver inhabit the wet ditches. Moose, timber wolves, deer, mink, bobcat, and fox all reside here; you may see any of them along this stretch of highway, particularly in early morning and evening hours. Great Gray Owl are common along this road (though not always visible), as are Northern Goshawk, Sharp-tailed and Ruffed Grouse, Common Raven, Black-billed Magpie, and Gray Jays; the best time to see these may be late fall when the foliage has dropped. Northern Hawk-Owl, Snowy Owl, and Snow Bunting are winter regulars.

Beltrami Island Forest and vicinity

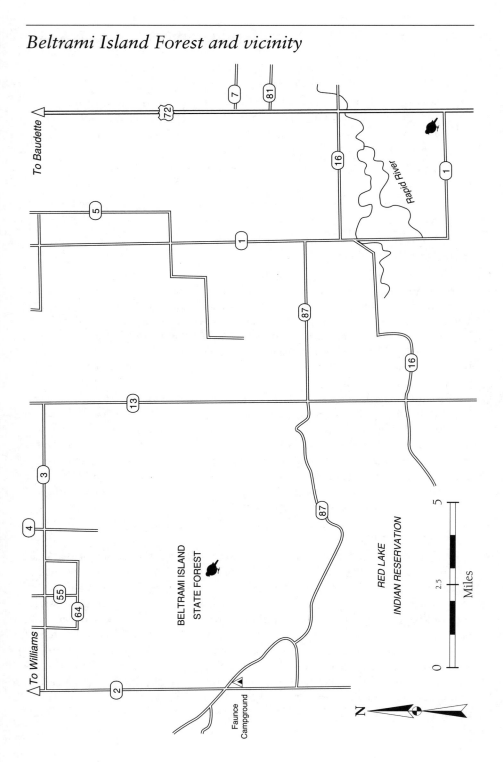

To Baudette

To Williams

Rapid River

BELTRAMI ISLAND
STATE FOREST

RED LAKE
INDIAN RESERVATION

Faunce
Campground

72 7 81 16 1 5 87 16 13 3 4 55 64 2

N

0   2.5   5
Miles

Most of the land supports tamarack and black spruce bog, sedge meadow, willow, and alder brush mixed with aspen. As you penetrate farther into Lake of the Woods County and closer to the town of Baudette, hayfields appear, mixed with peatland cleared to support crops of oats, corn, flax, and wheat. Check sedge meadows for Nelson's Sharp-tailed and Le Conte's Sparrows and Yellow Rails. Highway 72 is the quickest route to Lake of the Woods, but you may want to make a detour on **County Road 1** and angle up to County Road 87 to traverse the roads and trails of **Beltrami Island State Forest** with its stands of jack pine, balsam fir, aspen, and white cedar swamps as well as spruce bogs. All of the better roads are included in this map, but you may find other trails worth exploring.

This is Spruce Grouse country; the best time to see them is the first hour of daylight, picking gravel on these forest roads. Barred and Northern Saw-whet Owls are found here. Check the brushy boglands for Olive-sided, Yellow-bellied, and Alder Flycatchers and Palm Warblers. Other possibilities include Winter and Sedge Wrens; and Golden-winged, Cape May, Pine, Connecticut, Mourning, and Canada Warblers. Check pines specifically for kinglets, Boreal Chickadees, crossbills, and Evening Grosbeaks. As you move farther west, the forest composition changes to mixed deciduous. Look here for Black-billed Cuckoos, Eastern Towhees, and Philadelphia, Yellow-throated, and Warbling Vireos.

Additional help:

Minnesota Highway Map location: F,G-4

Hazards: Muddy roads, ice storms, blizzards, mosquitos, black flies

Nearest food, lodging, gas: Baudette

Camping: Faunce Campground (picnic sites but no running water)

Land ownership: State of Minnesota, private

Additional information: Area forestry office, (218) 634-2172

Recommended length of stay: 1 day

11. Lake of the Woods and vicinity ─────────

Habitats: Lakeshore, aspen forest, balsam fir stands, hay fields, brushland, mixed deciduous forest

Key birds: Double-crested Cormorant, American White Pelican, Common Goldeneye, Piping Plover, Caspian Tern, Common Tern, Black Tern

Best times to bird: April-June; October-November

Don't miss: Rocky Point; Pine, Currys, Sable islands (by boat)

General information:

We refer to most of Minnesota's lakes in acres, but reference to a body as large as Lake of the Woods must be made in miles. This lasting vestige of Glacial Lake Agassiz spans more than 2,000 square miles. The lake receives its name for its many wooded islands; some have estimated as many as fourteen thousand charted islands, lying primarily in the Canadian portion of the lake. The name was passed to the French by the native Crees, who inhabited the lake's north side, and the explorer Verendrye translated their words as "Lac des Bois" (Lake of the Woods) on the first maps.

A natural route for the early fur traders, Lake of the Woods was connected to Montreal by the Rainy River, Pigeon River, and St. Lawrence Seaway, and

Lake of the Woods is special for many reasons, including its nesting colonies of American White Pelicans and Double-crested Cormorants.

Lake of the Woods and vicinity

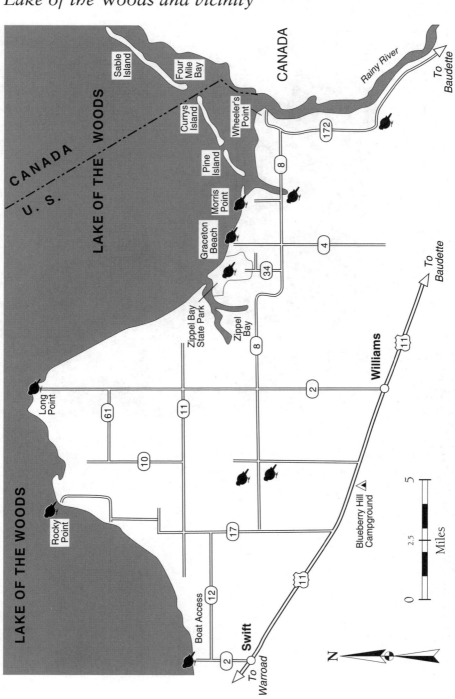

The Great Gray Owl is a large and elusive nesting bird usually found in the northern boreal region, although winter movement sometimes results in birds showing up as far south as the Twin Cities. Clearcut edges and remote roadways in spruce bogs are likely places to spot them. BILL MARCHEL

to Hudson Bay and the rich fur country to the northwest by its outlet, the Winnipeg River. Because the English controlled the northern route, all French trade returning from the northwest had to cross this lake. Verendrye, along with fifty men, established Fort St. Charles in 1732 at the top of Minnesota's Northwest Angle, which today is the northernmost point in the continental United States. From here Verendrye supervised exploration as far west as the Rocky Mountains.

Lumber fueled the early economy of this area. The great fire of 1910, which killed forty-three people, also opened up lands and enriched the soil with ash for farming. During the following decade, a settlement boom saw immigrants claim nearly every section of land in the county, much of which was too wet for agriculture. Funded by state loans, Lake of the Woods County undertook a ditching plan, but when struggling settlers' taxes became delinquent en masse, the county defaulted on its loan and had to forfeit thousands of acres to the state. As a result, more than half of the county's 840,000 acres are today state owned.

Birding information:

Northern Lake of the Woods County (some 320 miles north of the Twin Cities) may be one of the state's most exciting birding areas, not because it offers the most unusual or largest number of species, though it has its specialties. Rather, this area is enchanting for its remote character, decent roads, and spectacular lake vistas. This map section deals with birding sites west and northwest of the town of Baudette, north of Highway 11. To reach the lake itself, take Highway 11 west from downtown Baudette. Just outside of town you'll see the turnoff for State Highway 172. Turn right and drive about 12 miles to reach Wheeler's Point.

Like most of Minnesota, spring birding here is best in the forests and field margins where the you can count the songs of bog, brushland, and woodland species by the scores. However, summer and fall offer special birding opportunities on and around the lake.

In early spring, check the hayfields and fallow fields along **State Highway 172**, between Baudette and the lake, and along **County Road 8** running west off Highway 172, for shorebirds, geese, and swans. In wet years, waterfowl (including many species of ducks) and shorebirds may concentrate around temporary ponds in the fields. Check here in fall for the above species, as well as Sandhill Cranes.

In May and June, the forests of **Zippel Bay State Park** (take County 8 west about 6 miles from the intersection of Highway 172 and turn north on County Road 34), and the aspen forests between the town of Williams (16 miles west of Baudette on Highway 11) and the lake can be good places to look for many of the species mentioned in the previous section (for Beltrami Island State Forest). Be alert for Great Gray Owls, which are common here, especially during early spring and fall when trees are bare of leaves. The lake shoreline and sandbars around Zippel Bay also provide good shorebird habitat during spring and early fall migrations.

In summer, Lake of the Woods itself offers interesting birding, and the best way to enjoy it is from a boat. Four Mile Bay, protected by the sandbar **Pine, Currys,** and **Sable islands,** can be accessed from either **Wheeler's Point** or **Morris Point;** at last count at least a dozen resorts here offered boat and motor rentals. The large, shallow bay (the mouth of the Rainy River) is a good place to see Osprey and Bald Eagle, especially on the Canadian side. Also look for Common Loon; Herring, Ring-billed, and Franklin's Gulls; and Black, Common, and Caspian Terns. If you prefer a landbound view of the bay, try the docks of Trail's End Resort at the end of Wheeler's Point.

For a quicker access to the islands, depart from Morris Point Resort, just a short jaunt by water from Pine Island. Weather comes up fast on the lake, and strong winds from the northwest or west can be notoriously dangerous, but you can always duck behind the islands if necessary. Cruise the lake-side shoreline of Pine and Currys islands and watch for the state's endangered Piping Plover, easy to spot on the open sand beaches (be careful not to disturb this nesting species).

While you're on the lake, keep an eye out for the large feeding flocks of American White Pelicans and Double-crested Cormorants which frequent this shoreline. The best place to observe them is from the northernmost point of Currys Island (even better from Sable Island, but check with the resort to find out if the Canadians are enforcing immigration laws aimed at U.S. anglers or you may find yourself entering Canada illegally). The pelicans and cormorants have a large nesting colony on one of the tiny Three Sisters Islands about 14 nautical miles due north of here.

In fall, enormous rafts of Lesser Scaup build up on the open waters of the lake, staying as late as November 1, in some years, but usually departing earlier. Watching these flocks in the tens of thousands mill about over the endless lake horizon on an October morning is a sight to behold. Other common Minnesota waterfowl use the lake as a migratory feeding and resting spot, including Tundra Swan; unusual species such as Red-throated Loon and scoters can be spotted from time to time. The best lake viewing is from **Graceton Beach** (take County 4 north from County 8 to its end), **Long Point** (take County 2 north from Highway 11 to its end), **Rocky Point** (take County 17 north from Highway 11 to its end), and the boat access north of Swift (take County 2 north from Highway 11 to its end).

Additional help:

Minnesota Highway Map location: G-3

Hazards: Northwest winds, poison ivy

Nearest food, lodging, gas: Baudette, Wheeler's Point, Morris Point, Zippel Bay Resort

Camping: Blueberry Hill Campground, Wheeler's Point, Morris Point

Land ownership: State of Minnesota, private

Additional information: Area forestry office, (218) 634-2172; Zippel Bay State Park; (218) 783-6252

Recommended length of stay: 2 days

12. Bemidji and vicinity

Habitats: Lakeshore, bog, mixed deciduous forest, hay fields, wetland, brushland

Key birds: Common Loon, Red-necked Grebe, Redhead, Bald Eagle, Osprey, Black Tern, Black-backed Woodpecker, Yellow-throated Vireo

Best times to bird: April-June

Don't miss: Mississippi River Outlet, Three Island County Park

General information:

If you have trouble tracing the Mississippi River to its source in northern Minnesota, you are not alone. The "Father of Waters" winds and wends its way through bogs, deep forests, and lakes—and even flows north in some sections. No wonder early explorers bent on discovering the river's source were baffled. Its myriad tiny tributaries create a veined web through nearly impenetrable bogs, and lie in close proximity to a major watershed which drains north to Hudson Bay.

However, the difficulties in finding the river's source did not dampen the obsessions of those who pursued it. In 1700, the Frenchman Du Charleville reached little farther than the Twin Cities' St. Anthony Falls, declaring the river's source to be near the Arctic Ocean. Lieutenant Zebulon Pike, in 1805, declared Cass Lake the source, as did Lewis Cass in 1820. Giacomo Beltrami, in 1823, settled on Lake Julia as the source. Unfortunately, he missed the discovery narrowly, as he wrote that a western tributary stream of the Mississippi originated in Elk Lake (Lake Itasca).

Henry Rowe Schoolcraft solved the puzzle in 1832, setting out from Lake Bemidji by canoe, but not up the Mississippi, which does feed this lake. Rather, he followed what is now called the Schoolcraft River, south of Bemidji. Schoolcraft recorded the name for Lake Bemidji using the old Ojibway name "Pamitchi Gumaug," meaning to "cross or transect," referring to the Mississippi River's obvious entry and exit across the center of this lake. Nicollet mapped the lake as Pemidji a few years later.

Several lakes east and southeast of Bemidji were noted on the earliest maps of the region because of their sheer size, including Winnibigoshish, Cass, Bowstring, and Leech. These large bodies of water were important to early travel and settlement. Today they lie within the Chippewa National Forest, an area that includes some 700 lakes and more than 900 miles of streams and rivers, including the fledgling Mississippi.

Birding information:

Situated at the northern fringe of the glaciated lake country with which Minnesota is so often associated, the Bemidji area (214 miles north of the Twin Cities) is representative of so many similar vacation areas in the state such as Brainerd, Walker, Alexandria, and others. All feature well-developed

Bemidji and vicinity

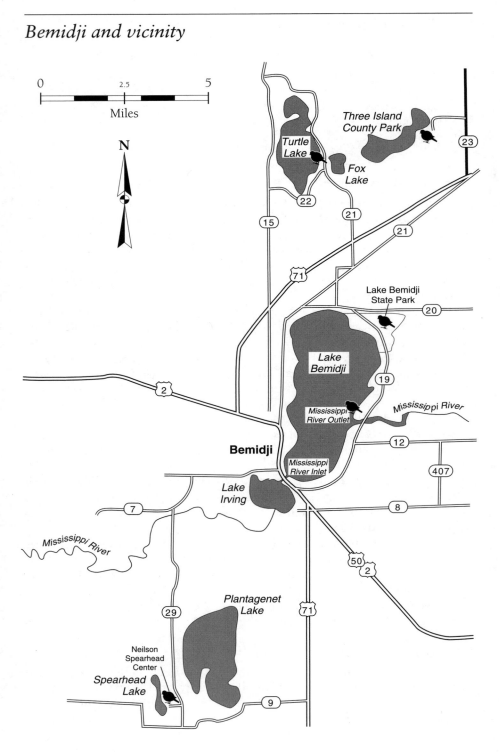

0   2.5   5
Miles

N

Three Island
County Park

Turtle
Lake

Fox
Lake

23

22

21

15

21

71

Lake Bemidji
State Park

20

Lake
Bemidji

19

2

Mississippi River

Mississippi
River Outlet

Bemidji

Mississippi
River Inlet

12

407

Lake
Irving

8

7

50
2

Mississippi River

Plantagenet
Lake

29

71

Neilson
Spearhead
Center

Spearhead
Lake

9

road systems, beautiful lakes, and plentiful services, but Bemidji and vicinity also offers birds. To reach Bemidji, take U.S. Highway 10 west from the Twin Cities to Little Falls, then take U.S. Highway 371 north.

The Bemidji area marks the western side of the largest nesting concentration of Bald Eagles in the lower 48 states—the Chippewa National Forest and vicinity, which has hosted as many as 189 breeding pairs in recent years. The best eagle viewing is on the larger lakes: Leech, Winnibigoshish, Cass, and Bowstring, the Mississippi River between Cass and Bowstring lakes, and the Leech Lake and Winnie Dams. Osprey have become increasingly common in recent years and a number of the area's lakes are home to nesting Red-necked Grebes.

Bemidji lies in a transition zone where northern boreal forest yields more and more to deciduous tree species, and finally, farther west, to prairie; the bird species found here reflect those habitat changes. Nesting species here include Redhead Duck, Mourning Dove (notable because they are absent in the northeast), Black Tern, Sandhill Crane, Upland Sandpiper, Yellow Rail, Yellow-throated and Warbling Vireos, Eastern Towhee, and Pine Warbler.

In spring and fall, start by checking the **Mississippi River inlet and outlet** of **Lake Bemidji** for waterfowl, loons, grebes, terns, and gulls. The inlet can be viewed from the public boat access at the southeastern edge of the lake. If you're unfamiliar with the town, the easiest way to reach the outlet is to take Main Street south from downtown, which turns into Highway 50. Follow

The recreational trail bridge at the outlet of Lake Bemidji provides a good look at the lake's shallows and possibly Red-necked Grebes.

Highway 50 to County 8 east, then proceed to County Road 407 and north to County Road 12, then west again to County 19 and right to the river bridge. Park at the edge of the road on the south side of the bridge. A trail on the south side of the river leads to an old railroad grade, now a hiking trail, which crosses the river as a foot bridge and provides a good overlook of the lake. A spotting scope would be helpful. Walking north or south on the railroad grade could produce some interesting forest birds.

Farther north on County Road 19 is **Lake Bemidji State Park**, another good place to view the lake. A short hike inside the park to the bog boardwalk is worth the effort (about 2 miles round-trip). Besides Common Veery, sapsuckers, and Red-eyed Vireo, you may see such specialties as Boreal Chickadee and Black-backed Woodpecker. Carnivorous pitcher plants and sundews grow here, as well as wild orchids.

North of the park on County Road 21 you'll encounter the Tri-Lakes area, particularly **Turtle Lake**, a nesting area for Common Loon, Red-necked Grebe, and Black Tern. Turtle Lake can also be viewed from its west side along County Road 15. East of here is the almost 2,900-acre **Three Island County Park** (turn north off County 23 about 12 miles north of Bemidji onto County 21, then left at the park sign), where Bald Eagles and Osprey nest, offering good forest trails and camping and picnic sites.

Finally, the **Neilson Spearhead Center**, south of Bemidji on a 460-acre tract surrounding Spearhead Lake (take Highway 71 south about 6 miles to County 9, then west about 3.5 miles and turn north on County 29), is owned and managed by the Mississippi Headwaters Audubon Chapter. The resident caretaker can answer questions about the Bemidji area in general; (218) 759-9335 or (218) 751-4454.

Additional help:

Minnesota Highway Map location: F,G-7,8

Hazards: Poison ivy, biting insects

Nearest food, lodging, gas: Bemidji

Camping: Lake Bemidji State Park, (218) 755-3843

Land ownership: State of Minnesota, private

Additional information: Minnesota Department of Natural Resources, (612) 296-6157; Bemidji Area Information Center, (218) 751-3540

Recommended length of stay: 1 day

13. Itasca State Park and vicinity ─────────

Habitats: Lake; jack pine barrens; spruce and tamarack bog; virgin pine stands; mixed pine, birch, aspen forests

Key birds: Common Loon, Red-necked Grebe, American White Pelican, Bald Eagle, Common Tern, Ruby-throated Hummingbird, Black-backed Woodpecker, Least Flycatcher, Red-breasted Nuthatch, Sedge and Winter Wrens, Hermit Thrush, 15-20 species of breeding warblers, Swamp Sparrow

Best times to bird: April-June; October-November; December-February

Don't miss: Upper Rice Lake, Kabekona Rookery

General information:

The word "Itasca" may sound like it has Native American origins, but it is a contrived composite of the Latin "Veritas Caput," or "true head," as its discoverer Schoolcraft christened it in 1832. Schoolcraft may have the distinction of discovering the source of the 2,500-mile Mississippi River, but Jacob Brower must be credited with conserving this 32,000-acre park. He rallied citizens to establish the park to protect remnant stands of virgin timber and the wildlife within. He served as the park's first commissioner, battling logging interests, politicians, and poachers while personally paying many of the costs associated with these efforts. He negotiated and acquired more than half the park's lands.

The Mississippi is no more than a creek where it leaves the inviting birding forests, bogs, and marshes of Itasca State Park.

Itasca State Park and vicinity
Lake Alice Bog

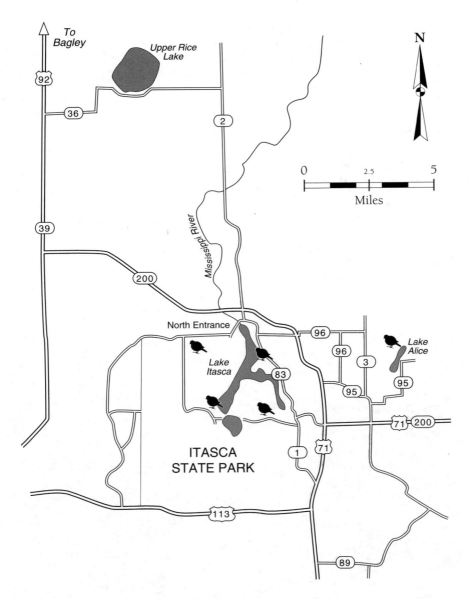

Itasca may be the longest-studied of any birding site in the state. The naturalist Elliot Coues, accompanying the roving Zebulon Pike, visited the area in 1894. Dr. Thomas Roberts (author of *Birds of Minnesota*, 1932) studied birds in the park during the early 1900s. Other ornithologists who have worked in and studied the park include Gustav Swanson, Donald Lewis, Joseph Hickey, John Emlen Jr., S. Charles Kendeigh, David Parmelee, and Dwain Warner, long-time curator of the University of Minnesota's bird collection who taught summer sessions to university students here for many years.

The vast Leech Lake, Cass Lake, and Lake Winnibigoshish, east of Itasca, were traditionally important to Native Americans for their wild rice beds and fisheries as well as their position as flowages of the Mississippi River and its many connecting streams. Many of the names in this central lake country were adapted from the Ojibway, who had already established names for the lakes, points, and islands. The first French maps refer to Leech Lake as "Lac Sangsue," a translation of its native title, which in English means "bloodsucker."

Birding information:

You can reach Itasca State Park from Bemidji by taking Highway 71 south/southwest, or from the Twin Cities by taking U.S. 10 west to Little Falls, then north on U.S. 371 to Walker and west on State Highway 200. From Duluth, take U.S. 2 to Bagley and turn south on State 92. Signs mark your way into the park.

Between Itasca State Park and the town of Bagley (east on County 36 from State 92) lies one of those unique, undeveloped lakes that for some reason attracts a number of interesting birds. **Upper Rice Lake** is not large, but that doesn't seem to bother the Red-necked Grebes that nest here. Western Grebes have also been seen on the lake of late. As you head west toward the lake on County Road 36, you'll pass some nice alder swamps (home to Alder Flycatchers) and mixed conifer and deciduous forest. Northern Goshawks are occasionally seen perched on the dead tree limbs along this road as they watch the openings for Ruffed Grouse and snowshoe hares. Park on either side of the band of trees on the south side of Upper Rice Lake for a good view of the lake. In addition to grebes you're likely to see American White Pelicans, Black Terns, Franklin's Gulls, and Ring-billed Gulls.

Traveling southeast toward Itasca on State Highway 200, the Clearwater County Campground (west side) is a great lunch spot, and in spring offers some relaxing birding right from your picnic table. Although **Itasca State Park** receives more visitors than any other state park, and at times can be downright crowded, don't be discouraged; the park is large enough that the birds don't seem to mind. Evening Grosbeaks nest here in the tops of mature conifers within sight of busy park roads, and Common Loons, Bald Eagles, and Osprey haunt the lakes. Other interesting breeding birds which commonly nest here include Barred Owl; Pileated Woodpecker; Olive-sided, Yellow-bellied, Alder, and Least Flycatchers; Red-breasted Nuthatch; Hermit Thrush; and more than a dozen wood warblers. The Itasca species list totals 211 birds. Though considered rare, Black-backed Woodpeckers have been observed nesting here in recent years.

You can pick up a bird list in the interpretive center (just inside the north entrance from Highway 200) at the headwaters for about $1, and the summer trails map available at the entrance information office is especially helpful.

Itasca State Park and vicinity
Kabekona Rookery/Leech Lake and vicinity

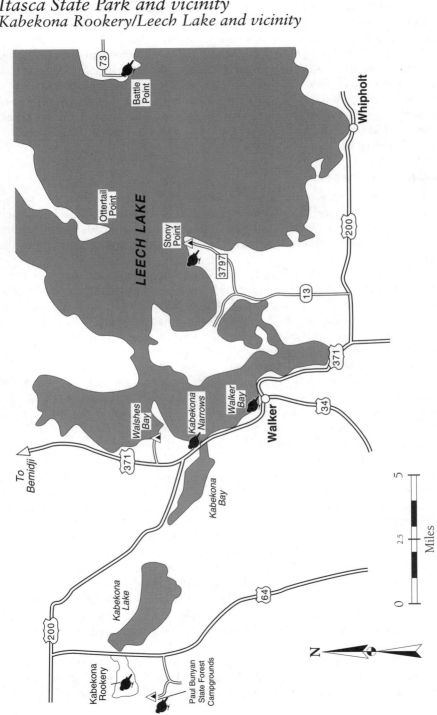

The Kabekona rookery between Itasca State Park and Leech Lake can easily be viewed from the roadway.

The Wilderness Drive loop and its associated trails provide a good glimpse of the park and its habitats. For the winter birder, Rough-legged Hawk, Ruffed Grouse, five types of woodpecker (including Three-toed), both Red and White-winged Crossbills, Evening Grosbeak, Purple Finch, American Tree Sparrow, Northern Shrike, Snow Bunting, Red-breasted Nuthatch, and Brown Creeper are among the possible sightings. Also be sure to check the forest in the vicinity of the University of Minnesota's biological station.

Just east of the state park are a series of bogs long-visited by university ornithology classes. The **Lake Alice** area bogs offer viewing of many of the lowland species described within Itasca—without the tourists.

A comfortable ride east from the bogs brings you to a unique heron rookery, which can be easily viewed without leaving the pavement of State Highway 64 (take Highway 71/200 east to about 3 miles past the town of Kabekona, then turn south on State 64). Situated over a large wetland surrounding Gulch Creek, the **Kabekona Rookery** can be seen with the naked eye, but binoculars are useful and a spotting scope even better. Notice the artificial platforms built to replace trees and branches lost to wind, ice storms, and age. Keep an eye out for Bald Eagles and Osprey, which frequent this area. Just south of the rookery is a trail that leads west off the highway into the **Paul Bunyan State Forest**, the Gulch Lakes campgrounds (five), and myriad forest roads and spurs worth investigating.

Following State Highway 200 east will lead you to Leech Lake and the town of Walker. The first glimpse of Leech comes at the **Kabekona Narrows**; a

Itasca State Park and vicinity
Eagle viewing areas

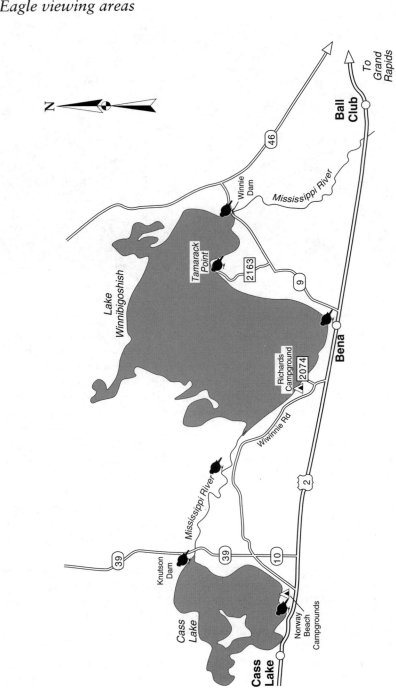

Eagles are often seen hunting along the shorelines of larger lakes near the Chippewa National Forest. This is Leech Lake.

public boat access on the north side offers a welcoming foot bridge which spans the narrow and gives a good view of the large **Walker Bay,** worth scanning for gulls and loons.

While the Itasca area forests feature a mix of boreal and deciduous, those around the southern end of Leech Lake (southern Cass County) exhibit more predominantly deciduous characteristics, and the list of birds opens up accordingly. Species such as Red-shouldered Hawk, Yellow Rail, Great-crested Flycatcher, Wilson's Phalarope, and Eastern Screech-Owl become possibilities here.

Highway 200/371 southbound leaves Walker and Highway 200 heads east below Leech Lake. Take County Road 13 north to reach the expansive vistas of **Stony Point,** one of the best places in the state to view migrating loons and waterfowl in spring or fall. Habitat along roads to the point is dominated by ash, mixed birch, and conifers. The boat launch offers a good view of the lake to the east; you can also go through the campground to the point to get a view of the lake to the north. Another good Leech Lake viewing area lies across the lake to the northeast. A Common Tern colony on Pelican Island can be viewed by boat from Whipholt, on the south shore. **Battle Point** (across the lake, northeast of Stony Point) can be reached by taking Highway 200 east to County Road 8, then proceeding north across the Boy River and turning east on County Road 73.

The points on the north side of Leech Lake offer opportunities to view eagles, especially in late fall and very early spring, as does the Federal Dam area on the northeast side of the lake. Good summer, spring, and fall eagle viewing areas (see map) can be found north of U.S. Highway 2 (west of Grand Rapids, between the towns of Ball Club and Cass Lake) around Cass Lake and **Lake Winnibigoshish.** Check the **Mississippi River** between the two lakes, including the **Knutson Dam** on County Road 39 (northeast corner of Cass Lake); West Winnie Road (which loops off Highway 2 between Bena and Cass Lake); Forest Road 2074 and the Richards Campground, just west of Forest Road 2074; and County Road 9, east of Bena (north from Highway 2), including **Tamarack Point** (Forest Road 2163) and the **Winnie Dam.** Some of the good lake vistas provide viewing for loons and waterfowl in early spring and late fall, including **Norway Beach Campground** on County Road 10 (on the southeast shore of Cass Lake) and the lakeshore in **Bena** itself.

Additional help:

Minnesota Highway Map location: E-8, 9

Hazards: Poison ivy, mosquitos, black flies, deer flies, black bears, icy roads

Nearest food, lodging, gas: Itasca State Park Entrance, Bagley, Walker, Bena

Camping: Itasca State Park, Gulch Lakes Campgrounds, Stony Point Campground, Norway Beach Campground, Richards Campground, City of Bena Campground

Land ownership: State of Minnesota, private

Additional information: Itasca State Park manager, (218) 266-3654; Paul Bunyan Forest/Gulch Lakes Campgrounds, (218) 755-2890; Leech Lake Area Chamber of Commerce, (218) 547-1313; Cass Lake Area Civic & Commerce, (218) 335-6723; Federal Dam Area Recreation Association, (218) 654-3135

Recommended length of stay: 3 days

14. Brainerd and vicinity ──────────────

Habitats: Mixed deciduous forest, lake, bog, pine stands

Key birds: Common Loon; Red-necked Grebe; Red-shouldered Hawk; American Woodcock; Red-headed, Red-bellied, and Pileated Woodpeckers; Yellow-bellied Sapsucker; Alder Flycatcher; Yellow-throated and Warbling Vireos

Best times to bird: April-June; December-February

Don't miss: West end of North Long Lake (Red-necked Grebes)

Brainerd and vicinity

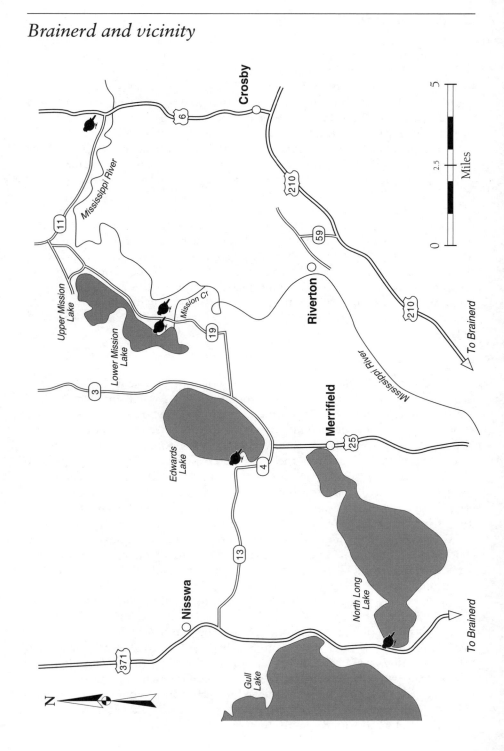

General information:

Early explorers adopted the name Crow Wing from the Ojibway description of an island at the junction of the present Crow Wing and Mississippi rivers. The French translated the name to mean "River of the wing of the Raven," later referred to as Crow Wing. Today it remains the name of the county that hosts some of the most beautiful—and most developed—areas in the state, outside of the Twin Cities area.

The name first suggested for the town of Brainerd was "Ogemaqua," meaning "chief woman," a name the Ojibways had given the beautiful early settler Emma Beaulieu. But Brainerd was chosen, honoring the maiden name of the wife of J. Gregory Smith, then president of the Northern Pacific Railroad Company.

One of the most interesting area names belongs to a road which runs west from U.S. Highway 371 along Gull Lake. The name "Hole In The Day Road" has left more than a few tourists scratching their heads in wonder. The name honors Ojibway Chief Puk-O-Nay-Keshig (Hole-In-The-Day), a brave warrior and later a skilled spokesman for his people. Hole-In-The-Day was greatly respected by all who knew him, and traveled to Washington D.C. many times. In 1868, one year after negotiating the most important treaty in the state's history between the Ojibway and the U.S. government, he was assassinated, at only about forty years of age.

Birding information:

Some say the Brainerd area (125 miles north of the Twin Cities) has too many tourists and lake cabins to offer good birding—a statement disproved by the increased population of nesting Common Loons and Red-shouldered Hawks, and regular occurrence of many worthy species including Ruffed Grouse, American Woodcock, Saw-whet Owl, Whip-poor-wills, all of the state's woodpeckers including Three-toed and Black-backed, all the vireos (except Bell's), all the flycatchers (except Acadian), and warblers including Connecticut, Golden-winged, and Mourning (even a Blue-winged reported in the southern part of Crow Wing County). To reach Brainerd, take U.S. 10 west from the Twin Cities to Little Falls, then U.S. 371 north.

This area not only has birds and beauty, its abundance of paved secondary roads makes for easy, year-round travel and birding through and around the forests, marshes, and lakes. There are enough pine stands in the area to attract decent numbers of winter finches.

Crow Wing County lacks any specific famous birding spots (although the corner of Mille Lacs Lake at Garrison is one of the state's best spots to watch the fall gathering of loons in October), but it does have some sites worth pointing out. First among these is the easily reached west shore of **North Long Lake** (on U.S. Highway 371, about 7 miles north of its intersection with Highway 210 in Brainerd), where cooperative Red-necked Grebes nest in the long, open bullrush beds. They can be easily viewed in spring and summer from the east side of Highway 371. The grebes also nest on nearby **Edwards Lake** (take Highway 210 west from Brainerd, turn north on Highway 25 at the west end

American Woodcock are common spring and fall migrants in about the eastern third of the state and breed most commonly in the same areas. They become especially active during the hours of dusk and dawn.

of town, continue north past Merrifield about 2 miles to the "Y," then go west and north on County 4 less than 1 mile), and can often be viewed from the boat access on the lake's west shore. Upper and Lower Mission lakes are drained by **Mission Creek**, on the east side of the lower lake. The wildlife area surrounding the creek bears investigation (turn right at the above-mentioned "Y" on County 3, then right again on County 19; turn north/left at the "T" on County 19 and go about 1.5 miles).

For the more adventurous, the **Mississippi River** can be boarded by boat or canoe north of Crosby and offers an easy, scenic birding trip down to the take-out point at Riverton. Check with local merchants for river conditions and access information.

Additional help:

Minnesota Highway Map location: G-11

Hazards: Poison ivy, mosquitos, black flies, deer flies

Nearest food, lodging, gas: Brainerd, Nisswa, Crosby

Camping: Gull Lake, North Long Lake, Edwards Lake, Mission Lake

Land ownership: State of Minnesota, private

Additional information: Brainerd Lakes Area Chamber of Commerce, (218) 829-2838; Nisswa Area Chamber of Commerce, (218) 963-2620

Recommended length of stay: 1 day

15. Aitkin/McGregor, Mille Lacs, and vicinity ⎯⎯⎯⎯

Habitats: Marsh, ash and alder swamp, bog, mixed deciduous and conifer forest, hayfields/pasture, wild rice beds, open water

Key birds: Common Loon (fall), Ring-necked Duck, Sharp-tailed Grouse, Yellow Rail, Great Gray Owl, Snowy and Northern Hawk-Owls (winter), Yellow-bellied Flycatcher, Gray Jay, Black-billed Magpie, Boreal Chickadee, Sedge Wren, Connecticut and Mourning Warblers, Nelson's Sharp-tailed and Le Conte's Sparrows

Best times to bird: April-July; October-November

Don't miss: Rice Lake National Wildlife Refuge, McGregor Marsh

General information:

Aitkin has been the scene of commerce for hundreds of years. A fur post on Cedar Lake, just west of the present city, was built by the British in the mid-1700s. The post sat on the main Ojibway route to the Mississippi River. Following the War of 1812, with foreign enterprise banned from American soil, John Jacob Astor's American Fur company purchased trade districts in the newly independent country's interior, including the Cedar Lake trading post. The largest of Astor's districts, the Fon Du Lac, stretched from Grand Portage to Pine County to the Red River. It was placed in the charge of William Aitkin, a naturalized citizen and native of Scotland.

Aitkin based his operation on the shores of Sandy Lake, then a cornerstone of travel connecting the Mississippi River north and south with Lake Superior via the long Savanna Portage along the St. Louis, Savanna, and Prairie rivers. Later, Aitkin operated a Mississippi River post at the site of the town that today bears his name.

Herring Gulls call Minnesota's northern boreal region home, commonly nesting on islands where chicks are safe from landbound predators. In spring and fall, these gulls are common migrants in eastern and central portions of the state.

The Mississippi River, always an important regional travel route, became especially significant in the great logging boom of the late 1800s. The settlement that is now Aitkin became established as a river transportation center where steamboats served and supplied upstream logging camps. Settlers moved into the clearings created by the timber cutters, and steamboats carried the wave of woodsmen and pioneers, eventually as far as the first great rapids upstream: now the city of Grand Rapids.

Mille Lacs Lake covers about 200 square miles in central Minnesota. Its sheer size and unique, almost round, shape make it easily identifiable—even in a satellite photo of the United States shot from hundreds of miles away in space. For more than four thousand years, Native Americans established permanent villages along the shores of Mille Lacs Lake, traveling farther north and west to gather rice and hunt. The name "Mille Lacs" is somewhat a misnomer, stemming from the Ojibway "many lakes," the title they gave the adjoining lake country. The French defined it the "thousand lakes area," thus Mille Lacs.

Birding information:

To reach the Aitkin area from Leech lake, travel west on State Highway 200, then south on U.S. Highway 169; from Grand Rapids, travel south on Highway 169; from the Twin Cities, take Highway 169 north past Mille Lacs Lake. Except for logging, this portion of Minnesota has seen little significant change over the decades. Although agriculture is practiced successfully here, it is diversified and lends itself to wildlife; the forests, bogs, marshes, and meadows here lend themselves to birds.

In addition to being in the transition of the northern deciduous region to the west, thus sharing a large number of that region's birds, the lands between the city of Aitkin and State Highway 200 have the distinction of hosting many bird species only seen much farther north. If you don't have time to travel from the Twin Cities to Waskish or Isabella to see a Great Gray Owl, you might want to set your sights here. Other examples of interesting species include Sharp-tailed Grouse, Black-billed Magpie, and Connecticut and Mourning Warblers, to name a few.

About 90 percent of Minnesota's designated Wildlife Management Areas lie outside the northern boreal region, but they begin to appear more frequently from here to the south and west. One of the best for birding is the **Moose-Willow Wildlife Management Area**, about 5 miles south of Hill City on U.S. Highway 169 (on the east side of the highway). Trumpeter Swans nest on the lakelike pool of the Moose River. You may also find Boreal Chickadee, Great Gray Owl, Yellow-bellied Flycatcher, Connecticut Warbler, and Le Conte's Sparrow. Spring and early summer, when birds are most vocal, are the best times to be here.

Another good area to check is **County Road 18** (drive about 11 miles south of Moose-Willow WMA on Highway 169, then turn east) where you'll find the species mentioned above (no swans). The road here is maintained year-round for residents, which provides the opportunity to check for winter specialties such as Sharp-tailed Grouse, Great Gray and Northern Hawk-Owls, Northern Shrike, Pine Grosbeak, White-winged Crossbill, Common and Hoary Redpolls, and Snow Bunting. Precisely 4.1 miles east of Highway 169 on County 18, an unimposing driveway marked by a dead-end sign heads north for 2.1 miles. This is one of the

Aitkin/McGregor, Mille Lacs and vicinity
Moose-Willow WMA/Aitkin County Road 18

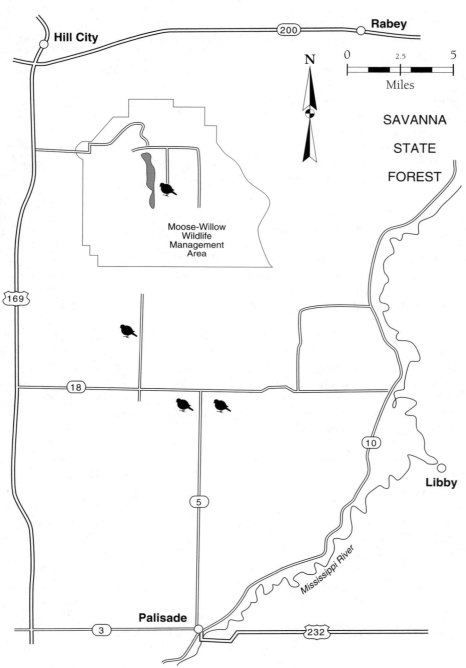

state's more famed birding stretches, often called "Pietz's Road." Its tamarack and balsam fir give it the appearance of a place farther north, and it is a reliable place to see Great Gray Owls, particularly in late winter.

Also along County 18, check the wet meadows on the south side near County Road 5, where Yellow Rails occasionally nest and can be heard calling in early spring, and the open terrain lends itself to sightings of grouse, hawks, and owls, especially in winter.

Farther south, just west of U. S. Highway 169 on County Road 3, you'll find the **Little Willow Wildlife Management Area**, habitat which supports nesting Bald Eagles and Osprey. Stop also on the north side of **Gun Lake**, where Black-billed Magpies have nested in recent years (most easily reached by taking Highway 210 west from U.S. 169, 8 miles north of Aitkin, turning north on Township Road 78, and following the road left around the lake). This is an excellent place to view Sharp-tailed Grouse in spring; look from the roads here at any time, or in the first couple of hours of daylight, when you may be able to see them trading back and forth to the lek which sits north of the lake.

As you travel south on U.S. 169 toward the city of Aitkin, the amount of agricultural land increases. Just north of Aitkin, and north of **County Road 22**, are fields and brushlands where nesting Black-billed Magpies have been recorded.

Also worth a short visit are the forests and wetlands of the Kimberly Wildlife Management Area, or **Kimberly Marsh**, south of State Highway 210; it is a haven for biting insects, but also for birds including nesting ducks, Sandhill Cranes, and Black Terns. Follow the sign for Portage Lake Road (T245) from State Highway 210, and head south past the tamarack bog and deciduous forests. The sign for the marsh is 4.5 miles down the road. You can park here and walk into the area. Follow the old earthen dike that runs along the marsh to the north, a CCC construction project. When leaving the marsh, take a right at the "T" (past a tamarack swamp, some nice stands of red and white pine, and willow and alder swamps) to emerge at Kimberly, where a left or right at the "Y" will lead you back to Highway 210.

McGregor Marsh, just southeast of the city of McGregor (east on Highway 210 from Highway 169, or straight north from the Twin Cities on Highway 65) may not be as widely familiar to the average Minnesotan as Hawk Ridge, but the marsh is more important to visiting birders for one reason: Yellow Rails. This sedge marsh is the most consistent place in the state to see (hear) this elusive bird, though it also has the potential for American Bittern, Sedge and Marsh Wrens, Bobolink, and Nelson's Sharp-tailed and Le Conte's Sparrows. Weekend traffic on State Highway 65 can be distracting, but the rails don't seem to mind. There is good marsh on either side of Highway 65, just south of its intersection with Highway 210, which can be checked by walking the shoulders or along the old railroad grade (now a recreational trail), or by walking County Road 8 or Township 101, which skirt the marsh.

About 5 miles south of the intersection with Highway 210 on Highway 65 is the entrance to **Rice Lake National Wildlife Refuge**, an 18,000-acre preserve of woodlands, wetlands, meadows, and croplands. The refuge boasts a bird list of 219 species, but of primary interest are its Sharp-tailed Grouse, Sandhill Cranes, and abundant fall waterfowl concentrations (as many as 100,000 Ring-necked

Aitkin/McGregor, Mille Lacs and vicinity
McGregor, Aitkin, Rice Lake NWR

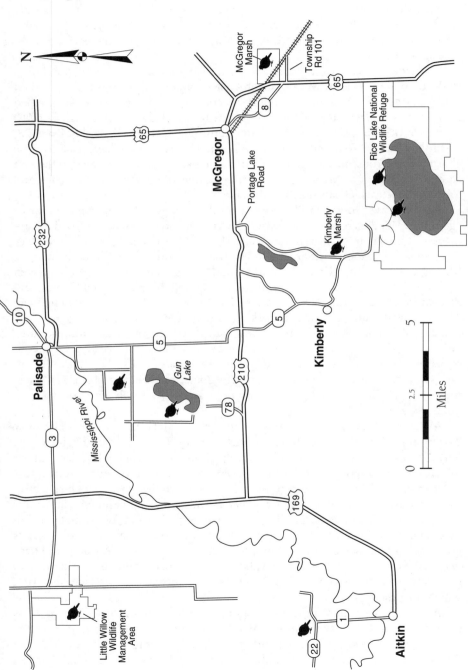

The lake observation deck at Rice Lake National Wildlife Refuge is a good place to view waterfowl and eagles in fall, when tens of thousands of Ring-necked Ducks stage here.

Ducks stage here in fall). Bald Eagles are attracted to the lake in both spring and fall. Check the forests along the main road for Black-billed Cuckoo, Wood Thrush, and Scarlet Tanager. The 0.75-mile Twin Lakes Loop trail on the north side of the lake is worth hiking, as is the 2.75-mile Rice Lake Pool Trail.

About 14 miles south of Aitkin on Highway 169 spread the broad waters of **Mille Lacs Lake.** The lake is large enough to attract birds you might not expect to find in central Minnesota, including Red-throated and Pacific Loons, sea ducks, and gulls as seemingly misplaced as the California Gull, which appeared here in the fall of 1976. Each fall (peaking in mid-October), migrating Common Loons gather here in large numbers to rest and feed. This is one of only four places in the state where Common Tern nest. As a point of trivia, the lake contains the smallest National Wildlife Refuge in the United States, less than 1 acre of land in the form of two rockpile islands far out on the lake: Spirit and Hennepin islands.

Prevailing northwest winds in fall (the best viewing season) make the protected west side of the lake the most likely place to view water birds close to shore. Try a stop along Highway 169 at **Garrison, Wigwam Bay,** or **Vineland Bay,** just south of the Mille Lacs Indian Museum.

You'll find the entrance to **Mille Lacs Kathio State Park** just south of Vineland Bay on County Road 26. This large park, the state's fourth largest with more than 10,000 acres, offers a number of good hiking trails through mixed deciduous woodlands of the raised glacial moraine which borders the lake's south side. Many of the park's trails allow horses, but a number of trails that radiate from the information center, and the campground at Ogechie Lake, are designated hiking only.

Aitkin/McGregor, Mille Lacs and vicinity
Mille Lacs Lakes Area

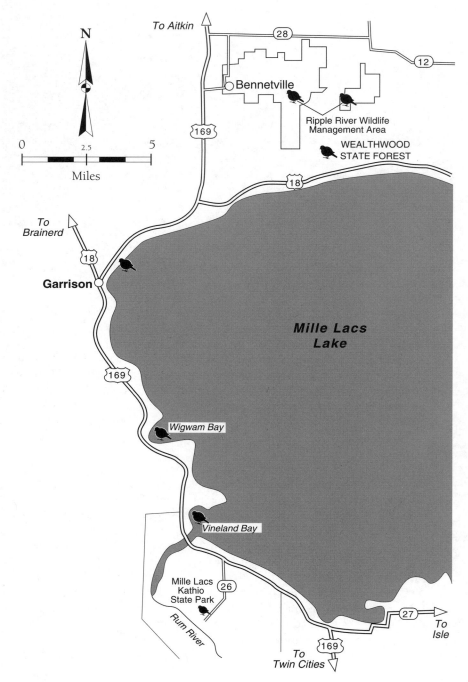

Southern Aitkin County reflects the transition between northern boreal and deciduous woodlands, including associated bird species.

The woodlands along State Highway 18 through the **Wealthwood State Forest** (follow Highway 169 northeast from Garrison and turn right on Highway 18) are worth a spring or early summer drive. In summer this road becomes enclosed by tree canopy and is quite picturesque. Although somewhat busy on weekends, it can be a quiet weekday birding spot. The extensive woodlands north of Highway 18 contain the **Ripple River Wildlife Management Area** (enter by turning east about 4 miles north of the intersection of Highways 169 and 18).

Additional help:

Minnesota Highway Map location: I-11,12

Hazards: Mosquitos, black flies, muddy roads

Nearest food, lodging, gas: Aitkin, McGregor, Garrison, Onamia

Camping: Mille Lacs Kathio State Park, Big "K" Campground (6 miles south of Aitkin on U.S. Highway 169), Bradley's Resort and Campground on Farm Island Lake (8 miles south of Aitkin)

Land ownership: State of Minnesota, U.S. Department of Interior, private

Additional information: DNR Information, (612) 296-6157; Rice Lake National Wildlife Refuge, (218) 768-2402; Aitkin Chamber of Commerce, (218) 927-2316 (Up North info line (800) 526-8342); Mille Lacs Area Tourism Association, (800) 346-7646; Mille Lacs Kathio State Park manager, (612) 532-3523; private campground association, (612) 432-2228

16. Nemadji State Forest ─────────────

Habitats: Aspen forest, spruce/tamarack bog, alder swamp

Key birds: Turkey Vulture, Ruffed Grouse, Alder Flycatcher, Gray Jay, Boreal Chickadee, Sedge Wren, Northern Shrike (winter), Golden-winged Warbler, Savannah Sparrow

Best times to bird: April-June; December-February.

Don't miss: Harlis Forest Road

General information:

When the Voyageurs approached what is now the port of Duluth/Superior after paddling their large canoes down the length of Lake Superior, their Native American guides directed them to the two rivers at the head of the lake. "Nemadji," or "left hand," referred to the first river on the left. The Frenchmen named the river on the right St. Louis.

Today the Nemadji river basin, which flows out of Minnesota and into Wisconsin, is nearly as quiet as it was when named. Like so many areas in this region of the state, the Nemadji State Forest lands met with loggers' hands in the 18th century, but since then little has changed. Once the big timber was

Portions of the northern boreal region's forests, especially along its southern boundary, are commonly broken up by hay fields, occasionally attracting plovers.

Nemadji State Forest

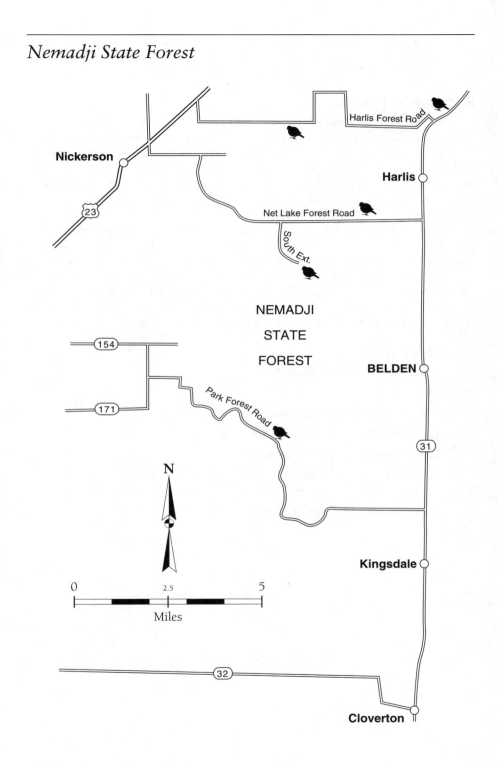

Nickerson

Harlis Forest Road

Harlis

Net Lake Forest Road

South Ext.

NEMADJI

STATE

FOREST

BELDEN

154

171

Park Forest Road

23

31

N

0   2.5   5

Miles

Kingsdale

32

Cloverton

gone, the land held little economic value. Area agriculture consists mostly of hay and pasture land, because soils here are generally too light to support grain crops. This land remains overlooked and little known, even today.

Birding information:

The Nemadji State Forest occupies the northeastern corner of Pine County, and a small portion of southern Carlton County. It is an area with few roads, little settlement, and lots of trees and bogs, but it is accessible enough to birders and worth a visit. This is one of the closest areas to the Twin Cities (certainly the quickest to reach) which holds several of the previously listed boreal species, including Boreal Chickadee, Gray Jay, Great Gray Owl, and winter forest specialties.

If you're traveling north on I-35 from the Twin Cities you can exit at Sturgeon Lake and go east to State Highway 23, then north to reach Nickerson, but for a more relaxed route, take the Askov/Finlayson, State Highway 23 exit. You can cross east to Cloverton on County Road 32 and take County 31 north into the forest, or stay on State Highway 23 heading northeast to Nickerson. Once you're in the forest area, check for birds on **Net Lake Forest Road, Park Forest Road,** and in the bogs along **Harlis Forest Road.**

Additional help:

Minnesota Highway Map location: L-12

Hazards: Mosquitos, black flies, muddy roads

Nearest food, lodging, gas: Sturgeon Lake, Moose Lake

Camping: Gafvert Campground on Pickerel Lake

Land ownership: State of Minnesota

Additional information: DNR information, (612) 296-6157; Area Forestry Office Information (Gafvert Campground info), (218) 485-4474

Recommended length of stay: 1 day

Minnesota
Prairie Region

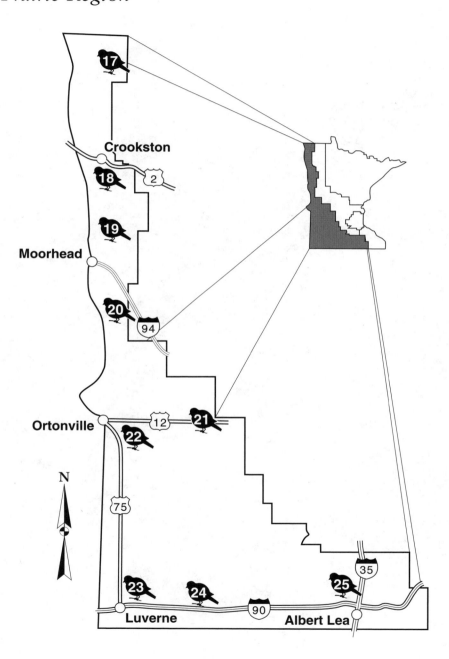

Crookston

Moorhead

Ortonville

N

Luverne

Albert Lea

Greater Prairie-Chickens courting

Prairie Region

Covering the western third of the state, and pocketed within adjoining regions, Minnesota's prairie grasslands easily stand as the state's largest single biome, and the one most changed by man. Prior to European settlement, the prairie region's vast plains supported bison, elk, wolves, and pronghorn antelope. Shallow wetlands formed a mosaic across the northern two-thirds of the prairie, producing ducks and geese in numbers incomprehensible by today's standards, as well as great flocks of Sandhill Cranes, Upland Sandpipers, Long-billed Curlews, Wilson's Phalaropes, Marbled Godwits, and Willets.

Shortly after the last ice age, early Native Americans took up a nomadic existence on the prairie; by about one thousand years ago, some tribes had established permanent settlements on major lakes and watercourses. Earthen lodges with river-bottom timber frames housed the residents of villages, which numbered as many as several hundred people. Their far-reaching trade network is apparent from artifacts which include seashells, copper, obsidian, and flint. In addition to hunting (primarily for buffalo), these natives tended crops, stored food underground, and buried their dead in ceremonial mounds. But tragedy lay around the corner, not only for the native culture, but for the prairie itself.

By the early 1800s, nomadic tribes were trading with Europeans for guns and horses. It became impossible for the permanent villages to defend themselves against attack by their traditional enemies, and the villagers returned to a nomadic lifestyle. Meanwhile, white traders and settlers were demanding more and more of the region's resources, including its abundant game and land. In 1851, a treaty with the Sioux ceded 24 million acres—including all of the southern prairie land in the state today—to the U.S. government. A new wave of settlement began.

By the late 1800s, the plow had already made vast inroads into the virgin prairie soils. A number of Minnesota's birds whose fate was tied to the prairie followed the grasslands' decline, including the now-extirpated McCown's Longspur and Long-billed Curlew, and former nesting birds that today are rare or uncommon visitors, including the Whooping Crane, Burrowing Owl, American Pipit, Sprague's Pipit, and Baird's Sparrow. Today, less than 1 percent of Minnesota's original prairie stands remain!

Tantamount to the rape of the prairie was the wholesale drainage of wetlands by agriculturalists bent on tilling everything in sight. The land was trenched and tiled, streams straightened and ditched, and potholes drained and plowed. As recently as 1967, one ditch project aimed at a small western Minnesota watershed eliminated more than 350 individual wetlands totaling almost 5,000 acres, sparing just 9 acres of publicly owned wetland. An estimated twelve thousand ducks annually were lost in this process, and grebes, wrens, rails, and other birds were also affected. And this in only a 100-square-mile area. Since settlement began, more than 9 million acres of Minnesota wetlands have been drained to accommodate agriculture!

In addition to habitat loss, human persecution wiped out some species. Although their numbers were never great, Trumpeter Swans, which once nested throughout this region, made easy targets for slaughter. Great Egrets, prized for their plumage, suffered similarly at famous Heron Lake and elsewhere, though they are common in the state today. Other species once abundant in Minnesota, including Sandhill Crane, Upland Sandpiper, Marbled Godwit, and even Canada Goose were persecuted to the point of elimination from most traditional breeding grounds.

Fortunately, remnant prairie habitat still supports many of the species originally found in the state including birds, though in much smaller numbers and sometimes frighteningly fragmented populations. Unfortunately, the bison, grizzly bear, antelope, and elk are long gone, and birds like Upland Sandpiper, Marbled Godwit, Greater Prairie-Chicken, and Wilson's Phalarope continue tentative existences.

Although the prairie region is large, its best native habitats remain local and isolated. As bird habitat goes, the remaining undisturbed tracts tend to be wetlands (usually within wildlife management areas) combined with temporarily set-aside croplands, and the few preserves established to protect or restore native grasslands and their associated plant and animal species.

One of the best times to visit prairie grassland habitats is the hours following a soaking rainstorm, when birds that normally hide in dense grass prefer to stand on the open roads and perch on powerlines, signs, and fenceposts, making them highly visible. Caution should also be exercised at these times, as unimproved roads may either contain deep mud, or be firm but as slippery as grease.

17. Karlstad and vicinity

Habitats: Aspen parkland, pasture, brushland, sedge marsh and meadow

Key birds: Northern Harrier, Sharp-tailed Grouse, Sandhill Crane, American Woodcock, Common Snipe, Snowy (winter) and Short-eared Owls, Whip-poor-will, Alder Flycatcher, Black-billed Magpie, Sedge Wren, Bobolink, Lapland Longspur (fall), Snow Bunting (winter), Savannah and Clay-colored Sparrows

Best times to bird: May, June; December, February

Don't miss: Twin Lakes Wildlife Management Area

General information:

With its broad, open lands bordering the Red River of the north, Minnesota's northwest corner has always been easily traversed. This flat valley, with its rich soils, is the former lake bed of the giant Glacial Lake Agassiz, which eventually drained northward, like the Red River itself. The river's connections—downstream to Lake Winnipeg and eventually Hudson Bay, upstream to the

Karlstad and vicinity

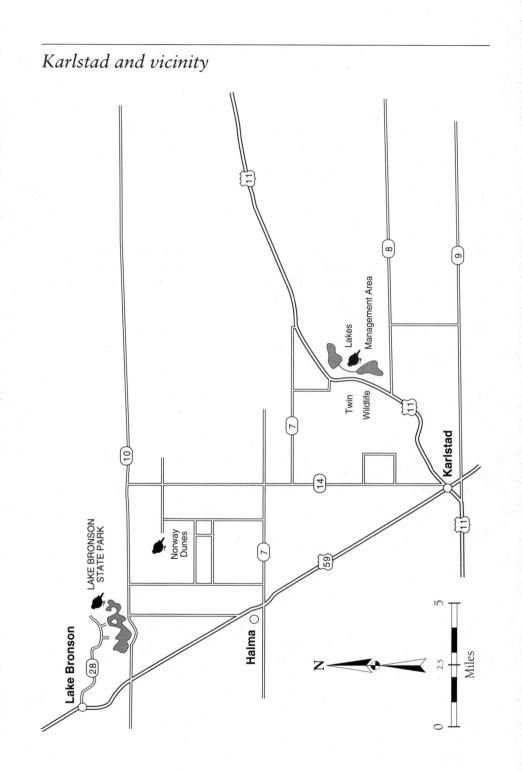

Minnesota and Mississippi rivers and the Gulf of Mexico, and east overland and via Lake of the Woods/Rainy River to Lake Superior and the St. Lawrence River—made it a virtual crossroads for early explorers, and an important link in the transport of valuable furs collected from the north and northwest.

Legend has it that in the mid-fourteenth century, Norsemen (or Vikings) trod the landscape of northwestern Minnesota. Records show that in the 1600s, the French explorers Radisson and Groseilliers discovered the region. When their venture was rejected by their crown, they returned a second time with British backing to claim the land for England.

In 1734, the son of the great explorer Sieur de la Verendrye, Pierre, claimed the Red River valley for France. Under the French, trade via the St. Lawrence River flourished. Following the Seven Year War, when the British took over France's claims in 1763, the northern trade route to Hudson Bay grew busy. By 1811, Americans controlled trade in the region, and the Red River became linked to Mississippi steamboats via the oxcarts of the Pembina Trail. By the 1850s, railroads from the south brought a flood of settlers, who subsequently ditched and cultivated across the Red River valley.

Birding information:

The town of Karlstad lies along the transition zone between aspen parkland and prairie. It holds the distinction of being the birding site in this book most distant from the Twin Cities metropolitan area (about 330 miles northwest). To reach Karlstad from the Twin Cities, take U.S. Highway 10 west to Detroit Lakes, then follow U.S. Highway 59 north to Karlstad. If you're in the Lake of the Woods area, take State Highway 11 west from Baudette. This may seem like the end of the world, but it offers some good birding.

The most interesting area habitat lies east and north of Karlstad, in the aspen parklands and mixed sedge meadows and brushlands. Notable nesting birds include Sharp-tailed Grouse, Least Bittern, Sandhill Crane, Marbled Godwit, Wilson's Phalarope, Alder Flycatcher, Black-billed Magpie, Sedge Wren, and Clay-colored and Le Conte's Sparrows. West of Karlstad, the endless croplands of the Red River valley should produce winter sightings of Gray Partridge, Lapland Longspur, and Snow Bunting.

A first stop might be **Twin Lakes Wildlife Management Area**, 2 miles northeast of Karlstad on both sides of State Highway 11. Any of the roads through and around the area are worth inspection. Viewing is not only good in early spring and summer, but winter should produce Snow Bunting, Lapland Longspur, and in some years Prairie Falcon and Snowy Owl. Different habitat can be found in the grasslands and oak savannah of the **Norway Dunes** area, 320 acres of Nature Conservancy land just northwest of here (follow Highway 59 north for 5 miles to Halma, turn right on County 7, and take either of the first two roads north). Look here for Upland Sandpiper and Marbled Godwit.

Lake Bronson State Park, just southeast of the town of the same name and 5 miles farther up Highway 59 from Halma, is a good spot to camp, picnic, or hike. The lake itself is actually a reservoir, created by a dam on the South Branch Two River built when local wells dried up in the dust bowl of the

1930s. If you're in a hurry, this may be one of the better places in the state to see a moose without much effort, as they are common in the park. Of the park's 14 miles of hiking trails, the best for birding is probably the Hi-Bank interpretive trail, which radiates from the east campground and skirts the lake.

Additional help:

Minnesota Highway Map location: C-3

Hazards: Mosquitos, ice storms, blizzards

Nearest food, gas, lodging: Karlstad, Lake Bronson

Camping: Lake Bronson State Park

Land ownership: State of Minnesota, The Nature Conservancy

Additional information: Minnesota DNR, (612) 296-6157; Lake Bronson State Park manager, (218) 754- 2200

Recommended length of stay: 1 day

18. Crookston and vicinity

Habitats: Aspen parkland, grassland, pasture, brushland, sedge marsh and meadow

Key birds: Greater Prairie-Chicken, Sandhill Crane, Upland Sandpiper, Marbled Godwit, Wilson's Phalarope, Veery, Sedge and Marsh Wrens, Yellow-throated Vireo, Chestnut-sided Warbler, Ovenbird, Savannah Sparrow

Best times to bird: May, June; mid-August-October

Don't miss: Prairie tracts at Pankratz, Tympanuchus, Pembina; Crookston sewage treatment ponds

General information:

Located in the heart of Minnesota's Red River valley, Crookston, like so many towns of this agricultural boom region, was named in honor of a railway man; in this case, Colonel William Crooks, an engineer responsible for routing the first railroad through this area. His father, Ramsay, may have been more significant; a former president of the American Fur company, he was a well-known citizen who held the trust of regional Native Americans during the early 1800s.

Once described as an "ocean of prairie," the Red River valley now stands as a carpet of cropland over some of the world's richest soils. It is a land where people once worried about frequent prairie grassland fires, but now worry about crop-eating insects. It is a land of wheat, sugar beets, potatoes, and sunflowers, and of the endless repetition of neatly planted rows.

Crookston and vicinity

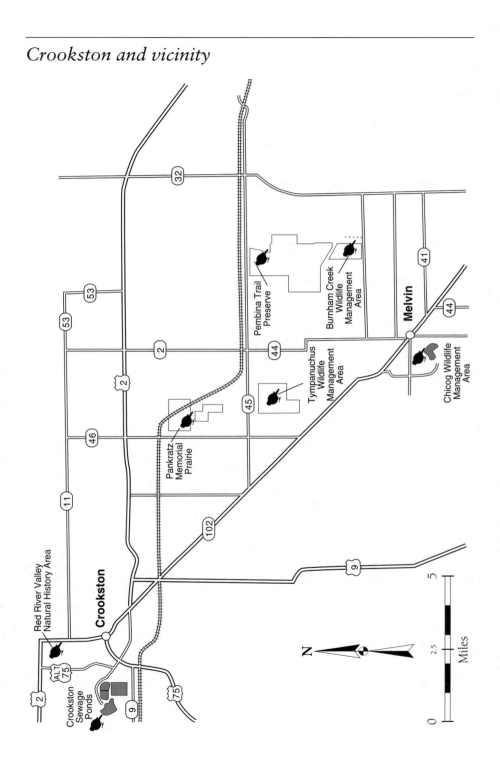

Red River Valley Natural History Area

Crookston

Crookston Sewage Ponds

Pembina Trail Preserve

Burnham Creek Wildlife Management Area

Melvin

Tympanuchus Wildlife Management Area

Chicog Wildlife Management Area

Pankratz Memorial Prairie

N

0   2.5   5

Miles

The horizon here probably appears much as it did hundreds of years ago. There is little to relieve the eye except the distant rows of trees lining the course of some stream. The only source of timber for both native and early settler, the dominant tree species are cottonwood, elm, green ash, and box elder.

The prairie and wetland sites preserved near Crookston would not be unique, were they not so rare today. One of the sites, the two units of the Pankratz Memorial Prairie, was acquired thanks to the farsighted thinking of a University of Minnesota-Crookston student, Norman Pankratz, who held a great love for nature. Pankratz named The Nature Conservancy as beneficiary of his life insurance policy. Following Pankratz' untimely and early death, the organization was able to purchase the two units in stages between 1973 and 1984.

Birding information:

For birders, the area in an around Crookston has a lot to offer. The series of prairie tracts southwest of Crookston are the main draw, and perhaps the state's best in one locale. The tracts are close together enough to make an attractive birding destination in themselves, especially in spring and fall when migrating ducks, geese, and Sandhill Cranes may concentrate. Keep a close watch when driving between sites, because interesting birds may be seen close to these little-traveled roads. To reach Crookston from the Twin Cities (about 287 miles), take I-94 west to Barnesville, then follow State Highway 9 north. From Karlstad, take State Highway 11 west to Donaldson and follow U.S. Highway 75 south.

Located just south of U.S. Highway 2 on County Road 46 is the **Pankratz Memorial Prairie**. These two tracts total 778 acres and offer birders a chance to see Greater Prairie-Chicken, Yellow Rail, Wilson's Phalarope, Upland Sandpiper, Marbled Godwit, Sedge and Marsh Wrens, and Savannah, Clay-colored, and Nelson's Sharp-tailed Sparrows, among other birds. Park on the unimproved township road at the preserve's southwest corner and walk in.

Just south of Pankratz on County Road 46 is the **Tympanuchus Wildlife Management Area**, named for the genus applied to the Greater Prairie-Chicken. This preserve is slightly drier than other area tracts, and is open to public hunting in fall, but it is a good place to check for prairie chicken, Upland Sandpiper, Marbled Godwit, and sparrows in spring and early summer.

Pembina Trail Preserve commemorates the ox cart trail along the remnant strand, or beach line, of Glacial Lake Agassiz, over which furs and buffalo hides from the hamlet of Pembina, North Dakota, were carried to St. Paul in the early 1800s. This 2,044-acre preserve (about 7.5 miles west of Highway 102 on the south side of County Road 45) contains large areas of sedge meadow, marsh, and shrub swamp, and is one of the very best places to see Sandhill Crane, Marbled Godwit, and many of the other species mentioned above. Look carefully along the south side of County Road 45, where cranes and godwits can often be seen. Sandhill concentrations here sometimes number in the thousands in both spring and fall.

Just south of the Pembina tract, **Burnham Creek Wildlife Management Area** supports at least sixty nesting species including a number of birds rating "special

Sandhill Crane

©Vera Mingwong 1995

concern" status in Minnesota: Least and American Bitterns, Greater Prairie-Chicken, Sandhill Crane, Upland Sandpiper, Wilson's Phalarope, and Nelson's Sharp-tailed Sparrow. Black Terns have nested here, and in a recent fall a Whooping Crane was spotted among a large flock of Sandhill Cranes. To reach the Burnham area from Crookston, follow Highway 102 southeast about 10 miles to Melvin, turn north on County 44, and take the second road to the right. About 3 miles in, look for an unimproved road heading north, which will take you along the east side of the management area (the lowland area with trees and brush, to your left).

The road that runs east/west on the south side of the management area is minimally maintained, but its primarily gravel surface remains passable in most weather; caution is advised. This road transects impressive birding habitat, and even cropland may produce an Upland Sandpiper for the observant watcher. The wet areas of Burnham Creek require a short hike and are most easily viewed in early spring, when surface water is at its highest and vegetation low. Park at the southeast corner of the unit to walk out. Wetlands surrounded by trees and brush will be apparent on your left as you head north. The area is closed to hunting from September 1 through the end of the waterfowl season, making it particularly attractive to ducks and geese.

Another area worth checking is the **Chicog Wildlife Management Area** near Melvin (from Crookston, follow Highway 102 southeast for about 10 miles, then turn south on County 44). Although fall hunting may disturb large numbers of cranes or waterfowl, many of the other species mentioned above may be encountered.

Another anomaly of the prairie region is the importance of abandoned gravel pits for wildlife. Often these areas collect water and are invaded by pioneering trees and shrubs (as well as those planted by man), making them ideal locations for a number of bird species which might otherwise not occur here. The 85-acre **Red River Valley Natural History Area** on the north side of Crookston, just south of State Highway 2, is one such site. It contains a mix of prairie grass, aspen stands, cottonwood forest, willow swamp, and cattail marsh, and is used by the University of Crookston as an outdoor environmental laboratory. Its network of forest trails are worth checking in spring for migrating passerines.

More popular among birders are the municipal **Crookston Sewage Ponds**, located at the city's southeast border. To enter the ponds, take Township Road 233 west from north Highway 73 and pass through the open gate. A dike road makes it easy to observe from a vehicle. The ponds are vast: one the size of a small lake, the other the size of a midsized lake. They lie just north of a large American Crystal Sugar pond that does not allow access. The west municipal pond is drawn down occasionally, making it especially attractive to shorebirds. Early autumn is the best time to be here, from mid-August through September, but spring offers good birding also. In summer, great numbers of Barn Swallows gather on the dikes to rest between feeding forays for the pond's many flying insects.

Additional help:

Minnesota Highway Map location: B,C-6,7

Hazards: Mosquitos, muddy roads

Nearest food, gas, lodging: Crookston, Erskine

Camping: Lake Cameron Campground, east on Highway 2 at Erskine

Land ownership: State of Minnesota, The Nature Conservancy

Additional information: Minnesota DNR, (612) 296-6157; Crookston Area Chamber of Commerce, (218) 281-4320; Erskine Development Corp., (218) 687-3826

Recommended length of stay: 2 days

19. Moorhead/Felton Prairie and vicinity ———————

Habitats: Wet prairie, sedge meadow, tallgrass prairie, dry upland

Key birds: Swainson's Hawk, Greater Prairie-Chicken, Upland Sandpiper, Marbled Godwit, Sprague's Pipit (rare), Loggerhead Shrike, Chestnut-collared Longspur, Baird's (rare) and Grasshopper Sparrows

Best times to bird: April-June; mid-August-October.

Don't miss: Felton Prairie complex, Moorhead sewage ponds

General information:

The Red River of the North separates the Minnesota city of Moorhead from its sister, Fargo, North Dakota. For about 400 winding miles it divides the two states themselves. The river begins at Lake Traverse, the former outlet of Glacial Lake Agassiz, which originally drained south through the Minnesota River valley. However, when receding ice and Agassiz's lowering waters finally receded far enough north, Lake Traverse became the headwater, rather than the foot, of the remnant river that would flow north.

The Red River flows north at a tortuously slow pace, dropping only about 6 inches per mile. It has no rapids, flows through no forests, and for the most part is muddy and uninviting. It has little recreational value, and several major character defects cause its cantankerous nature. First, because the river flows north, its lower reaches in Canada are typically ice-dammed in spring while at the same time its southern, upper reaches are rapidly melting. Major floods are a way of life in the Red River valley during most spring seasons. Second, the low, flat, former lake bed that is the river "valley" allows floodwaters to spread over lands far from the Red's banks. Finally, ditching and wetlands elimination throughout the watershed causes meltwater to pour toward the Red River unabated, further exacerbating the problem.

Given the Red River valley's wall-to-wall cultivation, it is remarkable that remnants of the prairie grasslands exist at all—but they do. The importance of these prairie tracts to species such as the Chestnut-collared Longspur, whose only Minnesota nesting spot is here at Felton Prairie, speaks to the critical need for such refuges, no matter how small.

Birding information:

Perhaps the most visited of any prairie site in Minnesota, the **Felton Prairie complex**, southeast of its namesake city, deserves attention not for its size, but for the interesting birds that occur here. Serious listers come to see nesting Chestnut-collared Longspur, as well as Baird's Sparrow, Loggerhead Shrike, and the fairly regular Sprague's Pipit. Three units make up the preserve: **Felton Prairie, Blazing Star Prairie**, and **Bicentennial Prairie**, totaling 410 acres. To reach the Moorhead area from the Twin Cities (about 231 miles), follow I-94 west. To reach the town of Felton, exit I-94 at Barnesville (23 miles before Moorhead) and travel 29 miles north on State Highway 9. The preserve lies 4 miles east of Felton, and the south units can be reached by driving about 1 mile south on the unimproved township road.

The Felton Prairie complex rests on a large, ancient beach ridge of the former Glacial Lake Agassiz, one of the highest areas in the Red River valley. In addition to the preserves, the area's associated pastures and unplowed acreages are worth investigating.

Prairie preserve habitat in Minnesota remains protected today thanks to private organizations like The Nature Conservancy. This is a typical tract in northwestern Minnesota.

Moorhead/Felton Prairie and vicinity

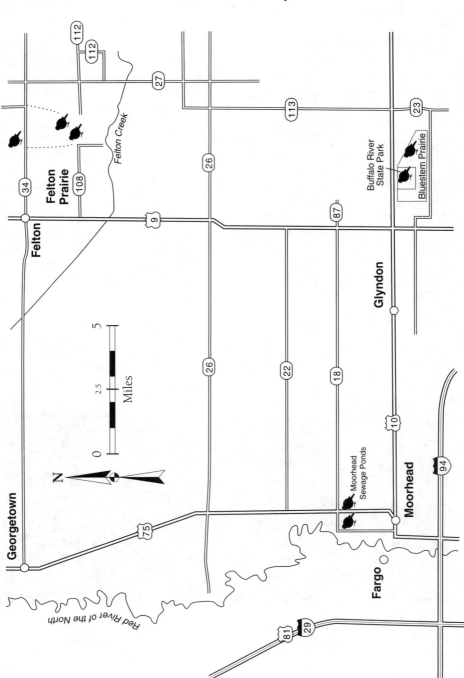

Spring and early summer are the best times to visit, when birds are on their nesting territories, singing consistently. Listen for booming Greater Prairie-Chickens at dawn in early spring, and watch for Swainson's Hawk, Upland Sandpiper, Marbled Godwit, Alder and Willow Flycatchers, Grasshopper Sparrow, and Orchard Oriole.

Farther south, where State Highway 9 intersects with U.S. 10, **Buffalo River State Park** (south side) can't claim any longspurs, but it does offer a bluebird trail and a wide area of grassland burned periodically since 1974, skirted by a dependable road. A small but interesting prairie demonstration site is maintained outside the nature center, with descriptions of many of the regional grasses and prairie flowers, including over fifty prairie plants. The associated 3,250-acre **Bluestem Prairie** site, bordering the park's south side, is the largest remnant of tallgrass prairie in the Midwest. The area is still under improvement through controlled burning and restoration efforts. Blinds for viewing booming prairie chickens are available by reservation only; call the prairie office in March at (218) 498-2679.

Moorhead's Sewage Ponds (a mile north of town on either side of U.S. Highway 75 at its intersection with County 18) are worth a visit in spring or fall. The ponds are extremely reliable for sighting migrating shorebirds in late summer and early fall, and rarities have been recorded here over the years. The ponds are owned by the American Crystal Sugar Company and should be respected as private property.

Additional help:

Minnesota Highway Map location: B,C-9,10

Hazards: Muddy roads

Nearest food, gas, lodging: Moorhead, Glyndon

Camping: Buffalo River State Park, (218) 498-2124

Land ownership: State of Minnesota, The Nature Conservancy

Additional information: Minnesota DNR, (612) 296-6157; Fargo/ Moorhead Convention & Visitors Bureau, (701) 282-3653

Recommended length of stay: 1 day

20. Rothsay and vicinity

Habitats: Tallgrass prairie, sedge meadow, pasture, cropland, open brushland

Key birds: Prairie Falcon, Greater Prairie-Chicken, Gray Partridge, Sandhill Crane (spring, fall), Upland Sandpiper, Northern Shrike (winter), Smith's and Lapland Longspurs (October), Le Conte's and Savannah Sparrows

Best times to bird: April-June; October; January-March

Don't miss: Rothsay Wildlife Management Area (I-94 to County Road 24, west to County Road 15 north)

General information:

Although the plow and axe pushed many birds and mammals out of their former range, these two settlement tools initially improved conditions for the Greater Prairie-Chicken in Minnesota. Prior to settlement, the prairie chicken's range was probably restricted to the southern portion of the state. By the 1880s, they could be found statewide, with the exception of the extreme northeast and north-central portions.

For the next several decades prairie chickens were so abundant that it was common to see flocks numbering in the hundreds migrating across southwestern Minnesota to wintering areas in Iowa. However, as agricultural practices became more intensive in the prairie and northern deciduous regions, and second growth timber replaced the forest clearings of the boreal region, prairie chicken numbers began to decline significantly. Today, remnant populations of Greater Prairie-Chickens exist in only a few areas of the state, dependent on undisturbed tracts of grassland combined with a mix of pastureland, hayfields, and open brushland.

The state's only areas meeting these unique habitat requirements are the beach ridges of the former Glacial Lake Agassiz in the prairie region, where remnant prairie tracts provide adequate undisturbed grassland cover for nesting. The Rothsay area marks the southernmost portion of one of these well-known beach lines.

Over the years, giant icons (statues embodying a town or regional mascot) have sprung up across Minnesota, and some of them are birds. Blackduck displays a stout black duck (of course), Belgrade boasts a giant crow, Fergus Falls exhibits a large loon, Frazee flaunts a big turkey, Remer has raised an oversized eagle, Pelican Rapids proudly proclaims its huge pelican, and Rothsay (appropriately) manifests its enormous prairie chicken.

Birding information:

No other birding area in Minnesota is as well known for booming prairie chickens as the **Rothsay Wildlife Management Area.** Although there may be equally good booming grounds farther north, Rothsay's lie in closest proximity to the Twin Cities. It is a convenient stop off Interstate 94, north of Fergus Falls; to reach the town, simply take I-94 west from the Twin Cities (about 198 miles) to the Rothsay exit. You might start by taking County Road 26 west 4 miles, then turning north on the gravel road that meets the wildlife management area in 2 miles. Go

Rothsay and vicinity

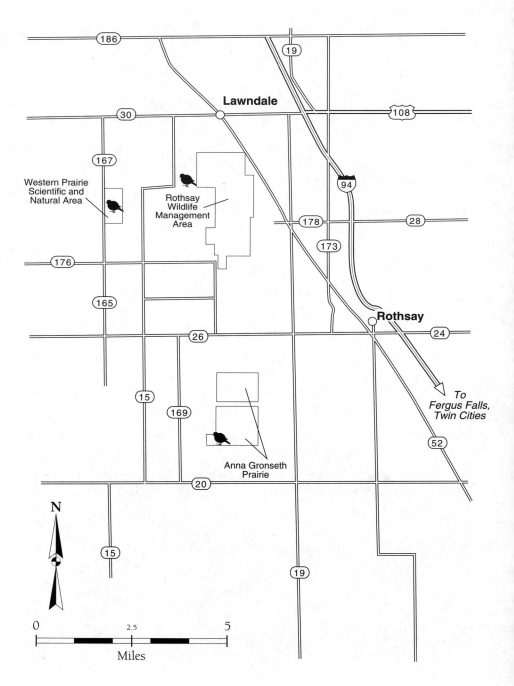

west here and north again to skirt the wildlife area, and view the pastures and hayfields for prairie chickens and other birds. Any of the roads in and around the wildlife management area, both north and south, are worth careful inspection; be sure to check the 320-acre **Western Prairie Scientific and Natural Area** and 911-acre **Anna Gronseth Prairie** lands (both worth hiking).

Prairie chickens aren't all the Rothsay area has to offer. Wilkin County is a major staging ground for Sandhill Cranes in spring and fall, and no other location in the state has as many records for Prairie Falcons. Other fall migrants include Smith's and Lapland Longspurs (October), and winter specialties include Snow Bunting and Northern Shrike. Willow Flycatchers are common here, as are Le Conte's Sparrows. Gray Partridge are seen regularly, and both Western Meadowlark and Eastern Kingbird are highly visible. Watch also for Upland Sandpiper, Marbled Godwit (sometimes in large numbers in spring), Wilson's Phalarope, nesting Black-billed Magpie, and Bobolink.

Additional help:

Minnesota Highway Map location: B,C-11

Hazards: Muddy roads

Nearest food, gas, lodging: Rothsay

Camping: Maplewood State Park (southeast of Pelican Rapids), (218) 863-8383

Land ownership: State of Minnesota, The Nature Conservancy

Additional information: Minnesota DNR, (612) 296-6157

Recommended length of stay: 1 day

Many prairie pothole wetlands are contained within Minnesota's wildlife management units, scattered across the west-central portions of the prairie.

21. Sibley State Park and vicinity

Habitats: Prairie grassland, hardwood forest, marsh, lake

Key birds: Common Loon (Mud Lake), Broad-winged Hawk, Great Egret, Black-crowned Night Heron, Pileated and Red-bellied Woodpeckers, Sedge Wren, Yellow-throated and Warbling Vireos, Yellow-headed Blackbird, Scarlet Tanager, Field Sparrow

Best times to bird: March-June; December

Don't miss: Fort Johanna historical marker vista, Timber Lake Road, Eagle Lake

General information:

Sibley State Park is a good birding site, and it is located in an area of closely located sites, which, in sum, offer excellent birding. The park was named for General Henry Hastings Sibley, a man who left a notable legacy in the state's early history.

Sibley came to Minnesota in 1834 at the age of twenty three, as an employee of the American Fur company. He represented the Minnesota Territory in the U.S. Congress, served as a regent of the state university, and became the state's first governor. But it was Sibley's role in the Sioux uprising that may have brought him the most glory.

In 1862, after more than a decade of treaty abuses, four Sioux Indians murdered five white settlers in Meeker County's Acton Township, less than 30 miles southeast of the present Sibley State Park. Fearing retribution, Sioux leaders chose to go to war, attacking and destroying two agencies along the Minnesota River. The Sioux uprising was under way. Settlers fled for their lives, abandoning their prairie homesteads and constructing hastily built stockades, such as Fort Johanna just north of here, for protection.

Colonel Sibley and his troops were sent from St. Paul to help quell the conflict. They rescued Fort Ridgely and defeated the Sioux at a number of key sites, including the final battle at Wood Lake in Yellow Medicine County, and later freed more than 260 prisoners held by the Sioux. Sibley went on to pursue the Sioux into North Dakota, but the damage in Minnesota was devastating. As many as eight hundred white settlers and soldiers had been killed, and the losses to the Sioux may have been even greater.

Perhaps it was appropriate that, some years later, Peter Broberg, a man with a great passion for the area's beautiful glacial moraine hills and lakes, suggested in the early 1900s that the land around Lake Sibley be protected as a park. Broberg was the sole surviving member of his family, victims of the Sioux uprising.

Kandiyohi County, which incorporates the city of Willmar, Sibley State Park, and most of the birding spots listed here, takes its name from the Sioux term "where the buffalo fish come" (kandi-ohi). The name refers to the big-mouthed buffalo fish, a member of the sucker family which reaches up to thirty pounds and is native to the Crow River drainage in this part of Minnesota.

Sibley State Park and vicinity

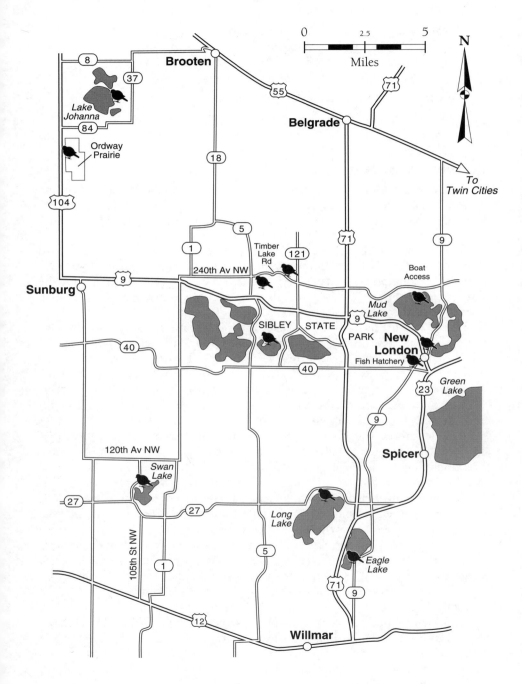

In springtime, buffalo fish run upstream to spawn, and in earlier times their masses choked lake inlets and provided easy food.

Birding information:

Although this area falls within the prairie region, the lands around Sibley State Park are a unique island of glacial hills, hardwood forests, and a few deep lakes more typical of the northern deciduous region farther east. As such, it stands isolated, an oasis for the likes of migrating passerines and nesting Broad-winged Hawks. Common Loons nest on Mud Lake. From the Twin Cities (about 100 miles), the quickest route to access the area is I-94 west to St. Cloud, then State Highway 23 to New London. For the scenic route, take Highway 23 to Paynesville, go right (northwest) to Brooten, then west on County 8 to 104 south.

To fully experience the biome change here, it is worthwhile to begin at the area's north side at **Ordway Prairie**, which can be reached by traveling west from State Highway 55 (Brooten) on County Road 8, then south on State Highway 104. The wayside along Highway 104 (a few miles south of County 8 on the left side), with its historical marker, provides a sweeping vista of rolling grasslands remindful of another time. Keep an eye out for hawks hunting the grasslands here. Also check the marshes on the east side of **Lake Johanna** for herons and egrets. A heron rookery on the lake once attracted such nesting species as Little Blue Heron, Cattle Egret, and Black-crowned Night Heron, as well as Great Blue Heron, Great Egret, and cormorant.

The view of Ordway Prairie, looking south from the Lake Johanna area. Sibley State Park's deciduous woodlands lie just over the horizon.

Following Highway 104 south from Lake Johanna, you will arrive at Sunburg. East of this village along State Highway 9 begin the hardwood forests and hills that make this area so unique. A good birding spot is **Timber Lake Road** (take County Road 1 north from Highway 9, then turn right on 240th Ave.), a picturesque drive through dense hardwoods that crowd this lane. This is one of the few places in the prairie region where you'll find Ruffed Grouse. It is a good spot for woodpeckers, including Pileated, Red-bellied, Red-headed, Hairy, and Downy, as well as spring warblers. All four thrushes have been found here, with Swainson's, Gray-cheeked, and Hermit most common and Wood Thrush less common. Black-billed and Yellow-billed Cuckoos and Scarlet Tanager also can be found.

Turn right from Timber Lake Road on County 121 to reach **Sibley State Park**, which offers more hardwoods and 18 miles of hiking trails. Some good birding may be found in and around the Cedar Hill Picnic Area, where a Yellow-throated Warbler was found summering at least two years in a row. Look for Barred Owl, Scarlet Tanager, warblers, thrushes, Turkey Vulture, and Eastern Towhee during spring and fall migration. The interpretive center's bird feeding stations are worth viewing during winter, and the park occasionally offers winter bird feeding seminars.

Farther west on 240th Ave. lies the boat access on the north side of **Mud Lake**, the home of nine pairs of Common Loon with young during a recent survey. State Highway 9 and County Road 9 also provide views of the lake. Watch for Bald Eagle around the lake.

The town of **New London**, on the south side of Mud Lake on State Highway 9, is quaint, mostly due to the surrounding water. Open water can be found here in November and December, and so can Bald Eagles and a variety of waterfowl. The **Fish Hatchery** in town utilizes fifteen rearing ponds, and the water is raised and lowered periodically (regularly lowered in fall), attracting shorebirds. Gain permission before entering the hatchery area.

Farther south toward Willmar is **Long Lake** (from New London take County Road 9 to County Road 27, then go west across U.S. Highway 71; Long Lake will be on your left). The mechanically aerated water here makes this the county's best spot for observing waterfowl during spring migration. Unfortunately for birders, the reconstructed roadway takes travelers farther from the lake than it once did. The best viewing time is mid- to late-March, before ice-out. An island in the lake supports one of the largest multispecies heron rookeries in Minnesota, where over 1,750 nests have been located in a single year. Great Blue and Black-crowned Night Herons, Great Egrets, and Double-crested Cormorants nest here, but a colony this size has the potential to attract less common species such as Little Blue and Yellow-crowned Night Herons. Cattle Egrets have nested here and Snowy Egrets have also been seen. A good spot to look for herons and egrets is the east side of nearby **Eagle Lake** (south of County 27, on County 9 again), where a new impoundment structure empties a large slough.

Swan Lake (northwest of Willmar, reached from 105th Street) is another good place to look for Bald Eagles, especially in early and late winter. As many as fifteen have been observed here at one time. The lake is also an excellent place to view waterfowl in spring. Red-necked Grebes nest here in summer.

Additional help:

Minnesota Highway Map location: E,F-15

Hazards: Mosquitos, poison ivy

Nearest food, gas, lodging: New London, Spicer, Willmar

Camping: Sibley State Park, (612) 354-2055

Land ownership: State of Minnesota, The Nature Conservancy

Additional information: Minnesota DNR, (612) 296-6157; Sibley State Park, (612) 354-2055; Willmar Chamber of Commerce, (612) 235-0300

Recommended length of stay: 2 days

22. Big Stone/Lac Qui Parle and vicinity ──────────

Habitats: Wetland, lake, prairie grassland, floodplain forest, granite outcrops, wood lots

Key birds: Western and Eared Grebes, American White Pelican, Double-crested Cormorant, Bald Eagle (fall), Upland Sandpiper, Willow Flycatcher, Marsh Wren, Orchard Oriole, Grasshopper and Clay-colored Sparrows

Best times to bird: March-June; September-early November

Don't miss: Big Stone National Wildlife Refuge Auto Tour, Louisburg Road across upper Marsh Lake, Salt Lake

General information:

The headwater of the Minnesota River, Big Stone Lake stretches 26 miles from Brown's Valley to Ortonville, never more than 1.5 miles wide. Once the lower outlet of Glacial Lake Agassiz, the river today is cut off from that watershed (Red River valley), meandering alone through the massive, former valley of the Glacial River Warren, 355 miles to its junction with the Mississippi.

The names of this area's central landmarks provide a legacy of the past and references to the present. Big Stone was named "Inyan tankinyanyan" ("very great stone") by the Sioux, for the prominent granite outcroppings of this part of the river valley (over 100 acres of exposed granite on the Big Stone National Wildlife Refuge alone). The Antelope Hills, and Stony Ridge, refer to a course of low hills and ridges that slant through Augusta, Mehurin, and Greeland townships near the famous birding site of Salt Lake (often called Rosabel Lake). Herds of pronghorn antelope were said to have roamed here, but were extirpated by the mid-1800s.

Lac Qui Parle Lake also takes its name from the Sioux, who described it to early French explorers as "the lake that talks." Various interpretations of the naming have cited the groaning of winter ice, the musical chant of waves breaking against shoreline stones, and the echo of voices thrown back from the

Big Stone/Lac Qui Parle and vicinity
Big Stone National Wildlife Refuge

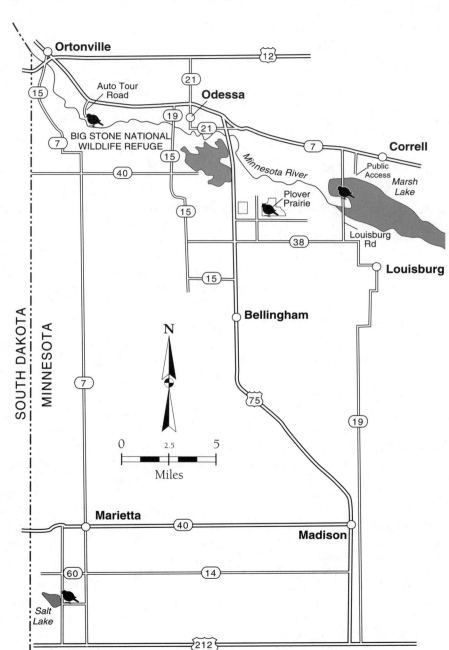

lake's bluffs. Today one might add the nightly clamor of ducks, geese, and cormorants to Lac Qui Parle's legacy. Artichoke Lake, several miles north of Marsh Lake (a good place to look for migrating waterfowl and shorebirds), shares its namesake with the Pomme de Terre River which feeds Marsh Lake. Both refer to the Sioux's prairie turnip, a tuber of a wild sunflower once widely used as a staple. Finally, the village of Odessa was named for the city in southern Russia that supplied the original seed for wheat grown in this vicinity.

Birding information:

No other place in Minnesota can claim the waterfowl numbers that frequent Big Stone, Marsh, and Lac Qui Parle lakes and the surrounding counties. The waters here are large enough to provide plenty of safe resting areas, and surrounding croplands provide an abundance of food. Mallards and Canada Geese are the most common visitors, but any duck or goose common to the state uses these waters at one time or another. Tundra Swans rest here on their way to and from the Arctic and shorebirds, given proper water levels, can be found in good numbers during migration peaks.

Each fall the traditions of these long-distance migrants guide them here from the Canadian prairies, northern tundra, and Arctic shorelines; each spring they return en route from their southern winter homes. Lac Qui Parle may be best known for its staging Canada Geese, a modern tradition created by wildlife managers who sought to establish flocks, although smaller numbers of Canadas always used the area. Snow Geese also stop here, along with White-fronted and even scattered Ross' Geese. To understand the essence of this area, pause in spring or fall during the last half-hour of daylight to view the movement of waterfowl as they trade between feeding field and lake.

In addition to the ubiquitous Mallards, American Wigeon, Gadwall, Northern Shoveler, and Redhead are common. Diving ducks prefer deeper lakes generally, but they frequent the bigger lakes here. Artichoke Lake hosts particularly strong numbers of diving ducks and several local preserves protect migrating Canvasback. Even sea ducks such as scoters occasionally make appearances in this area.

Rising and falling water levels on these large lakes associated with the Minnesota River create variously good and superb conditions for shorebirds. The many prairie pothole wetlands of Big Stone and Stevens counties attract large flocks of shorebirds during migration in low water years. Although dams have been built on all three of the major lakes in the river course, they were at one time naturally dammed by outwash from their feeder rivers.

Due to its location along Minnesota's western border, both eastern and western bird species may be observed here. For example, Eastern Bluebirds nest here, but Mountain Bluebirds have also been observed. The American Avocet has been seen in Lac Qui Parle County enough times to be almost predictable, though rare. Although the area's lakes and marshlands are impressive, it is the generous mix of floodplain woodlands and upland habitat that make for such "total" birding in this area. Perhaps the quickest route into the area from the Twin Cities (about 160 miles) is to follow U.S. Highway 12 west to Willmar, then State Highway 40 west to Milan, then right (west) on State Highway 7 to Odessa. Or, take State Highway 7 from the Twin Cities west all the way to Odessa.

Big Stone National Wildlife Refuge, 5 miles west of the Highway 7 Odessa turnoff, covers more than 11,000 acres of the Minnesota River valley, providing habitat ranging from grassland to floodplain forest to open water. At least seven different parking areas access a variety of habitats, which can be entered on foot. One of the better is the Rock Outcrop Hiking Trail, an easy 1-mile route. The Auto Tour, a 4-mile route accessible from Highway 7 on the north side, provides a look at the major habitats of the refuge. Upland Sandpiper, Marbled Godwit, Le Conte's and Grasshopper Sparrows, Orchard Oriole, and Willow Flycatcher are found in good numbers on the prairie areas. Don't forget to stop by the dam on Highway 75 on the east side of the refuge, featuring the East Pool Wildlife Observation Drive.

The **Louisburg Road**, which intersects the backwaters of Marsh Lake, offers a chance to view grebes, terns, gulls, waterfowl, herons, egrets, and pelicans. To the east, the public boat access on Marsh Lake's north side has a high knob which provides a good lake overlook. As you head west from Correll on Highway 7, the access road is the first to the left.

Southeast of the Big Stone refuge is the 655-acre **Plover Prairie** (take U.S. Highway 75, 4 miles south of Highway 7, and travel 1.5 miles east). Upland Sandpiper, Marbled Godwit, Loggerhead Shrike, Wilson's Phalarope, Short-eared Owl, and Burrowing Owl have been seen here over the years.

Even farther south, just below the town of Marietta, sits small-but-significant **Salt Lake** (from Highway 7, take Highway 75 south to Madison, then take Highway 40 west to Marietta; head south for 3 miles on County 7, and turn right on the township road). The lake's slightly saline waters support large populations of copepods, which in turn attract both waterfowl and shorebirds. Spring or fall migration periods are the best times to be here (particularly spring). A group of birders gathers annually to visit the lake near the end of April; for information about this trip, call the Minnesota Ornithologists Union (MOU). Salt Lake has accounted for a number of interesting birds over the years, including nesting American Avocet and a long list of other shorebirds and waterfowl, including Tundra Swan, White-Fronted and Ross' Geese, and Western and Eared Grebes. The lake is best viewed from the east side.

Marsh Lake Dam, at the lake's southeast end, is a good place to scan for Western Grebe, American White Pelican, and waterfowl (turn off County Road 51, southwest of Appleton). A good view of the head of Lac Qui Parle Lake and its associated backwaters can be had from **State Highway 119**. To reach the 11,000-acre **Chippewa Prairie**, take County Road 30 south from Highway 7. Short-eared Owls may be seen hunting during the day, and Upland Sandpipers are common. The bluffs above the marshes at the area's west end offer good vistas.

Father southeast, **Highway 40** from Milan (pronounced "mylan") bisects Lac Qui Parle Lake. Depending on water levels, the crossing's southwest corner can provide mudflats attractive to shorebirds. Finally, County Road 33, which leads south along the lake from Highway 40, is a pleasant drive that leads to **Lac Qui**

Big Stone/Lac Qui Parle and vicinity
Marsh Lake/Lac Qui Parle Lake and vicinity

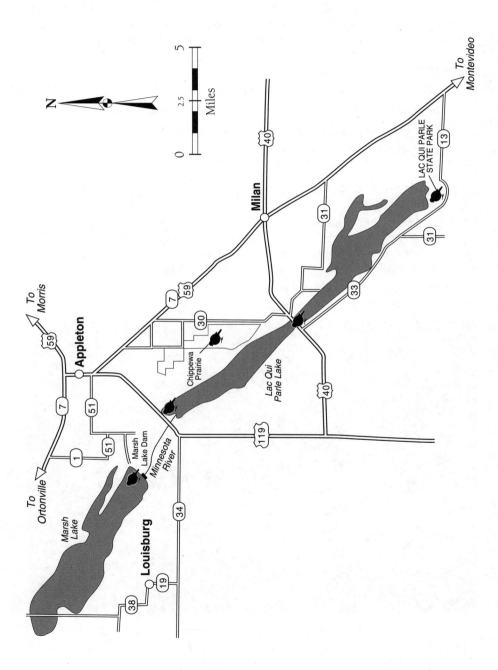

Parle State Park. To reach the lake, head north from the park entrance to the public boat access and picnic area. The park contains dense woodlands that often attract migrating warblers in spring.

Another area worth a visit is Big Stone Lake State Park, north of Ortonville on Highway 7. The north unit of the park (second entry, just south of County Road 6) is an excellent place to see Eastern Towhee and Yellow-throated Vireo.

Additional help:

Minnesota Highway Map location: B,C,D-15,16

Hazards: Stinging nettle, poison ivy, mosquitos, unimproved roads

Nearest food, gas, lodging: Ortonville, Appleton, Milan

Camping: Lac Qui Parle State Park, (612) 752-4736; Big Stone Lake State Park, (612) 839-3663

Land ownership: U.S. Dept. of Interior, state of Minnesota, The Nature Conservancy

Additional information: Big Stone National Wildlife Refuge, (612) 839-3700; Minnesota DNR, (612) 296-6157; Big Stone Lake Area Chamber of Commerce (Ortonville), (612) 839-3284, (800) 568-5722; Western MN Prairie Waters (Appleton), (800) 269-5527

Recommended length of stay: 2 days

Lac Qui Parle Lake shows a shoreline that reflects its changeable water levels. When water levels are low in August, good numbers of shorebirds can be expected around lakes and potholes in surrounding counties.

23. Blue Mounds State Park and vicinity ————————

Habitats: Prairie grassland, woodlots, gravel pit ponds

Key birds: Swainson's Hawk, Upland Sandpiper, Willow Flycatcher, Sedge Wren, Orchard Oriole, Blue Grosbeak, Dickcissel, Grasshopper Sparrow

Best time to bird: March-June

Don't miss: Prairie Coteau

General information:

Just when the prairie looks like it has nothing more to offer, something new captures the horizon. So it is with Prairie Coteau, or as the French named it, "Coteau des Prairies" ("Highland of the Prairies"), an approximately 40-mile-wide area rising 500-800 feet above the flatland, running southeast to northwest through southwestern Minnesota and into South Dakota. Underlain with Sioux Quartzite, the coteau primarily resisted the glacial forces that shaved flat surrounding areas, and its surface is marked by lakes and wetlands. A good example of the rising coteau can be seen between the towns of Tracy, in Lyon County, and Walnut Grove, in Redwood County.

For early settlers, the coteau signified the final edge of the great eastern forests and the beginning of the seemingly endless grasslands leading to the Rocky Mountains. This high ground acts as a divide for the southwestern Minnesota watersheds. Rock Creek, for example, is Minnesota's only major stream feeding into the Missouri River drainage; the Des Moines River feeds the Mississippi; and the Lac Qui Parle, Yellow Medicine, Redwood, and Cottonwood feed the Minnesota River. On the coteau's east side, deep wooded valleys, historically protected from prairie fires, provided homesteaders with their westernmost source of hardwoods. On its west side, the "West" truly begins, dominated by vast grasslands and even isolated populations of prickly pear cactus.

Outside the coteau, other Sioux Quartzite sites swell up on the flat prairie, and they are well known today. Blue Mounds State Park marks a rise where grasslands appear blue from a distance under the heat of a summer sky. Pipestone marks the best-known Sioux Quartzite site, where Native Americans have traditionally gathered the ochre-colored stone that forms the bowls of ceremonial pipes.

Birding information:

Although more than 230 bird species have been recorded at **Blue Mounds State Park,** its list of regulars is probably much shorter than that of many other sites listed in this book, primarily due to its uniform, rather than mixed, habitat types. What makes Blue Mounds and its surrounds special are the unique bird species found here. To reach Blue Mounds from the Twin Cities (about 200 miles), take U.S. Highway 169 south to Mankato, then State Highway 60 south to Worthington, then I-90 west to Luverne. It's also an easy drive down U.S. Highway 75 from the aforementioned Big Stone area.

Mention Blue Mounds and most birders think of Blue Grosbeak and Burrowing Owl (although the latter haven't nested here in recent years), but the park is

Blue Mounds State Park and vicinity

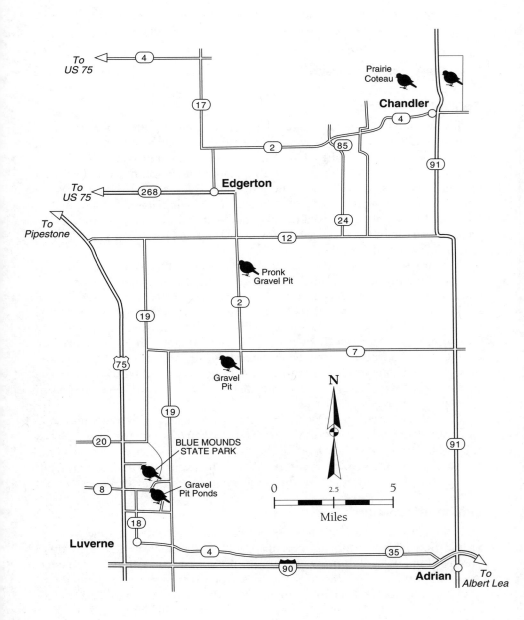

To US 75 ← 4

17

Prairie Coteau

Chandler

4

85

2

91

To US 75 ← 268

Edgerton

To Pipestone

24

12

Pronk Gravel Pit

2

19

7

75

Gravel Pit

N

19

20

BLUE MOUNDS STATE PARK

91

8

Gravel Pit Ponds

0   2.5   5

Miles

18

Luverne

4

90

35

Adrian   To Albert Lea

also home to Swainson's Hawk, Gray Partridge, Upland Sandpiper, American Woodcock, both Black- and Yellow-billed Cuckoos, Sedge Wren, Dickcissel, Grasshopper Sparrow, Bobolink, Yellow-headed Blackbird, and both Baltimore and Orchard Orioles.

From Luverne, take Highway 75 north. The park can be entered from either the north (the main entrance) on County Road 20, or from the interpretive center road up the hill from County Road 8. From the north entrance, turn north to visit scenic Upper Mound Lake and scan its surface and cattail marshes. A waterfall on its south side rushes gently over the red Sioux Quartzite, providing a welcoming cascade of falling water in such dry country. Next, check the trees at the picnic area, especially in spring, when any of about thirty warbler species may be found. A buffalo prairie overlook might provide a view of the small herd here, or the grassland birds. Also worth checking is the prairie hillside trail on the north side of Lower Mound Lake.

The best hike in the park traverses the Lower and Upper Cliffline trails. The upper trail courses the grassland and along the upper side of the cliff's oak trees, while the lower trail offers views across meadow (to the east) and up into the oak-covered slope. Although Blue Grosbeaks may be encountered anywhere in the park, the most likely place to see them is near the interpretive center or on the dead-end road that enters the park from Highway 75, 1 mile south of the main entrance. Scan for grosbeaks on the roadside wires or along brushy edges, and listen for their warbling, Purple Finch-like song.

The Prairie Coteau, west of Chandler, offers some rare, undisturbed grassland areas in southwestern Minnesota. Upland Sandpiper should be present here throughout spring and summer. This is also a good place to look for hawks.

Water is relatively scarce in this part of the state, so the rare lake, marsh, or gravel pit pool deserves attention. The unnumbered, east-west gravel road south of Blue Mounds (head south on Highway 75 from the park, then turn left 1 mile south of County 8) is a good place to listen for screech-owls during spring and early summer; it leads to a series of **gravel pit ponds,** which commonly attract shorebirds in migration. Other good gravel pits include the **County Road 7 pit,** northeast of the park, and the **Pronk Gravel Pit** farther northeast on County Road 2. The pits offer especially good birding when bars and shorelines become exposed in periods of low water. Trucks are busy hauling here during the week. The area can be viewed from the road; gain permission to access the area.

Other good birding spots close to Blue Mounds are the Luverne City Park, at the west edge of town on County Road 4, and Edgerton's Rock River Park. The parks' trees attract warblers during spring migration. In addition, the meadows around Edgerton should offer up Blue Grosbeak and Upland Sandpiper, particularly during spring and early summer.

A fascinating landscape of steep, hillside grasslands resembling those of eastern Montana, or some ancient river valley, can be found on the **Prairie Coteau** on both sides of County Road 4 west of Chandler (20 miles north of I-90 and Adrian on State Highway 91). A number of gravel roads alternately radiate uphill, and any one of these should offer the chance to see Swainson's Hawk, Upland Sandpiper, Sedge Wren, Dickcissel, Grasshopper Sparrow, or Bobolink, in addition to abundant Tree Swallows and Western Meadowlarks; this also is a good area to see Blue Grosbeak. Less than 2 miles northeast of Chandler (east of Highway 91 and north of County 4) is a wetland complex worth viewing.

Several other worthwhile area birding spots are: Pipestone National Monument (more grassland and some inviting riverine woodland), 21 miles north of Blue Mounds on Highway 75, just north of the town of Pipestone (check the ponds behind the monument near the cemetery); and Split Rock Creek State Park (the largest body of water in Pipestone County, which attracts waterfowl including swans and pelicans in migration), 13 miles north of Blue Mounds and 7 miles west of Highway 75 on County Road 2.

Additional help:

Minnesota Highway Map location: C-20,21

Hazards: Poison ivy, tapwater high in nitrates

Nearest food, gas, lodging: Luverne, Edgerton, Pipestone

Camping: Blue Mounds State Park, (507) 283-4892; Split Rock Creek State Park, (507) 348-7908

Land ownership: U.S. Dept. of Interior, state of Minnesota

Additional information: Minnesota DNR, (612) 296-6157; Luverne Area Chamber of Commerce, (507) 283-4061; Pipestone Chamber of Commerce, (507) 825-3316

Recommended length of stay: 1 day

24. Heron Lake and vicinity ─────────────

Habitats: Marsh, lake, upland forest, floodplain forest

Key birds: American White Pelican, Black-crowned Night Heron, American Bittern, Least Bittern, Franklin's Gull, Forster's Tern, Marsh Wren

Best times to bird: March-June; September-October

Don't miss: Duck Lake, Lindgren-Traeger Bird Sanctuary

General information:

Jackson County's Heron Lake owns a storied past when it comes to birds and birders. The Sioux referred to this lake as "Hokabena," "the nesting place of herons." A derivation of the name was applied to the nearest town, Okabena, at its founding in 1879. Heron Lake is the second largest Minnesota lake south of the Twin Cities (Swan Lake in Nicollet County is larger) and its shallow marshlands and luxuriant emergent and submergent vegetation were historically attractive to wild birds.

As a premier wetland for ducks, geese, herons, egrets, and other associated birds, Heron Lake was much studied by the preeminent Minnesota ornithologist Dr. Thomas Roberts. He reported that Trumpeter Swans bred at the lake until the 1880s. Roberts took many field trips to view the lake's "teeming bird life," befriending local residents like Tom Miller, a market hunter who lived on the lake from 1883 to 1899 and was ". . . surprisingly well-informed," according to Roberts. Miller sent migration records to the U.S. Biological Survey for a number of years, and often guided and advised Roberts about the marsh.

In addition to Trumpeter Swans, Heron Lake once boasted nesting White-faced Ibis and American White Pelican. Those species persevered into this century, but eventually ceased breeding at the lake. This was also a fabled migratory stop for great flocks of Canvasbacks for many decades.

Although still a great birding site, Heron Lake has suffered from habitat alteration. Water is both channeled into and pumped out of the lake, causing water levels to fluctuate with the weather. Silt levels from runoff are high. Water clarity and submergent vegetation have suffered from the invasion of rough fish, particularly carp and bullheads. Heron Lake once hosted a colony of 300,000 Franklin's Gulls, a symbol of the lake's decline, but that number has declined to about 15,000.

Today, efforts are under way to restore Heron Lake's "teeming" bird life, through habitat improvement and other measures, such as the release of twelve Trumpeter Swans in 1995. These now join the more than 255 swans that have been released elsewhere in the state since the early 1980s.

Birding information:

Although the grandeur of its bygone days has somewhat diminished, **Heron Lake** continues to be a worthwhile spot for birders today. The town of Heron Lake can most easily be reached from the Twin Cities (about 145 miles) by

Heron Lake and vicinity

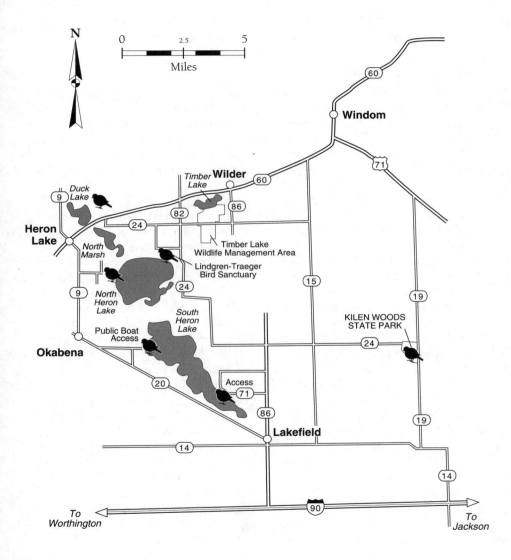

N

0   2.5   5
Miles

60

Windom

71

Timber **Wilder**
Lake   60

82   86

Duck
Lake
9

**Heron
Lake**

24

Timber Lake
Wildlife Management Area

North
Marsh

Lindgren-Traeger
Bird Sanctuary

15

9

North
Heron
Lake

24

KILEN WOODS
STATE PARK

South
Heron
Lake

19

Okabena

Public Boat
Access

24

20

Access

71

19

86

Lakefield

14

19

14

90

To
Worthington

To
Jackson

taking U.S. Highway 169 south to Mankato, then State Highway 60 south. Franklin's Gulls nest here in large numbers; grebes, herons, and egrets are easily observed; and Least Bitterns, American Bitterns, Common Moorhen, Osprey, Wilson's Phalarope, Forster's Tern, American White Pelican, and King Rail are all possibilities. Heron Lake's location and size continue to make it attractive to rarities such as the Glossy Ibis, Common Black-headed Gull, and Little Gull, which have been viewed in recent years.

Of the four associated lakes, **North Heron Lake** is probably the most attractive to the greatest variety of birds, but it is also the most difficult to view. The **Lindgren-Traeger Bird Sanctuary**, a 91-acre marsh on the north side, provides a fair vantage point to view birds (take Highway 60 north 1.5 miles to County Road 24, then go right 2 miles and take the township road south 1 mile). For another vantage point, follow County Road 9 south from the town of Heron Lake for 1.3 miles; the left-turn, dead-end road leads to the west side of Heron Lake.

Some other wetland complex spots to check include **Duck Lake** (from County Road 9, 1 mile north of the town of Heron Lake), and both the west public boat access on **South Heron Lake** (first left turn on County 20, 0.33 mile southeast of Okabena) and the other east side boat access (on County 71, 2 miles north of County 14 in Lakefield). During periods of low water, mudflats in the area can provide good shorebird numbers.

About 8 miles east of Heron Lake is **Kilen Woods State Park**, a 200-acre oasis of forest along the Des Moines River. The park is an excellent place to view warblers in spring migration as they move along the river's wooded corridor. The park's entrance is along County Road 24 (follow State Highway 86, 4 miles north of Lakefield, then take County 24 east 6 miles).

Additional help:

Minnesota Highway Map location: E-21

Hazards: Poison ivy, stinging nettle, mosquitos, tapwater high in nitrates

Nearest food, gas, lodging: Jackson, Windom, Lakefield, Heron Lake, Okabena

Camping: Kilen Woods State Park, (507) 662-6258

Land ownership: State of Minnesota, private

Additional information: Minnesota DNR, (612) 296-6157; Jackson County Tourism, Inc., (507) 847-4235

Recommended length of stay: 1 day

25. Albert Lea and vicinity ————————————

Habitats: Lake, wetland, deciduous forest, oak savannah

Key birds: Western Grebe, American White Pelican, Sedge Wren, Orchard Oriole, Dickcissel, Grasshopper Sparrow

Best times to bird: March-April; November-December

Don't miss: Helmer Myre State Park

General information:

Southeastern Minnesota, with its beautifully wooded hills and hollows, has been described as "little Switzerland." The area gets attention for its long, rolling grasslands, unusual "blue" coteaus, and "western" flavor. But what about the land in between?

It is hard to picture what today's cultivated prairie might have looked like in its virgin cloak, before the coming of Europeans. We know from archaeological records that the area around Albert Lea was inhabited for more than 9,000 years. Artifacts tell us the area must have been rich in natural resources, and able to support thriving encampments of native peoples.

We also know that the area was much richer in lakes than it is today. Freeborn County's Lake Geneva, for example, is the sole survivor among a number of shallow lakes in the Turtle Creek watershed that were drained for cultivation. Minnesota Lake, a sizable body of water, was listed as a "former" lake in 1920, when the lake bed was reported to be growing crops, though it is obviously restored today.

This area was favored among early explorers who climbed up out of the Mississippi basin onto the game-rich Minnesota prairies. Many of the earliest exploring parties, financed and outfitted by foreign crowns, gained the favor of their sponsors through reports of promise in this rich country of prairie lakes and streams.

Birding information:

Once upon a time, the rich grasslands and game-filled lakes and marshes of this part of southern Minnesota were a destination for hopeful settlers. Today, the bulk of travelers pass through at interstate highway speeds. But those who choose to stop will be rewarded. Although bird rarities seldom are reported in these portions of Faribault, Freeborn, and Blue Earth counties, the few area lakes and relative absence of woodlands make the good birding spots that much more attractive to migrants. To reach Albert Lea from the Twin Cities, follow I-35 south about 95 miles to the Albert Lea exit.

Minnesota Lake, on the Blue Earth county line, is broad and shallow enough to attract loons, ducks, gulls, and pelicans during both spring and fall migration. The best time to visit is around the April ice-out and again in early November, just before freeze-up. The best lake view is from County Road 20 on the north side, or from the town of Minnesota Lake itself. To reach Minnesota

Albert Lea and vicinity

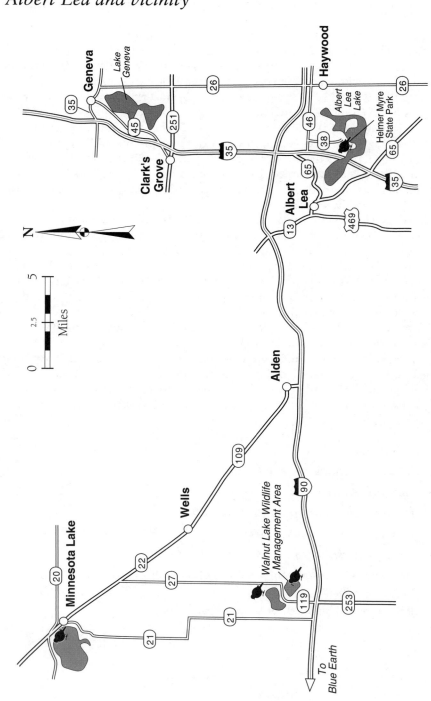

Geneva

Lake Geneva

Haywood

26

35

45

251

26

Clark's Grove

35

Albert Lea Lake

46

38

Helmer Myre State Park

65

35

65

Albert Lea

N

13

469

5

2.5

Miles

0

Alden

109

90

Wells

Walnut Lake Wildlife Management Area

Minnesota Lake

20

22

27

119

253

21

21

To Blue Earth

Lake from Albert Lea, follow I-90 west to the Alden exit, then take State Highway 109 northwest to Wells, and State Highway 22 northwest to Minnesota Lake.

Walnut Lake Wildlife Management Area is best known for hunting, but it has plenty of good habitat for nesting birds, including Orchard Oriole, Sedge Wren, Dickcissel, and Grasshopper Sparrow. The lakes here also are good places to view waterfowl migrants in spring. To reach Walnut Lake, take I-90 west to the State Highway 253 exit, then take County Road 119 north 1.5 miles, where it passes between the areas two units.

Covering more than 1,600 acres, **Helmer Myre State Park** (better known locally as "Big Island") encompasses part of the shoreline and the prominent island-peninsula on **Albert Lea Lake**. The park lies 3 miles southeast of the town of Albert Lea on County Road 38. Signs on both I-90 and I-35, which intersect just north of Albert Lea, will direct you to the park. Use exit 11 on I-35 for the most direct access.

The park's hardwood forest, primarily on the island, has been able to maintain itself for centuries because of its isolation from fire. It is reminiscent of those seen farther north in the northern deciduous region, and attracts a number of interesting woodland birds in migration, particularly warblers. The park also includes oak savannah and wetland habitats. Albert Lea Lake has become a consistent place to view pelicans, especially during fall migration, and its open water attracts waterfowl and an occasional Bald Eagle in winter.

Northwest of Albert Lea, **Lake Geneva** has hosted a number of interesting birds over the years, not the least of which are nesting Western Grebes. The lake is best viewed from County Road 45 on the west side, including the public boat access area. To reach the lake from I-35, take the Clark's Grove exit (State Highway 251) and go west into Clark's Grove, then take County Road 45 northeast past the interstate about 1 mile and look for the public boat access sign on your right.

Additional help:

Minnesota Highway Map location: E-21

Hazards: Poison ivy, mosquitos

Nearest food, gas, lodging: Albert Lea

Camping: Myre-Big Island State Park, (507) 373-5084

Land ownership: State of Minnesota, private

Additional information: Minnesota DNR, (612) 296-6157; Albert Lea CVB, (800) 345-8414

Recommended length of stay: 1 day

Minnesota
Southern Hardwood Region

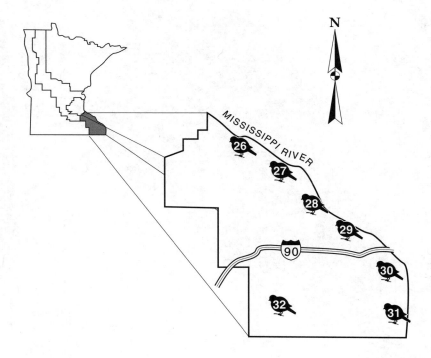

Broad-winged Hawks

Southern Hardwood Region

Radiating away from the Mississippi River as it traces its 125-mile course from the Twin Cities to Iowa, Minnesota's southern hardwood region encompasses floodplain, wetlands, wooded bluffs, and ravines more characteristic of places like the hill country of Missouri than Minnesota. But this *is* Minnesota, and this region comprises a small but very special part of the state. Drained by four major waterways—the Cannon, Zumbro, Whitewater, and Root rivers—the region contains about seventy five designated trout streams.

The species and character of the southern hardwood region differ considerably from Minnesota's northern deciduous region. Here the hills, hollows, and river bottoms nurture hickory, butternut, black walnut, and swamp white oak; a more southerly climate brings an early spring and lingering fall; and the landscape is carved by countless streams and almost no lakes. It is a land inhabited by opossum, turkey, quail, and even rattlesnakes.

The Mississippi River here became the gateway through which countless explorers and pioneers entered Minnesota. It became the watery highway it remains today, first transporting people north, and later carrying logs, grain, and other important products south.

One of the region's most important features, Lake Pepin is a broad, 20-mile-long pool formed by the outwash of Wisconsin's Chippewa River, a natural resting area for large flocks of migratory waterfowl and major concentrations of Bald Eagles in March and November. Another landmark is the Upper Mississippi Wildlife Refuge. Its northern edge borders Lake Pepin, and it incorporates river bottom and associated habitat for the next 300 miles downstream (to Rock Island, Illinois), providing important wetland habitat for migrant waterfowl and shorebirds, and floodplain forest nesting sites for a variety of bird species. East of the deeply cut bluff country, the rolling lakeless area of mixed prairie and oak woodland was untouched by the last glaciers, and today supports handsome farms and important southern Minnesota cities such as Rochester, with its large wintering flock of giant Canada Geese.

One of the things that makes the southern hardwood region so special is its bird life, species with limited range in the state, but all uniquely associated with this small region, including Great Egret, Turkey Vulture, Eastern Screech-Owl, Red-bellied Woodpecker, Willow Flycatcher, Blue-gray Gnatcatcher, Wood Thrush, Loggerhead Shrike, Northern Cardinal, Eastern Towhee, Lark Sparrow, Eastern Meadowlark, and Orchard Oriole.

There are also species that occur *only* in this region (although some of their ranges may extend slightly beyond), including Wild Turkey, Northern Bobwhite, Common Moorhen, Acadian Flycatcher, Tufted Titmouse, Bell's Vireo, Blue-winged Warbler, Cerulean Warbler, Prothonotary Warbler, and Louisiana Waterthrush. And this is one of the best parts of the state to get an up-close-and-personal look at birds in migration, especially eagles, waterfowl, and wood warblers. Fall colors in this region usually peak in the first two weeks of October.

26. Frontenac State Park

Habitats: Hardwood forest, floodplain forest, lake shoreline

Key birds: Bald Eagle (late fall, late winter), Turkey Vulture, migrating hawks (fall), Blue-gray Gnatcatcher, migrating warblers (May), Prothonotary and Cerulean Warblers (nesting)

Best time to bird: April-mid June

Don't miss: In-Yan-Teopa overlook

General information:

Rarely is a birding area extremely productive of species, yet charming and scenic at the same time. Frontenac State Park is such a place, and it is well known to Minnesota birders.

Perched on a point of the Mississippi River's Lake Pepin, Frontenac seems to have had a siren's charm since the earliest times. Native peoples built their encampments and buried their dead here as long ago as 400 B.C. Father Louis Hennepin visited this section of the Mississippi River in 1680, followed in the early 1700s by Rene Boucher, who built a log stockade on this site, naming it Fort Beauharnois. The first settler to build his home here was James "Bully" Wells, who operated a trading post.

In 1854, Israel Garrard bought the site, joined a few years later by his younger brother Louis. They named it Frontenac, in honor of the former governor of New France who initiated many important New World explorations. Shortly after the Civil War the Garrards began construction of many of Frontenac's buildings, using local hardwood lumber and quarried rock. St. Hubert's Lodge, the Lake Side Hotel, and Christ Episcopal Church can still be viewed in the old town today. During the late 1800s, prior to the coming of the railroad, Frontenac was a nationally known resort for the savoir faire river traveler.

Frontenac rests on Point No-Point, named because this promontory can be seen for 8 miles on the lake, yet seemed to appear no closer for those approaching on river craft until its shore was reached. Certainly it was this visible point of land that attracted so many travelers over the ages. Perhaps it was the enormous rock seated atop the bluff—In-Yan-Teopa, as the Sioux called it—that lured so many to Frontenac.

Birding information:

Frontenac State Park is as traditional a spring site for birders as it is for birds. For many years Twin Cities warbler-watchers have gathered here during the last week of April and first weeks of May (depending on developing spring-like weather) to view the parade of fully plumaged wood warblers on their way north. To reach Frontenac from the Twin Cities (about 60 miles) follow Highway 10/61 south from I-94 in St. Paul (or from I-494 south of St. Paul), remain on Highway 61 south past Red Wing, and look for the Frontenac sign after about 10 miles. Enter the state park by turning east on County Road 2.

166

Frontenac State Park

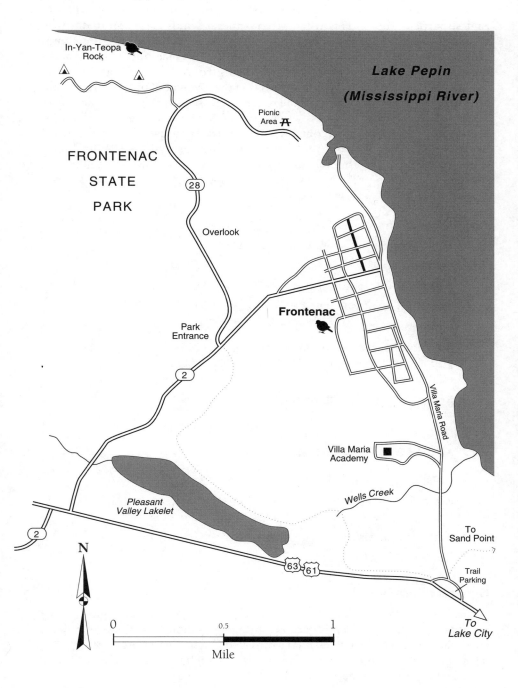

In-Yan-Teopa Rock

Lake Pepin
(Mississippi River)

Picnic Area

FRONTENAC
STATE
PARK

28

Overlook

Frontenac

Park Entrance

2

Villa Maria Road

Villa Maria Academy

Wells Creek

Pleasant Valley Lakelet

2

N

63 61

To Sand Point

Trail Parking

To Lake City

0   0.5   1

Mile

The park's high bluff area (reached by taking County 28 inside the park, from County 2), where camping and picnic grounds are located, offers a good view of the lake, a chance to see warblers, and also a chance to see hawks and eagles, particularly on days when rare northeast winds create an updraft on the bluff. The prominent rock outcrop, **In-Yan-Teopa**, is located near the campground. Switchback trails descend the bluff below the picnic area, and concentrations of warblers may occur along the trails from May 1 to May 15.

Another good place to view warblers is in the low woodlands in and around the village of **Frontenac**. Some of the roads are closed to through traffic; walking is advised. Scan the trees between Villa Maria and the old village of Frontenac, and keep an eye out also for Tufted Titmouse. The trail toward Sand Point, accessible from the parking area just as you enter Villa Maria road, may produce Prothonotary Warblers, or in years of low water, gulls and shorebirds. Enter the Villa Maria road by turning left from Highway 61 about 1.5 miles south of County 2.

Additional help:

Minnesota Highway Map location: M-18

Hazards: Cool, wet weather

Nearest food, lodging, gas: Red Wing, Lake City

Camping: Frontenac State Park, (612) 345-3401

Land ownership: State of Minnesota

Additional information: Minnesota DNR, (612) 296-6157; Red Wing VCB, (612) 385-5934; Lake City Area Chamber of Commerce, (800) 360-4123

Recommended length of stay: 3 hours

27. Wabasha and vicinity

Habitats: River backwater, marsh, lake

Key birds: Tundra Swan (November), Bald Eagle (winter), Great Egret, Herring Gull, Willow Flycatcher, Orchard Oriole

Best times to bird: November, December; February-March

Don't miss: Swan migration (November)

General information:

Wabasha is taken from the Sioux "Wapasha," or "red cap," the names of three hereditary chiefs whose bands occupied the country along the Mississippi River and Lake Pepin. The first chief, it is told, visited Quebec in the late 1700s, receiving from the British a red hat and English flag. Upon his return he was lauded by his tribe for possessing these great gifts, and thus named.

Wabasha and vicinity

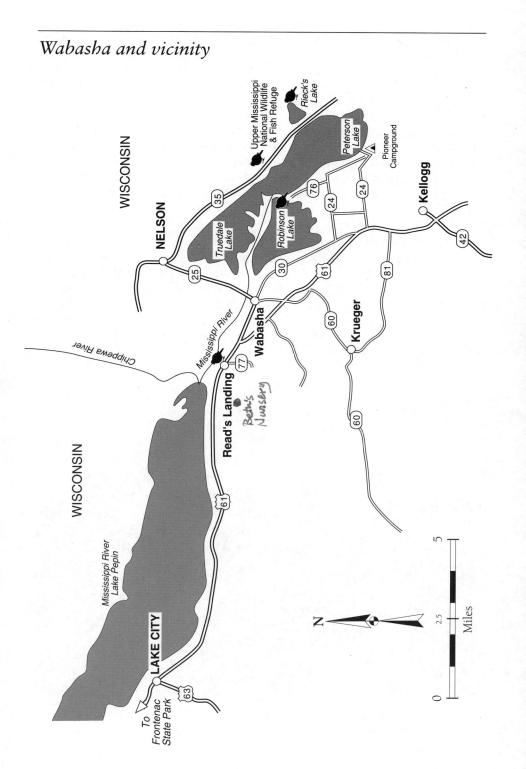

WISCONSIN

Upper Mississippi
National Wildlife
& Fish Refuge

Rieck's
Lake

Peterson
Lake

Pioneer
Campground

Kellogg

35

76

24

24

NELSON

Truedale
Lake

Robinson
Lake

25

30

61

81

Mississippi River

Wabasha

Krueger

60

60

Chippewa River

77

Read's Landing

Beth's Nursery

61

WISCONSIN

Mississippi River
Lake Pepin

LAKE CITY

63

To
Frontenac
State Park

N

0   2.5   5

Miles

Read's Landing, north of Wabasha, was first established as a Sioux trading post in about 1810, and continued operations until about 1880. Its last proprietor was Charles Read, who came from England as a youth, but served America as a soldier in the service of the Canadian Rebellion against the British. Ironically, Read was captured by the British and sentenced to be hanged. He was later pardoned, after which he returned to the United States.

Like Big Stone, Marsh, and Lac Qui Parle in the west, Lake Pepin is a natural flowage lake, formed by the outwash of one river entering another. In this case, Wisconsin's Chippewa River enters the Mississippi. Like the others, Lake Pepin's level has been stabilized with control structures. In addition, its channel has been dredged to accommodate the barge traffic that courses the river today.

Birding information:

Lake Pepin, stretching along the east side of Highway 61 from Red Wing to just north of Wabasha, is a magnet for waterfowl, particularly those birds drawn to big water. Each November thousands of big Common Mergansers (estimates of as many as 100,000 at one time) raft up on the lake, and their uniformed ranks are fascinating to watch as they follow the schools of shad. Loons, grebes, scaup, and gulls also use the lake at this time, when its current, and more southerly location, keep it open long after most of the state's lakes have frozen over.

Birders enjoy eagle watching throughout the winter at places like Read's Landing north of Wabasha, but especially in February and March.

No, it isn't Minnesota, but it's just across the river. Rieck's Lake is the best place to get a close look at wild Tundra Swans.

To reach Lake Pepin from the Twin Cities, follow Highway 10/61 south from I-494 and stay on Highway 61 through Red Wing (it's about another 15 miles south to Lake City). The Lake City Marina, 2 blocks east of Highway 61 at the end of Park Street in downtown Lake City, offers a chance to check out gulls that frequent the docks and breakwater areas. **Highway 61**, all along Lake Pepin's west shore, provides many observation points where one can park and scan the water for gulls and waterfowl.

Read's Landing (about 10 miles south of Lake City on Highway 61—watch for the County Road 77 sign) is one of few spots providing all the ingredients to serve as a funnel for migrating and wintering Bald Eagles. As such, it has become familiar to Minnesota birders, and naturalist-led trips from the Twin Cities are offered during the peak eagle-viewing seasons (primarily late winter). The constricted flow of the Mississippi River, plus the inflow of the Chippewa River from Wisconsin, provide open water most of the winter, and as many as several hundred eagles have been known to occupy the waterway between here and Lake Pepin at one time (with counts of up to fifty birds typical in the vicinity of Read's Landing). County Road 77 drops directly into the landing area, or the river can be scanned from the highway just north of here.

The backwaters south of Wabasha around **Robinson Lake** and **Peterson Lake** become home to Minnesota's greatest concentrations of Tundra Swans during fall migration. Following County Road 30 south out of downtown

Tundra Swans nest in the Arctic but pass through Minnesota each spring and fall on the way to and from their Eastern Seaboard wintering grounds. Spring migration peaks during the first half of April. Fall peaks occur about the third week of November. BILL MARCHEL

Wabasha to County Road 24 east, then on to County 76 north will wrap you around Robinson Lake. Another good place to see Tundra Swans in late fall (and a few in early spring) are the Weaver Bottoms (see next map section). Although it's not Minnesota, a spot just across the river offers the best swan viewing in the Midwest. South of Nelson, Wisconsin, the **Upper Mississippi River National Wildlife and Fish Refuge** offers a handicap-accessible viewing platform perched over **Rieck's Lake** at the mouth of the Buffalo River, providing a good look at hundreds of resting swans. Cross the Mississippi River at Wabasha on east Highway 25 to Nelson, Wisconsin, and take State Highway 35 south about 6 miles to reach the bridge at Rieck's Lake.

Additional help:

Minnesota Highway Map location: M,N-18,19

Hazards: Cold

Nearest food, lodging, gas: Lake City

Camping: Pioneer Campground (6 miles southeast of Wabasha on Co. Rd. 24), (612) 432-2228

Land ownership: State of Minnesota

Additional information: Minnesota DNR, (612) 296-6157; Lake City Area Chamber of Commerce, (800) 360-4123; Wabasha Area Chamber of Commerce, (612) 565-4158

Recommended length of stay: 1/2 day

28. The Whitewater

Habitats: Wetland, sedge meadow, oak savannah, deciduous forest, creek margins

Key birds: Golden Eagle (winter), Red-shouldered Hawk (nesting), Wild Turkey, American Woodcock, Black- and Yellow-billed Cuckoos, Eastern Screech-Owl, Sedge Wren, Louisiana Waterthrush, Lark Sparrow

Best times to bird: May-June; October-December; February-March

Don't miss: Highway 74 from Weaver southwest to Elba

General information:

Looking at the beautiful timbered hills and pastoral valleys of Minnesota's southeastern counties, it's hard to imagine the area as a wasteland, but that is the picture that began to emerge only half a century after settlement. Along with receiving the earliest settlers in Minnesota, the southern hardwood region also fell victim to some of the worst conservation practices anywhere in the state.

While the recipe for disaster lay right under the pioneers' noses, none seemed to have the foresight to envision it: steep slopes, thin soils, and an abundance of streams with the potential to flood. The rich valley soils withstood cultivation, until flooding washed loosened soils into the creek beds. In an effort to put more land into production, slopes were cleared of timber, terraces plowed, and the fragile hillsides grazed.

Without the protection of stabilizing vegetation, flash floods carried huge amounts of topsoil, followed by sand and gravel, down the slopes and onto the valley floors, clogging and muddying creek beds and burying homesteads. Whole communities were abandoned, and although the term had yet to be coined, the area had become an ecological disaster.

Fortunately, one man with vision and a great love for these bluffs and valleys identified the practices that had led to such decline, and set out to promote ecological order. Richard J. Dorer began a farsighted conservation movement in the 1930s, first concentrating its efforts on the Whitewater Valley. One look today at the beauty of this valley and surrounding lands confirms that Dorer's efforts to restore the region to its former splendor were not in vain. The Memorial Hardwood State Forest, which spreads across this region, was established in 1961, taking under its care about 2 million acres—the largest of the state forests. In 1976 it was appropriately renamed the Richard J. Dorer Memorial Hardwood Forest.

Birding information:

Six miles below Wabasha (65 miles southeast of the Twin Cities) on Highway 61 lies the small town of Kellogg. Southeast of Kellogg are several areas comprising thousands of acres of undisturbed land. The largest, **McCarthy Lake Wildlife Management Area,** is difficult to access, but County Road 84 southeast out of Kellogg does a decent job of skirting the area. You can probe

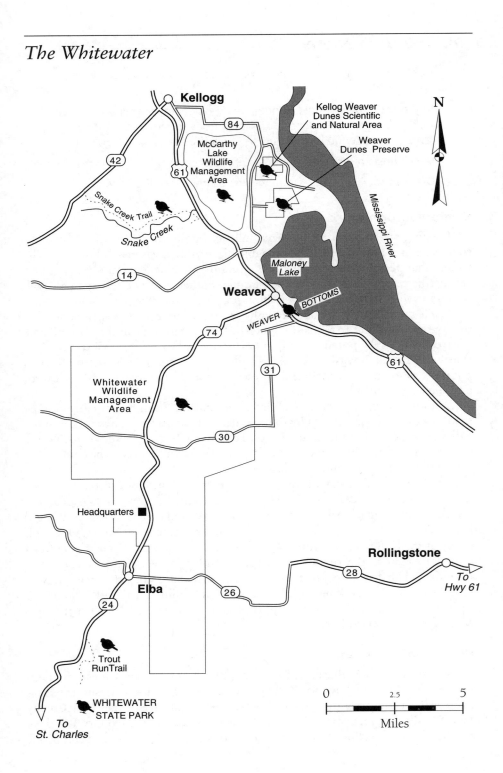

certain portions from the management area's east side, where wet meadows and a mix of dry brushland habitat should produce Great Egret, Black- and Yellow-billed Cuckoos, Willow Flycatcher, Orchard Oriole, American Woodcock, Sedge Wren, and Field, Lark, and Grasshopper Sparrows. Bell's Vireo, though rare, also nests here.

A piece of fine woodland habitat can be found along the **Snake Creek Trail**, which leaves the west side of Highway 61 about 4 miles south of Kellogg (just south of Snake Creek) and wends its way up to State Highway 42. Be sure to take the first right turn on the trail that crosses the creek.

Nearby are two preserve tracts, the **Weaver Dunes Preserve** and north of it, the **Kellogg Weaver Dunes Scientific and Natural Area**, both also accessed from County Road 84. These areas of sand prairie feature oak savannah, swales, and grassy dunes. The most important resident of the 697-acre Weaver Dunes Preserve is the endangered Blanding's Turtle ("Rare Turtle Crossing" signs can be seen on the roadsides). You may also see Loggerhead Shrike, Upland Sandpiper, and Western Meadowlark here, in addition to some of the species listed above.

About 7 miles south of Kellogg, just below the town of Weaver, lies the **Weaver Bottoms,** a good place to see Tundra Swans in late fall. Lesser numbers of swans make an appearance in the backwaters between Weaver and the town of Minneiska in spring, as do a wide variety of other waterfowl species. The bottoms lie on both sides of Highway 61. This is also a good place to see Forster's Tern during spring migration (May).

Comprising more than 27,000 acres, the heavy woodlands and water impoundments in the **Whitewater Wildlife Management Area** offer some of the best year-round birding in Minnesota. State Highway 74 southwest from Highway 61 in Weaver leads through the heart of the management area and to Whitewater State Park itself, about 3 miles southeast of the town of Elba. (The heart of the wildlife management area is outlined on this map, but its various tracts radiate widely.) Along its timbered valley flanking the Whitewater River, the area maintains fourteen artificial wetlands and over six hundred planted food plots. This is the area where Wild Turkeys were first released when the state program to re-establish the birds began in 1964. Today the flocks are common to the valley. Although turkeys have recently been transplanted to areas farther north in the state, the southern hardwood region is currently the only area where they thrive, along with a healthy population of Ruffed Grouse.

Check along the streams and wetlands for herons, egrets, ducks, Sedge Wren, Louisiana Waterthrush, Willow Flycatcher, and perhaps Bell's Vireo. The creek margins and nearby uplands should hold nesting (and courting in spring) American Woodcock. The uplands offer Wild Turkey, Ruffed Grouse, Red-shouldered Hawks, and Barred, Great Horned, and Eastern Screech-Owls. Winter Whitewater specialties include Golden Eagle, American Black Duck, Northern Shrike, American Tree Sparrow, and Common Redpoll, as well as the more common visitors to winter bird feeders mentioned earlier. A feeder is maintained at the area headquarters.

Also worth a visit is **Whitewater State Park**, on the south end of the management area, which offers camping, good hiking trails, and a visitors' program with organized birding trips throughout the year. The park also has an excellent nature center and maintains winter bird feeders. Louisiana Waterthrush have consistently been sighted along its streams in recent years. One of the park's best trails is the **Trout Run Trail**. If you're heading south on Highway 74, look for the old buildings of the former park entrance (south picnic area) on your left, 1 mile south of the new information center. Park here and walk in on the trail that makes a loop before heading south along Trout Run Creek. The dead-end trail through a lush valley takes about 1.5 hours to walk in its entirety and offers Louisiana Waterthrush habitat as well as excellent warbler habitat during spring migration.

Just a short drive southeast of the park (go to St. Charles and travel 10 miles east on U.S. Highway 14) is the town of Lewiston and its sometimes-productive sewage lagoons. The city of Rochester, with its large flock of wintering Giant Canada Geese, lies just 21 miles west of St. Charles on Highway 14.

Additional help:

Minnesota Highway Map location: M,N-19,20

Hazards: Poison ivy, biting insects, rattlesnakes, cold

Nearest food, lodging, gas: Lake City

Camping: Whitewater State Park, (507) 932-3007

Land ownership: State of Minnesota, The Nature Conservancy

Additional information: Minnesota DNR, (612) 296-6157; Wabasha Area Chamber of Commerce, (612) 565-4158; Rochester Convention and Visitors Bureau, (800) 634-8277; Winona Convention and Visitors Bureau, (800) 657-4972; Whitewater Wildlife Management Area Office, (507) 932-4133; Whitewater State Park manager, (507) 932-3007. For information on birding in Rochester and Olmstead County, contact Bob Ekblad, 5737 Shern Drive NW, Byron, MN 55920.

Recommended length of stay: 1 day

29. Winona and vicinity

Habitats: Floodplain forest, lake margin, brushy upland, parkland, hardwood forest

Key birds: Greater and Lesser Scaup (fall migration); Great Egret; Bonaparte's Gull (late April to early May); Caspian and Forster's Terns (spring); Black- and Yellow-billed Cuckoos; Willow Flycatcher; Sedge Wren; Field, Lark, and Grasshopper Sparrows

Best times to bird: March-June; September; November

Don't miss: Prairie Island Road

General information:

Despite its gentle, feminine name, the lore surrounding the site of this beautiful river city reads like an historic soap opera. The Indian maiden Winona was the cousin of the last of the Sioux chiefs named Wabasha. The name, meaning "first born," was actually common in usage among Sioux families. It is pronounced correctly with the soft sound "win" on the first syllable and accented on the second syllable.

According to the tale, Winona, distressed by demands she give herself to a betrothed marriage, threw herself from a precipice overlooking Lake Pepin rather than comply with the arrangement. The same site, on the lake's east shore, is today known as "Maiden Rock."

The site of the city of Winona was called "La Prairie aux Ailes" by the French, meaning "Wing's Prairie." The name referred its former occupants, the Mdewakanton Sioux, of whom four successive chiefs bore the name Red Wing—that title gained by the first chief for his habit of carrying a swan's wing dyed scarlet under his arm.

Wabasha's band was the last to occupy this site, however. The Sioux themselves referred to Wabasha's village here as "Kiyuksan," which has been translated as "breakers in two," or "violators," referring to this band's breach of custom forbidding relatives to marry. In 1848, both the last chief Wabasha and Winona were reported to have played important roles in the relocation of the Winnebago band from Iowa to this site, "Wabasha's Prairie," and later to Long Prairie, some 200 miles northwest.

Birding information:

A pleasant place to visit (famous for its Winona Knits woolen mills, and an outlet store in town worth finding), Winona also offers birds and plenty of habitat, from the high, wooded parkland above the city to the wetlands, backwaters, and floodplain forests along the river—there's plenty to see. Winona lies on U.S. Highway 61 about 110 miles southeast of the Twin Cities.

The best place to start birding in Winona is the well-known **Prairie Island Road**, which transects the backwater channels and floodplain forests of the Mississippi River. From Highway 61 in Winona, take Huff Street northeast to Riverview Drive, turn left, continue to Prairie Island Road, and turn right. This area has lots of low, floodplain sideroads, which can be walked, and has produced sightings

Winona and vicinity

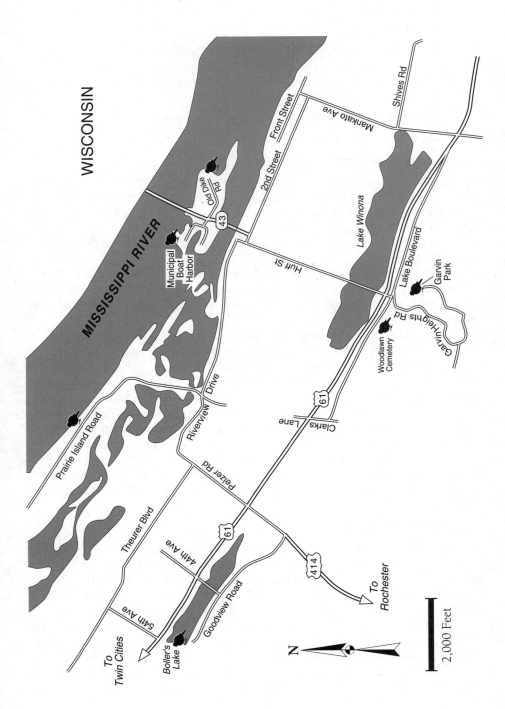

WISCONSIN

MISSISSIPPI RIVER

Old Dike Rd

43

Front Street

2nd Street

Municipal Boat Harbor

Huff St

Lake Winona

Mankato Ave

Shives Rd

Riverview Drive

Prairie Island Road

Pelzer Rd

61

Clarks Lane

Lake Boulevard

Garvin Park

Garvin Heights Rd

Woodlawn Cemetery

61

Theurer Blvd

44th Ave

54th Ave

Goodview Road

To Twin Cities

414

To Rochester

N

2,000 Feet

Boller's Lake

178

as unusual as a White Ibis in 1995, in addition to the eagles, herons, egrets, water-fowl, gulls, woodpeckers, and warblers commonly seen.

A couple of other quick places to visit along the river are the **Municipal boat harbor** (Huff Street northeast from Highway 61 to 2nd Street, right one block and left on Highway 43) and the **Old Dike Road** across Highway 43 from the boat harbor. The harbor is a good place to watch gulls, and the dike offers good places to look for the same birds you might find on Prairie Island Road. Before leaving this side of town, it might be worth a walk on the short stretch of the paved Winona Hike & Bike Trail, which can be reached from the extreme southeast end of the Fleet Farm parking lot in front of the lumber building. Take the trail back as far as Shives Road and watch for Black- and Yellow-billed Cuckoos, Willow Fly-catcher, Orchard Oriole, American Woodcock, Sedge Wren, and Field, Lark, and Grasshopper Sparrows. Bell's Vireo has also been spotted here in recent years.

Another good Winona spot is small **Boller's Lake,** just off Highway 61 on 44th Avenue on the northwest side of town, which may attract wading birds, gulls, waterfowl, or shorebirds. Father east, off Lake Boulevard (reached by turning southeast off Highway 61 from Clark's Lane or Huff Street), is Garvin Heights Road. The road begins by passing **Woodlawn Cemetery** (on your right as you leave Lake Boulevard), a good place to look for migrating warblers in spring, and ends up the hill (take a left at the "Y") at **Garvin Park,** which offers a spectacular view of the city and the river beyond, as well as some picturesque woodlands prime for spring warbler watching and many of the common upland forest birds of the southeast.

Additional help:

Minnesota Highway Map location: M,N-18,19

Hazards: Cold

Nearest food, lodging, gas: Winona

Camping: Winona KOA (south of the city on Highway 61), (612) 432-2228

Land ownership: State of Minnesota, city of Winona

Additional information: Minnesota DNR, (612) 296-6157; Winona Convention and Visitors Bureau, (800) 657-4972

Recommended length of stay: 1/2 day

30. La Crescent and vicinity

Habitats: Wetland, floodplain forest, brushy borders

Key birds: Bald Eagle (nesting, Blue Lake); Wild Turkey; Great Egret; Least Bittern; Sora Rail; Virginia Rail; Common Moorhen; Willow Flycatcher; Tufted Titmouse; Sedge Wren; Wood Thrush; Prothonotary, Cerulean, and Blue-winged Warblers

Best time to bird: May-June

Don't miss: O.L. Kipp State Park

La Crescent and vicinity
O.L. Kipp State Park, Mound Prairie Marsh

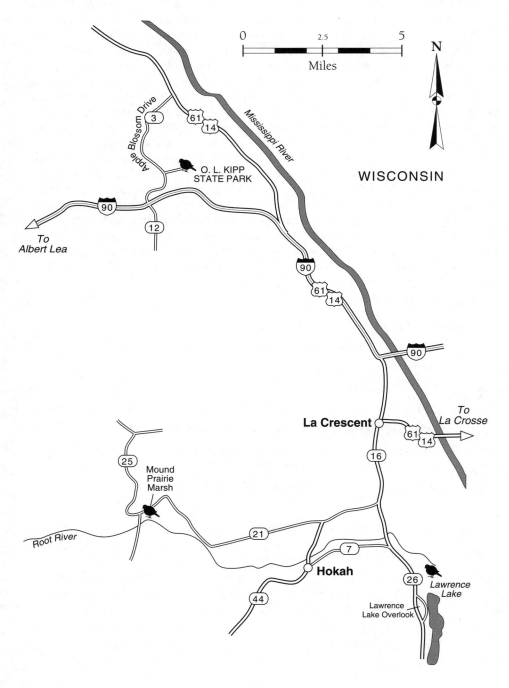

General information:

The river town of La Crescent need not envy the larger La Crosse, Wisconsin, that rests across the river. La Crescent is charming enough in its own right, and it certainly attracts more birders than its neighbor. Nevertheless, La Crescent earned its name somewhat by default to La Crosse, owing to a long-standing rivalry between the two town sites.

The first French explorers, entering the new lands that would be named Wisconsin, witnessed a spirited game of ball and stick played by the Sioux on the prairie here, a favorite field for the sport. That prairie was given the name La Crosse, referring to the bat used in playing ball, a name later applied to the game itself. Later, La Crosse Prairie became the site of the city of La Crosse.

Misinterpreting these words, La Crescent's founders assumed La Crosse to mean "the Cross," which actually would have correctly been termed "La Croix." According to some accounts, these same founders associated "the Cross" with the Crusaders who battled the Turks in their quest for the Grail, battles that became symbolized by Cross versus Crescent. As a symbol of defiance—rather than deference—to its river rival, La Crescent smugly adopted its present name in 1856.

Birding information:

The La Crescent area holds the distinction of producing an interesting array of hard-to-find birds, all in one place. Least Bittern, King Rail (rare), Yellow-crowned Night Heron (rare), Common Moorhen, and Prothonotary, Cerulean, and Blue-winged Warblers all have been found here, in addition to the more common regional wetland and forest bird species. La Crescent lies 134 miles south of St. Paul on State Highway 61, just 23 miles north of the Iowa border. Interstate 90, which runs all the way across southern Minnesota, enters Wisconsin just above La Crescent.

Approximately 8 miles north of La Crescent, **O.L. Kipp State Park** occupies 3,000 acres on the river bluffs. The park can be reached from the intersection of I-90 and U.S. 61, by traveling west on I-90 to the County Road 12 exit, then traveling back east on County Road 3 (Apple Blossom Drive) to the park's entrance. This is one of the younger state parks, but in an elite category when it comes to bluff country birds. Formerly the most dependable site in the state to find the rare Henslow's Sparrow, it has been less productive for this bird in recent years.

Six miles south of La Crescent (3.3 miles south of the junction of Highway 26 and County Road 7) is a nice little drive that leaves the highway to the east for about 200 yards and overlooks **Lawrence Lake** before returning to the highway again. This is a good place to use a spotting scope to scan for waterfowl and wading birds, especially in March when migrants use the marsh.

About 10 miles west of La Crescent is **Mound Prairie marsh**, which recently has become a dependable spring birding site for Sandhill Crane and Common Moorhen. To reach the marsh, take State Highway 16 south from La Crescent and follow it toward Hokah, turning right on County Road 21 on

La Crescent and vicinity
La Crescent

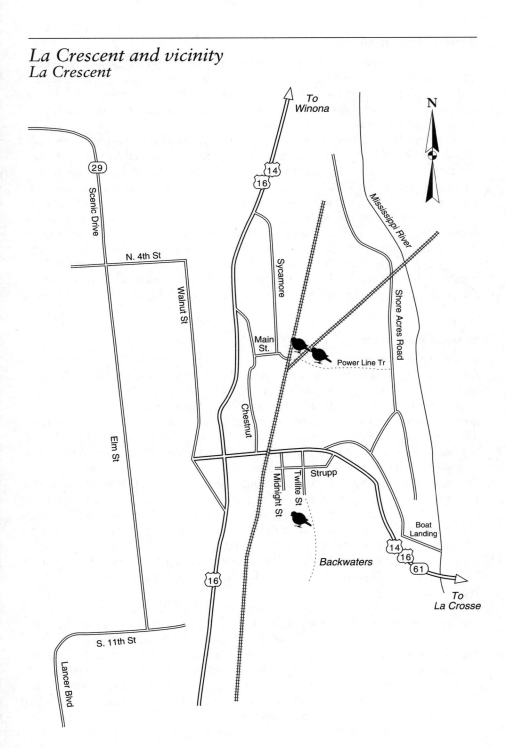

the north side of the Root River. The marsh lies at the intersection of County 21 and County 25, in a place called Mound Prairie.

One of the best places to find Willow Flycatchers in **La Crescent** is the Brush Dump just east of the car wash at the end of the very short Main Street. Park at the dump and listen for flycatchers. A walk from here along the railroad tracks could produce rails, moorhens, egrets, and herons. With consent, cross the truss storage lot to view excellent marsh habitat north of the tracks. The trail through the open gate to the east has been a great area to find Prothonotary Warblers; this powerline trail ends at Shore Acres Road.

Another good place to view the Mississippi River backwaters is just south of Highway 61/14/16 as it heads toward the river and Wisconsin. Watch for **Twilite Street** and follow it south 1 block to its dead end; a trail goes down through the willows to the backwaters. On the opposite side (north) of the highway is **Shore Acres Road,** which views some excellent shallow water areas. Bear left on this road and drive 0.4 mile past the second "Y" to the powerline that comes in from the west. You can park here and follow the powerlines back to the Brush Dump area mentioned earlier.

Additional help:

Minnesota Highway Map location: O-21

Hazards: Poison ivy, stinging nettles, biting insects

Nearest food, lodging, gas: La Crescent

Camping: O.L. Kipp State Park, (507) 643-6849

Land ownership: State of Minnesota, City of La Crescent

Additional information: Minnesota DNR, (612) 296-6157; La Crescent Chamber of Commerce, (800) 926-9480; O.L. Kipp State Park manager, (507) 643-6849. For guided birding (advance notice preferred) contact: Fred Lesher, 509 Winona Street, La Crosse, WI 54603; (608) 783-1149.

Recommended length of stay: 1/2 day

31. Reno and vicinity ─────────────────────────

Habitats: Wetland, floodplain forest, hardwood forest

Key birds: Turkey Vulture; Sharp-shinned, Cooper's, and Broad-winged Hawks and Peregrine Falcon (Oct.-Nov. migration); Wild Turkey; Black- and Yellow-billed Cuckoos; Wood Thrush; Cerulean and Prothonotary Warblers; Louisiana Waterthrush; Orchard Oriole; Eastern Towhee

Best times to bird: Late April-June; September-October

Don't miss: Beaver Creek Valley State Park

Reno and vicinity

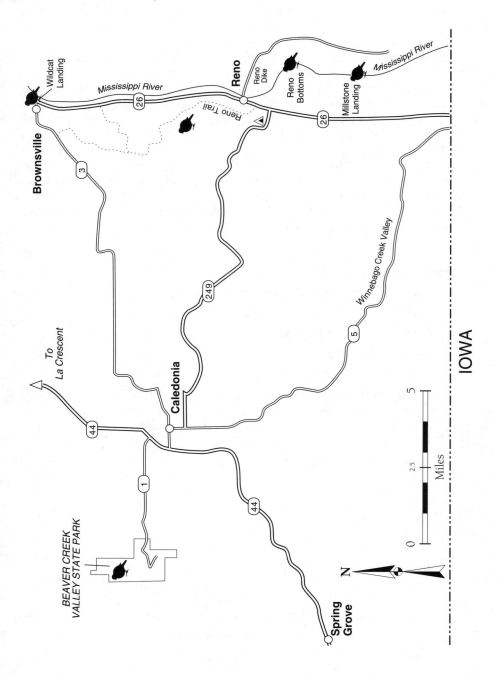

General information:

When railroads reached the Mississippi River from the east and steamboat travel was at its peak, the valleys of southeastern Minnesota were some of the first lands in the state to receive the flood of settlers. Many villages and townships were incorporated during this period of the middle 1800s, their names derived from a familiar local landmark, the memory of a former homeland, or in honor of an important founding figure.

Samuel Houston never served as President of the United States, as had the namesakes of Fillmore, Jackson, Lincoln, and Washington counties; nor had he even visited or played any role in the establishment of this county. Nonetheless, he was a popular enough American figure to merit recognition in this corner of Minnesota.

Admittedly, Houston lived a colorful life. As a boy, he spent several years living with the Cherokee Indians in his native Tennessee. He fought in the Creek War, showed bravery when severely wounded, and won the favor of General Andrew Jackson. Five years later he began a law practice, became a member of Congress, and by the age of forty-four was Governor of Tennessee. He resigned the governorship, some say because of marital problems, and moved to Arkansas to resume life with the then-relocated Cherokee tribe.

Houston was once again thrust into the spotlight when President Jackson commissioned him to travel to Texas, to inquire into its purchase. He eventually became Commander-in-Chief of the Texas Militia. Houston captured the Mexican General Santa Anna in the Battle of San Jacinto, ending the war with Mexico, and later became President of the Texas Republic. Just prior to the Civil War, in 1854, he unsuccessfully bid for the Presidency of the United States, the same year Houston County was established. It is possible that some of Houston County's founders, or their sons, fought with Houston in the Mexican War. It has been reported that he was a popular presidential candidate in Minnesota.

The village of Reno, in Houston County, was likewise named for a soldier who served in the Mexican War, who also had no direct ties to Minnesota. Jesse Lee Reno was a West Virginia native who, as a Major General of United States volunteers, died in the Civil War battle at South Mountain, Maryland, in 1862.

Birding information:

Even without seeing a bird, a springtime trip to remote and beautiful Houston County would be worthwhile. But there are plenty of birds to see, attractively surrounded by rich river-bottom wetlands, quiet glens of spring creeks, and enveloping wooded bluffs.

The town of Reno, perched along the Mississippi River on State Highway 26, just 7 miles from the Iowa border in the extreme southeastern corner of Minnesota, is small enough to miss if you're not paying attention, but it is a good focal point for birders in this far corner of the state. Approaching Reno from the north on Highway 26 (just south of the town of Brownsville) is Wildcat County Park and **Wildcat Landing**, which offers a good view of the river bottoms, camping, and a public boat access. The confluence of Wildcat Creek and the Mississippi River is a hotspot for early- and late-season shorebirds.

Closer to Reno a wide portion of the river is visible, and several pulloffs provide safe views of the river bottoms. Huge rafts of Lesser and Greater Scaups and Canvasbacks gather here in November. A few blocks north of Reno, on the east side of Highway 26, is the access to the **Reno Bottoms**. The public access gate is often locked, but you can walk down a trail onto the long dike that extends into the river bottom to the east. This is an excellent spot to carry-in a canoe and explore the backwater sloughs and floodplain forests among the many river channels; look for wading birds, waterfowl, woodpeckers, and warblers. Stick to the channels with current to avoid dead ends. Two public access points downstream provide take-out spots.

Just south of Reno, about 0.5 mile north of Highway 249, the **Reno Trail** heads inland. This is the entrance to the Reno Management Unit of the state forest, where there are picnic tables and a primitive campground. The White-eyed Vireo has nested near the campground in the past. At the top of the camp-ground is a pump that draws fresh, cold spring water. Trails radiate up into the hills from here, or you can drive or walk up the main road to the north through beautiful hardwood forests and steep bluffs. Rose-breasted Grosbeaks com-monly nest near the campground, as do Orchard Orioles, and both Yellow- and Black-billed Cuckoos and Eastern Towhees are fairly common.

Also found in proximity to the Reno Trail are Wood Thrush, Yellow-throated Vireos, Blue-winged Warblers, and Scarlet Tanagers. This is a great springtime spot for warblers, a season when the Wild Turkey often responds to train whistles and owl hoots. Continue north up the bluff past the campground to reach a hawk viewing site. Park atop the bluff between the two radio towers; this is a premier place to watch for migrating hawks in September and Octo-ber.

About two-thirds of the way to the Iowa border, south of Reno on the east side of Highway 26, is **Millstone Landing**, another good, easily accessible birding site. A short road runs in from the highway to the landing. Millstone provides a good look at channels, backwater islands, and floodplain forests with lots of large silver maples. This is a favorite spot for viewing Prothonotary Warblers. The landing is a good lunch spot, with picnic tables and portable toilets.

A visit to Caledonia requires driving to the border town of New Albin, Iowa, to reach County Road 5, which heads northwest to Caledonia (State Highway 249 just south of Reno also leads here). However, County Road 5 is the better of the two routes, coursing the thickly wooded **Winnebago Creek Valley**. Caledonia features beautiful, well-kept homes and people who obvi-ously care a lot about their surroundings. Be careful not to do too much gawk-ing at the wonderful homes or you'll miss the well-marked County Road 1, just to the north.

County Road 1 leads into **Beaver Creek Valley State Park,** considered by some to be the best birding spot in the southern hardwood region. Certainly, it offers opportunities to see three species with extremely limited ranges in Min-nesota: Tufted Titmouse, Louisiana Waterthrush, and Cerulean Warbler. The park's namesake, Beaver Creek, is one of the state's clearest spring-fed trout streams, and this park is one of the loveliest. The Quarry Trail, which heads west from the park entrance and then northwest along the creek, provides miles of good birding. Other good spots can be found along the steep, wooded bluffs near the main campground and all the way to the park's south end, where the West Rim Trail climbs above the primitive group camp. Most of the southeast's common woodland bird species can be found here, but be especially alert for the rare and local Acadian Flycatcher, the more common Least Flycatcher, the Veery, and the Louisiana Waterthrush. Broad-winged Hawks probably nest in the park.

Additional help:

Minnesota Highway Map location: O-21

Hazards: Poison ivy, stinging nettles, biting insects, rattlesnakes

Nearest food, lodging, gas: La Crescent, Caledonia

Camping: Wildcat County Park, Beaver Creek Valley State Park

Land ownership: State of Minnesota, private

Additional information: Minnesota DNR, (612) 296-6157; La Crescent Chamber of Commerce, (800) 926-9480; Caledonia Chamber of Commerce, (507) 724-5477

Recommended length of stay: 2 days

32. Forestville State Park and vicinity _____

Habitats: Stream, floodplain, deciduous forest, prairie

Key birds: Red-shouldered Hawk, Wild Turkey, Eastern Screech-Owl, Whip-poor-will, Tufted Titmouse, Blue-gray Gnatcatcher, Eastern Towhee, Field Sparrow

Best time to bird: Late April-June

Don't miss: Root River State Trail (rent a bicycle)

General information:

One can only imagine what it might have been like for a Native American hunter to leave his Mississippi River encampment and enter the magnificent, serene valleys of the Root River in the centuries before settlement. Native people knew well the many deep hollows and high bluffs of the Root River drainage. Their name for "Root" was "Huktan," but the explorer Nicollet spelled it "Hokah," which survives today as the name of a town along the Root River.

These valleys saw the boom of settlement and the bust of exploitation—all within half a century after being populated by immigrants. Excessive logging, cultivation of steep slopes, overgrazing, and flooding caused massive soil deple-

Forestville State Park and vicinity

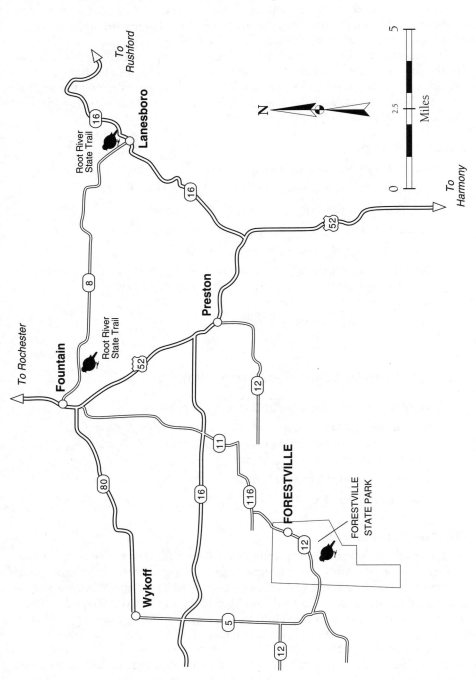

tion and erosion by the turn of the century, forcing the exodus of many home-steaders.

Although perhaps partially a victim of altered transportation routes, the town of Forestville, like much of this region, eventually suffered from failing agricultural productivity. The Forestville Store, whose last proprietor was Tom Meighen, was abandoned in 1910, and one can still view the dry goods and sundry items left by Meighen after he lost all hope of selling them. Today the Root River valley is a rich and productive land, with a healthy balance of forestry, agriculture, and watershed management—a testament to the benefits of wise land use. It is a beautiful area to bird.

Birding information:

No less than 166 bird species have been recorded in **Forestville State Park**. Even though it is probably the best-known birding site in Fillmore County, it may not get the attention that the Whitewater and Houston County receive. The number of species is impressive when one considers that this county has no lakes, nor does it have the Mississippi River and its backwaters. To reach Forestville from the Twin Cities, take U.S. Highway 52 south through Rochester, continue south to Fountain, then take State Highway 80 west to Wycoff and County 5 south to County 12 east. From La Crescent or Caledonia, take State Highway 44 west to Harmony, then U.S. Highway 52 north through Preston, State Highway 16 west to County 5 south, onto County 12 east.

Similar to Beaver Creek Valley State Park, Forestville State Park features clear trout-streams. Although not as heavily wooded, Forestville has about the same birding potential as Beaver Creek. It has more horse trails than hiking trails, but the best birding is on the hiking trail north from the campground nearest the park office and the trail at the north end of the park that goes to the Pioneer Cemetery atop the bluff. The park is within the easternmost range of the Swainson's Hawk in Minnesota.

North of Forestville (just southeast of the city of Fountain on County Road 8) is the west end of the 34-mile **Root River State Trail**, a paved biking/hiking route developed on a former railroad grade that roughly follows the Root River from here to Lanesboro, ending 6 miles east of Rushford. The trail offers many access points and can be birded by walking or biking portions, or the entire trail. You can rent bicycles from vendors in Lanesboro. Some common and highly visible birds along the trail include Turkey Vulture, Rough-winged Swallow, Red-bellied Woodpecker, Eastern Wood-Pewee, Eastern Phoebe, Belted Kingfisher, Northern Cardinal, and Field Sparrow. The trail also offers a good chance to see Tufted Titmouse and Bald Eagle. While you're in the area you may want to check out the feeders at Avian Acres, a commercial operation that sells bird seed and supplies and feeds wild birds year-round (1.5 miles southwest of Lanesboro off County Road 8; (507) 467-2996).

Additional help:

Minnesota Highway Map location: N-21

Hazards: Poison ivy, biting insects, rattlesnakes

Nearest food, lodging, gas: Preston, Lanesboro, Rushford

Camping: Forestville State Park, (507) 352-5111

Land ownership: State of Minnesota, private, cities of Lanesboro and Rushford

Additional information: Minnesota DNR, (612) 296-6157; Historic Bluff Country, (800) 428-2030. For guided birding (advance notice preferred) contact Fred Lesher, 509 Winona St., La Crosse, WI 54603; (608) 783-1149.

Recommended length of stay: 2 days

Minnesota
Northern Deciduous Region

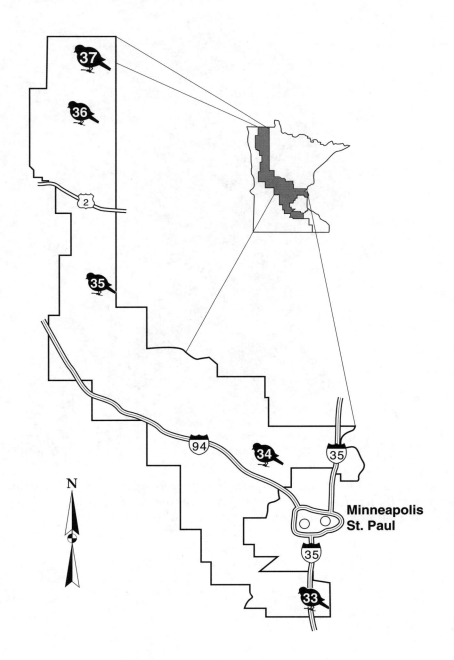

N

Minneapolis
St. Paul

Yellow-headed Blackbirds migrate and nest throughout the state, excluding most of the northern boreal region. They are common locally when nesting, and are best found where cattail habitat exists. BILL MARCHEL

Northern Deciduous Region

Encompassing a band of woodlands that runs from the lower Minnesota River to the Canadian border, Minnesota's northern deciduous region incorporates individual expanses of maple/basswood forest, oak savannah, and aspen parkland which separate the state's northern boreal region from the prairie region and provides habitat for its own unique variety of birds.

In presettlement times, this region may have been more purely defined by its dominant plant communities. Wildfires that swept off the prairies maintained the oak savannah (or "oak brushland," as it is termed in areas such as Sherburne County) and the aspen parkland, a mosaic of wetland, brush, sedge, and aspen groves in areas including Roseau County. The maple/basswood forest, or "big woods," existed in areas of rich soils, seen in Le Seuer County, where rivers and lakes protected trees from the reach of prairie fires. Although logging, fire suppression, and agriculture have changed the face of the region, the dominant forest types, though fragmented, remain.

The northern deciduous region is an extension of the great deciduous forest that extends from central Wisconsin into Minnesota, and once covered much of the eastern United States. It is difficult to clearly separate the boundaries of this region in Minnesota today, because the deciduous habitat type is often found transposed in portions of the prairie and boreal forest. In the region's southern two-thirds, the deciduous forest follows the rolling lake country of moraines left by glacial ice. In the northern one-third, it occupies a portion of the remnant lake bed of Glacial Lake Agassiz, today characterized by aspen parkland, with interspersed bogs and marshes separating prairie and boreal habitat types. Further confusing this region's boundaries are corridors of similar habitat types and associated nesting bird species that stretch far into the prairie region along the valleys of the Minnesota and Blue Earth rivers.

Most of the region's nesting birds have primary nesting ranges in the state's other regions, but these overlap into the northern deciduous zone. Birds whose ranges roughly center here include Horned Grebe (north), Red-necked Grebe, Double-crested Cormorant, Least Bittern, Red-shouldered Hawk (central), Sharp-tailed Grouse (north), Yellow Rail (north), Sandhill Crane (north), Whip-poor-will, Yellow-throated Vireo, and Eastern Towhee. Some birds, particularly those associated with the southern hardwood region, have recently been expanding their ranges here, including the towhee, Blue-winged and Golden-winged Warblers, and Red-shouldered Hawk.

The regional landscape today is dominated by small towns, lake cabins, and a hodgepodge of agriculture, forestry, and other rural ventures. Because of the overlap of bird species, the northern deciduous region is less important to visiting birders than other regions of the state. Also, this same deciduous habitat type dominates the Twin Cities metropolitan area, covered extensively earlier in this book.

33. Faribault, Northfield, and vicinity —————

Habitats: Deciduous woodland, oak savannah, lake, wetland

Key birds: Red-shouldered Hawk, American Woodcock, Willow Flycatcher, Black- and Yellow-billed Cuckoos, Orchard Oriole, Dickcissel, Grasshopper Sparrow

Best time to bird: Late March-June

Don't miss: Nerstrand Woods State Park

General information:

General Henry H. Sibley, the first governor of Minnesota, called him the most important pioneer. The Sioux respected him immensely, and his name was familiar to tribes from the Red River valley to the Missouri River. His name was Jean Baptiste Faribault, and he arguably did more to bring civilization to the Minnesota frontier than any other single individual.

Faribault was born in the Canadian province of Quebec, just a couple of years before this country gained its independence. He moved to Minnesota in 1803 and lived a long life as a trader with the Sioux. His first residence in the state was at the rapids on the Minnesota River, a few miles upstream from the present cities of Chaska and Carver. In addition to being well known as a trader, it is said he was the first to attempt agriculture in the state, and he worked to impart his knowledge about growing crops to the Sioux.

Faribault County was named for this great man in 1855, five years before his death at his final residence in the city of Faribault. It is an interesting footnote that Faribault's death came just two years before his friends, the Sioux, began their tragic uprising. Jean Baptiste's son, Alexander Faribault, established a trading post on the shore of Cannon Lake near the present-day city of Faribault.

Birding information:

This area contains the two major cities of Faribault and Northfield, and offers plenty of birding opportunities in the "big woods," the deciduous woodlands along the Cannon River and around area lakes. Faribault lies on I-35, 50 miles south of the Twin Cities. Northfield lies 12 miles northeast of Faribault on State Highway 3.

It's difficult to pick a starting point here, but the best-known birding site definitely is **Nerstrand Woods State Park**, south of Northfield on State Highway 246 (from Faribault take County Road 20 north to County 88 east to reach the park). Like most of this area, the very best birding comes in spring, when migrants—particularly wood warblers—are on the move and local nesting birds have arrived to claim territories. The original "big woods" in these rolling hills and valleys once covered about 5,000 acres; the park now preserves 1,280 acres of land.

Many of the birds common to the Twin Cities area are found here, but Nerstrand also has the potential for birds shared with the southern hardwoods

Faribault, Northfield, and vicinity

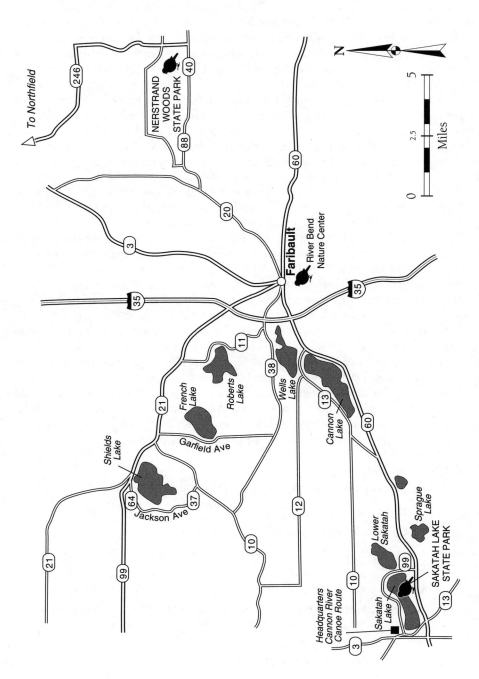

To Northfield

NERSTRAND WOODS STATE PARK

246

40

88

20

3

Faribault

River Bend Nature Center

60

35

35

11

French Lake

Roberts Lake

Wells Lake

38

21

13

Cannon Lake

60

Garfield Ave

Shields Lake

64

37

Jackson Ave

12

10

21

99

10

10

Lower Sakatah

Sprague Lake

99

SAKATAH LAKE STATE PARK

13

Headquarters Cannon River Canoe Route

Sakatah Lake

3

N

5

2.5

Miles

0

195

region that are more difficult to find in the Twin Cities, such as Red-shouldered Hawk, Ruffed Grouse, Wild Turkey, Acadian Flycatcher, Tufted Titmouse, Wood Thrush, Blue-winged and Cerulean Warblers, and Louisiana Waterthrush.

On the southeast side of Faribault is the **River Bend Nature Center**, a 661-acre preserve of woodland, prairie, and wetland habitats that claims a bird list of 244 species. Head east on Highway 60 to reach the nature center (on Rustad Road) by turning right at Shumway Avenue and left at Division Street, then right on 10th Avenue SE and left on 5th.

Sakatah Lake is a widening of the Cannon River that retains the Sioux word for the "singing hills" surrounding it. **Sakatah Lake State Park** occupies 3.5 miles of the lake's southern shoreline, covering some 840 acres of rolling deciduous woodland and oak savannah. Although it enjoys many of the birds mentioned above, its lake and wetlands also attract waterfowl in early-spring migration. A hiking trail that begins at the picnic area, follows the lake, and then loops back uphill provides good birding; the 39-mile Sakatah Singing Hills State Trail from Mankato to Faribault bisects the area. To reach the park entrance follow State Highway 60 west from I-35 in Faribault about 10 miles to the park signs.

On the northwest side of Sakatah Lake is the headquarters for the Cannon River Canoe Route, the most popular canoeing river in southern Minnesota. To reach the headquarters from Highway 60 just east of the state park, take County 99 north and follow it around the lake. Although the river is cold in May, and can be a busy thoroughfare on summer weekends, it cuts through some excellent birding areas on its 110-mile route to the Mississippi River. The stretch from Sakatah Lake to Faribault spans 15 miles, while the portion from Faribault to Cannon Falls measures about 30 miles, but there are access sites all along these routes.

Although this area lacks the interesting nesting species (such as Common Loon and Red-necked Grebe) found in the lake country farther north, it does offer a group of lakes in close proximity that are all worth a check during spring and fall peak migration times. **Shields Lake** (reached by taking State Highway 21, 9 miles northwest from its intersection with I-35, 1 mile north of Faribault) has long been a traditional nesting place for herons, egrets, and cormorants.

Additional help:

Minnesota Highway Map location: J-K, 19

Hazards: Poison ivy, mosquitos

Nearest food, gas, lodging: Faribault, Northfield

Camping: Nerstrand Woods State Park, (507) 334-8848; Sakatah Lake State Park, (507) 362-4438

Land ownership: State of Minnesota, private, city of Faribault

Additional information: Minnesota DNR, (612) 296-6157; Faribault Area Chamber of Commerce, (507) 334-4381; Northfield Area Chamber of Commerce, (800) 658-2548

Recommended length of stay: 1 day

34. Sherburne National Wildlife Refuge ——————

Habitats: Oak woodland and brushland, prairie, wetland

Key birds: Bald Eagle, Northern Harrier, Sandhill Crane, Whip-poor-will, Western Kingbird, Northern Shrike (winter), Lark Sparrow, Dickcissel, Clay-colored Sparrow, Grasshopper Sparrow

Best times to bird: Mid-April–early June; October–mid-November

Don't miss: Refuge Auto Tour Route (Sandhill Cranes, late October)

General information:

For anyone who has seen elk herds in the oak brush openings and on the aspen parkland slopes of Colorado, it's not hard to picture elk in Minnesota. Explorer Zebulon Pike wrote about the herds he encountered in 1805. The first map of the Minnesota Territory, in 1850, named the Elk River and Elk Lake, just east of what today is the Sherburne National Widlife Refuge.

Many people associate elk with the forested mountains of the West, but they actually are a prairie animal, whose high-pitched breeding whistle (or bugle) evolved as a means of communication over open country, where such sound frequencies carry farthest. The prairies and oak brushland transition zone of Anoka, Sherburne, Stearns, and Benton counties undoubtedly served these animals well. Elk were easy targets for hunters, however; by 1860 the large herds had disappeared from southern Minnesota and by 1900 were totally removed from their last vestiges in northwestern Minnesota.

The state has worked to reintroduce elk since animals from Wyoming were obtained in 1914. The only success has been in the Roseau County area, where animals were released in 1935. The herd at one time numbered as many as three hundred animals, but their shift westward into agricultural lands spelled their demise. Due primarily to poaching, the herd remaining in Marshall County has numbered only twenty to thirty animals for many years.

Birding information:

The 30,000-acre Sherburne National Wildlife Refuge lies within the prairie-deciduous forest transition zone north of the Twin Cities. Its vegetation was dominated by oak woodland and brushland (or oak savannah) in presettlement times, but fire suppression has allowed some of the woodlands to close or become more densely overgrown. The refuge also includes wet prairie and marshes. Expect to see birds typical of edge-type habitat in Minnesota. The refuge bird list contains 253 species, but that count may have been a bit generous and was being revised at last report. In addition to the more common deciduous forest, brushland, and wetland species of the Twin Cities region, this is a reliable place to see Sandhill Crane, Bald Eagle, Lark Sparrow, and wintering Northern Shrike. To reach the refuge from the Twin Cities, take U.S. Highway 10 west to Big Lake and follow County Road 5 north. After passing County Road 4 at Orrock, turn right on County Road 9 and proceed about 2 miles to headquarters.

Sherburne National Wildlife Refuge

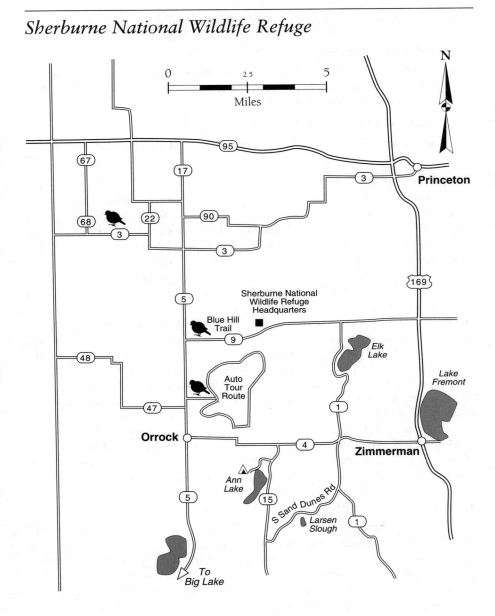

The best place to view songbirds on the refuge is the **Blue Hill Trail**, 1 mile west of refuge headquarters. The low, wooded, 75-foot rise was once called "Blue Mound" (like the state park near Luverne) because of its "blue" appearance from a distance.

The refuge's **Auto Tour Route**, a few miles south of County 9 on County Road 5, offers two short hiking trails, three wildlife management exhibits, and two observation decks to view waterfowl, cranes, and eagles. As many as six pairs of Bald Eagles have nested on the refuge in recent years. The primary habitat for nesting Sandhill Cranes here is cattail marsh. Trumpeter Swans have been reintroduced to the refuge, but a free-flying, breeding population has yet to be established. The auto tour covers 8 miles.

From early October through mid-November, depending on weather, the northwest corner of the refuge offers viewing of Sandhill Cranes as they leave their shallow water roosting areas and head out to cornfields to feed. The best viewing can be had during the first two hours of daylight near the intersection of **County Road 68 and County Road 3.**

Surrounding the refuge is Sand Dunes State Forest, a 10,000-square-mile area of mixed private and public land that has received thousands of tree plantings since the 1940s in an effort to stabilize the light, sandy soils that disastrously began to blow away during the 1930s. A forest campground is located on the west side of Ann Lake (go east from Orrock on County Road 4 and take County 15 south to the first right turn). Larsen Slough (County Road 4 from Orrock east to County Road 1, then south to South Sand Dunes Road) is always worth a look for nesting Sedge and Marsh Wrens, grebes, and water-fowl.

Additional help:

Minnesota Highway Map location: I-15

Hazards: Poison ivy, mosquitos

Nearest food, gas, lodging: Princeton, Elk River, Big Lake

Camping: Ann Lake campground

Land ownership: State of Minnesota, private, Department of Interior

Additional information: Minnesota DNR, (612) 296-6157; Sherburne National Wildlife Refuge, (612) 389-3323; Elk River Area Chamber of Commerce, (612) 441-3110; Princeton Area Chamber of Commerce, (612) 389-1764

Recommended length of stay: 1 day

35. Tamarac National Wildlife Refuge ─────────

Habitats: Deciduous forest, bog, wetland, lake, river

Key birds: Red-necked Grebe; Hooded Merganser; Bald Eagle; Ruffed Grouse; American Woodcock; Sedge Wren; Nashville, Chestnut-sided, and Mourning Warblers; White-throated Sparrow; Purple Finch

Best times to bird: Mid-April-early June; October-mid-November

Don't miss: Refuge Blackbird Auto Tour, Egg Lake Trail (fall)

General information:

Saying "all rivers lead here" may be an exaggeration, but certainly the lands of Tamarac National Wildlife Refuge rest upon a "height of land" that was important to Native Americans as well as early fur traders. From here one could reach, via water, the Mississippi River to the east and the Red River of the North to the west, separated by a portage between Shell and Height of Land lakes. The Ojibway called it by a name that roughly translates as "a divide separating water that runs different ways."

From here the Buffalo River leaves Tamarac Lake, the Pelican River leaves Detroit Lake, and the Ottertail River runs through Height of Land Lake—all major tributaries on their way to the Red River of the North. Nearby, the Shell River leaves Shell Lake on its way to the Crow Wing River and the Mississippi. Just a short distance north, the Wild Rice River is born on its way to the Red, as is the White Earth River at White Earth Lake. One can only guess about the colorful trading rendezvous that might have occurred here.

One rendezvous that was not overlooked here was that of the logger and settler, who cut the forests and carved farms from the once-productive wildlife lands. As early as the 1930s, plans were made to restore this once great wildlife area to its former grandeur, and in 1938 an executive order established Tamarac National Wildlife Refuge as a breeding ground for migratory birds and other wildlife. Tamarac's lands were purchased with funds from the sale of Federal Duck Stamps to hunters.

Birding information:

The 43,000-acre **Tamarac National Widlife Refuge** includes a mix of forests, bogs, wetlands, lakes, and rivers. To reach Tamarac from the Twin Cities, take U.S. Highway 10 west 197 miles to Detroit Lakes, then take State Highway 34 east about 5 miles and turn north on County Road 29.

The Tamarac area is managed primarily for waterfowl, but a wide variety of wetland and forest birds benefit from its prime habitats. Wood Duck, Mallard, Blue-winged Teal, Ring-necked Duck, and Lesser Scaup are abundant nesters here, while Canada Goose, Common Goldeneye, and Hooded Merganser are considered common nesters. Green-winged Teal, American Black Duck, Northern Pintail, Northern Shoveler, Gadwall, American Wigeon, Redhead, Bufflehead, and Ruddy Duck nest here in lesser numbers and are considered

Tamarac National Wildlife Refuge

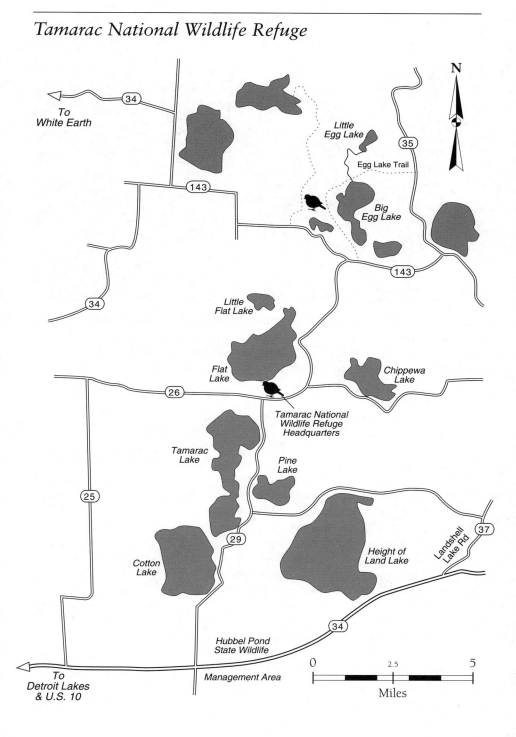

N

To
White Earth

34

Little
Egg Lake

35

Egg Lake Trail

143

Big
Egg Lake

143

34

Little
Flat Lake

Flat
Lake

26

Chippewa
Lake

Tamarac National
Wildlife Refuge
Headquarters

Tamarac
Lake

Pine
Lake

25

29

Cotton
Lake

Height of
Land Lake

Landshell
Lake Rd

37

34

Hubbel Pond
State Wildlife

Management Area

To
Detroit Lakes
& U.S. 10

0   2.5   5

Miles

Bald Eagles have become a fairly common summer sight in the extensive forests of the lake country in north-central Minnesota. During early spring and late fall migrations they gravitate toward open water, especially the Mississippi River south of the Twin Cities to the Iowa border. BILL MARCHEL

uncommon. Trumpeter Swans have been introduced here and are now considered a breeding bird on the refuge.

Other interesting nesting birds of the Tamarac refuge include Red-necked Grebe, Bald Eagle, Ruffed Grouse, American Woodcock, Black-billed Cuckoo, Least Flycatcher, Sedge Wren, Wood Thrush, White-throated Sparrow, and Purple Finch. Nesting wood warblers should include Golden-winged (perhaps), Nashville, Yellow, Chestnut-sided, Magnolia, American Redstart, Ovenbird, Mourning (perhaps), and the ever-present Common Yellowthroat.

Because of the presence of eagles on the refuge, the northern half is closed to visitors from March 1 to September 1. The refuge's 10-mile Blackbird Auto Tour, which is marked east of headquarters on County Road 26, is highly recommended anytime during the spring, summer, or fall. In the northern half of the refuge, the best birding road is probably the **Egg Lake Trail**, which runs north from County Road 33 back to County Road 35. The trail is open up to the boat access on Big Egg Lake, but beyond that must be walked.

Additional help:

Minnesota Highway Map location: D-9

Hazards: Poison ivy, biting insects

Nearest food, gas, lodging: Detroit Lakes

Camping: Long Lake Campsite (2 miles west of Detroit Lakes on U.S. Highway 10), (612) 432-2228

Land ownership: Department of Interior, state of Minnesota, private

Additional information: Minnesota DNR, (612) 296-6157; Tamarac National Wildlife Refuge, (218) 847-2641; Detroit Lakes Regional Chamber of Commerce, (218) 847-9202

Recommended length of stay: 1 day

36. Agassiz National Wildlife Refuge/Thief Lake ——

Habitats: Pools, marsh, grassland, brushland, aspen stands

Key birds: Pied-billed, Horned, Red-necked, Eared, and Western Grebes; American White Pelican; Northern Harrier; American Bittern; Sandhill Crane; American Woodcock; Franklin's Gull; Black Tern; Black-billed Magpie; Sedge Wren; Le Conte's and Nelson's Sharp-tailed Sparrows

Best times to bird: May-early June; October-early November

Don't miss: Agassiz's West Gate Road, view from Agassiz fire tower

General information:

This book has already discussed the scope of the former Glacial Lake Agassiz, which covered northwestern Minnesota, much of Ontario and Manitoba, as well as parts of Saskatchewan and North Dakota. It covered 200,000 square miles, was 700 miles long, and as much as 700 feet deep.

Glacial Lake Agassiz was first named in a report to the Minnesota Geological Survey in 1879, in honor of the eminent geologist Louis Agassiz who in the early 1800s put forth the first theories of land formation by the movement of glacial ice. Agassiz later undertook zoological research at Harvard College and founded the Museum of Comparative Zoology. Agassiz National Wildlife Refuge is named for the once great lake that bears his name.

Intense efforts were made in the early 1900s to drain the lands in and around what is now the Agassiz refuge, but the millions of dollars were no match for the size and scope of the bog lands east of here. The percolation capabilities and high water tables made the task an insurmountable one, and efforts were finally ceased. The ditches designed to drain the lands can still be seen today.

Agassiz National Wildlife Refuge/Thief Lake

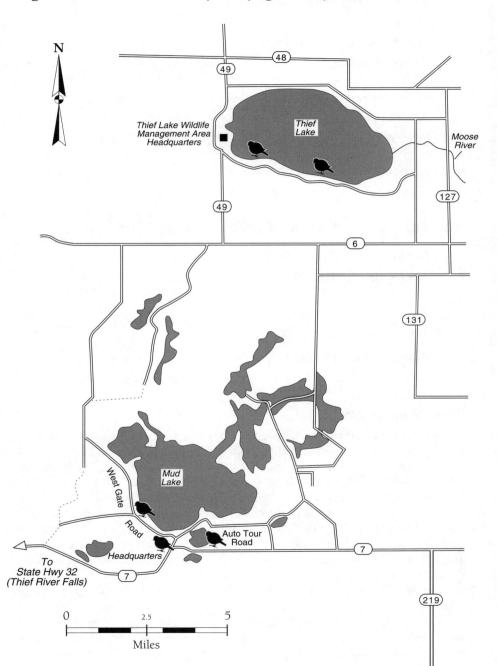

Birding information:

Agassiz National Wildlife Refuge is Minnesota's best. The visitor instantly knows why: It is big. It is wild. It is ultimately productive of habitat that can grow birds, and sustain them in migration. The 61,000-acre refuge isn't known for its deciduous woodlands, though they do exist here, but rather for its wetlands—miles and miles of wetlands. Agassiz lies a little over 300 miles northwest of the Twin Cities. To reach the refuge, take U.S. Highway 10 to Detroit Lakes, then follow U.S. Highway 59 north to Thief River Falls, and State Highway 32 north about 11 miles to County Road 7. Turn right here to enter the refuge.

The **Refuge Headquarters** (about 6 miles into the refuge, where County Road 7 turns right, proceed straight ahead, following the signs) can assist with information, if you arrive during regular business hours (closed weekends). During the long days of June, it's tempting to arrive late in the afternoon, and possible to get delayed along the entrance road by the swarms of Cliff Swallows and clear water beneath the Thief River bridge, or by the Pied-billed Grebes on the pool overlooked by the first observation stand.

Near headquarters, the old Forest Lookout Tower offers an unrestricted view of this beautiful refuge, and is a must for visualizing the size and scope of the pools, marshes, grasslands, brushlands, and aspen stands that make up this area. Those with a bit of luck might spot a moose, or simply an American

Agassiz National Wildlife Refuge is a sprawling area of bogs and marshes that make it a birder's paradise. In the foreground is refuge headquarters.

Bittern, Black Tern, Yellow-headed Blackbird, Northern Harrier, American White Pelican, or brood of Gadwalls amidst the yelling of the Sora Rails.

A unique feature of the refuge is the Franklin's Gull nesting colony, which may support up to 100,000 nesting birds in some years.

A walking trail leads northwest away from the tower, following the top of a dike. The wetlands along here provide relatively undisturbed cover (compared to roadsides) for a close-up look at birds. Agassiz's marshes enjoy a lot of bird traffic, with bitterns, terns, gulls, waterfowl, blackbirds, and hawks traveling back and forth between pools.

Some of the better birding roads at Agassiz require a gate key, which can be obtained from headquarters. However, the **Auto Tour Road** and the perimeter route of County Road 7 are open at all times. A gate key provides access to the dike roads, including the productive **West Gate Road**.

Less than 10 miles north of Agassiz is **Thief Lake Wildlife Management Area,** but it's farther if you wish to travel via an all-season road. The best all-season route requires returning via County 7 west to Highway 32, proceeding north about 10 miles to Middle River, then east about 10 miles on County Road 6 to County 49. Follow County 49 north to management area headquarters on the west side of Thief Lake. Or, take County 7 east out of Agassiz to State Highway 219/89 north, follow it to County 6 west, then follow that to County 49 north.

One of the larger state-operated management units, and a giant wild rice bowl that attracts swarms of waterfowl in the spring and fall, Thief Lake offers most of the same species as Agassiz, but is less accessible. Two public boat accesses on the lake's south shore provide opportunities for viewing the water; the brushlands and aspen stands north of Moose River on the lake's east side can provide good birding.

Additional help:

Minnesota Highway Map location: D-4,5

Hazards: Poison ivy, biting insects

Nearest food, gas, lodging: Thief River Falls

Camping: Check with Thief River Chamber of Commerce

Land ownership: Department of Interior, state of Minnesota, private

Additional information: Minnesota DNR, (612) 296-6157; Agassiz National Wildlife Refuge, (218) 449-4115; Thief River Falls Area Chamber of Commerce, (218) 681-3720

Recommended length of stay: 1 day

37. Roseau and vicinity

Habitats: Deciduous forest, coniferous forest, bog, wetland, hayfields

Key birds: Sharp-tailed Grouse; Great Gray Owl; Gray Jay; Black-billed Magpie; Boreal Chickadee; Nashville, Bay-breasted, Blackburnian, Connecticut, and Mourning Warblers; Snow Bunting (winter)

Best times to bird: May-early June; October-February

Don't miss: State Highway 310

General information:

Had the name Verendrye been that of an American, it would have been bannered across Minnesota, and a legend nationwide. But we seldom, if ever, hear of the dauntless French explorer who led the way across the American wilderness, probing the routes west and northwest nearly one hundred years before Lewis and Clark.

Sieur de la Verendrye opened the way for fur traders through Minnesota, Lake of the Woods, and beyond, into Manitoba and Saskatchewan. He searched the upper Missouri River and visited the Black Hills. He named and mapped more of northern Minnesota's major landmarks than any other single individual. One of Verendrye's sons was killed in a massacre by a Prairie Sioux war party. Two of his sons were the first white men to reach the Rocky Mountains. One of his sons claimed the Red River valley for France.

The elder Verendrye died in 1749 at the age of sixty-four. Shortly before his death, the King of France bestowed upon him the Cross of St. Louis. In 1874 a bill was introduced in the Minnesota Senate to name a northern county in honor of Verendrye, but the county was instead named "Cook," to commemorate a Minnesota casualty of the Civil War. It is fitting, if not a bit skewed, that the St. Louis River in Minnesota appears to have been named by Verendrye as a measure of gratitude for his king's blessing. Yet this, and the county of the same name, are the closest the state came to honoring his great sacrifices and achievement.

Verendrye named Roseau Lake on his 1737 map, translating into French the Ojibway word meaning "reed," referring to the bullrushes (or phragmites) common in shallow water here.

Birding information:

Despite its location so far north, Roseau County features not only deciduous woodlands, but also extensive bogs, wetlands, sedge marshes, and conifer forest, making it an excellent place for birding. Nearly three hundred species have been recorded in the county. Habitat here can be broken into three sections: the bogs and marshes northwest of the city of Roseau, the conifer forests north of town, and the deciduous woodlands to the southeast within the Beltrami Island State Forest. The town of Roseau lies some 320 miles north of the Twin Cities. From Thief River Falls, take State Highway 32 north to State Highway 11 east. From Baudette, take State Highway 11 west.

Roseau and vicinity

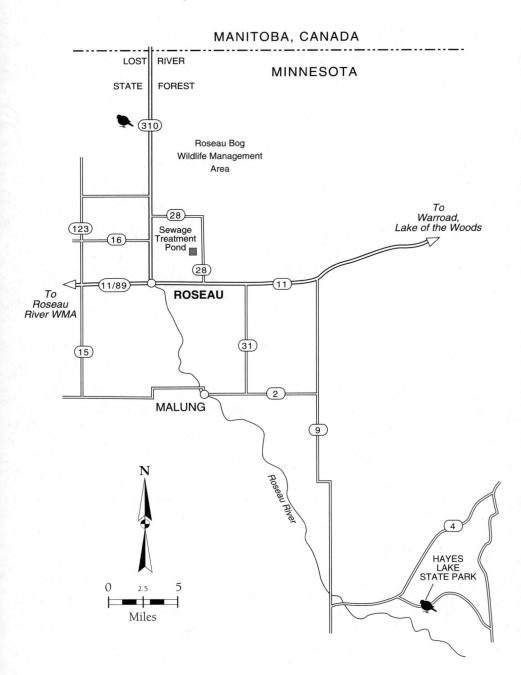

MANITOBA, CANADA

MINNESOTA

LOST | RIVER

STATE | FOREST

310

Roseau Bog
Wildlife Management
Area

123

16

28

Sewage
Treatment
Pond

28

11/89

ROSEAU

11

To
Warroad,
Lake of the Woods

To
Roseau
River WMA

31

15

2

MALUNG

9

Roseau River

N

0   2.5   5

Miles

4

HAYES
LAKE
STATE PARK

Any of the roads here that lead through open country and mixed brush-lands are good places to see Black-billed Magpie in spring, summer, or fall, or flocks of Snow Buntings in late fall and winter. Only about 10 miles of **State Highway 310** separate Roseau from the Canadian border. This stretch of road is reliable for birding, not heavily traveled, and worth a slow drive with plenty of stops for investigation. The roads that radiate away from the highway are also worth a drive, but some are low maintenance; proceed with caution during wet periods. Sprague's Pipits have been seen in several of the grassy fields east of the highway.

The bogs along the last 3 road miles have been consistent for observing Great Gray Owls over the years. These are the lands of the Lost River State Forest, which should provide opportunities to view Gray Jay, Common Raven, Boreal Chickadee, Black-backed Woodpecker, Yellow-bellied Flycatcher, Evening Grosbeak, Purple Finch, and Nashville, Magnolia, Bay-breasted, Yellow-rumped, Blackburnian, Connecticut, and Mourning Warblers, among others. With its stands of conifers, this area is also good for winter birding, when Spruce Grouse, Northern Goshawk, Northern Hawk-Owl, and winter finches might be more easily seen.

Northwest of Roseau, the Roseau River Wildlife Management Area offers excellent pools and wetlands for birding, and bogs and fen as far as the eye can see. Take Highway 11/89 west from Roseau to State Highway 89, then travel north 10 miles to County Road 3 and go west to reach the management area. Locked gates block many of the dike roads, but you can walk these roads and expect to see grebes, ducks, rails, bitterns, gulls, and terns.

Large tracts of deciduous forest begin just southeast of Roseau, and one of the best places to visit is **Hayes Lake State Park**. The park features a man-made flowage lake on the Roseau River and offers several good hiking trails through woodlands and bogs. Western Wood-Pewees were present in the park a few years ago. Take Highway 11 east from Roseau to County Road 9, then travel south 14 miles to County Road 4 west to the park entrance.

Additional help:

Minnesota Highway Map location: D-2,3

Hazards: Poison ivy, biting insects, some low-maintenance roads

Nearest food, gas, lodging: Roseau

Camping: Hayes Lake State Park, (218) 425-7504

Land ownership: State of Minnesota, private

Additional information: Minnesota DNR, (612) 296-6157; Roseau Civic and Commerce Association, (218) 463-1542

Recommended length of stay: 2 days

©Vera Ming Wong 1995

Snow Geese in flight

CHAPTER 4

Bonus birding / a guide to unique opportunities

Every once in a while the right mix of habitat and tradition brings together interesting species, or spectacular congregations of birds, in the same place at the same time. These *special situations*, reliable from year to year, are birding events not to be missed. The following is a month-by-month guide to unique birding opportunities in Minnesota.

January

Snowy Owls

Although in some years there are only a few of these emblematic owls haunting the shipping terminals of the Duluth harbor, they can be counted upon with some certainty here. In one year, as many as twenty-three individuals have wintered on the Duluth side of the port.

Snowy Owls usually appear in Duluth as early as mid- to late November, and stay until mid-March. It is believed they invade Minnesota to escape severe winters and short food supplies farther north. At least a few owls migrate south every year, and invasions, when large numbers appear, seem to take place about two or three times every ten years. The owls are attracted to the dependable food supply of rats and mice in the harbor area, and they may set up feeding territories if food supplies are good.

Snowy Owls feed at night and use the daylight hours to rest. They are least active on clear winter days, preferring to roost on the ground or on the bay ice, perhaps next to a drift or ice chunk—inevitably in a place a birder would not think of looking for them. They can occasionally be found on the ground near railroad tracks and, less often, atop buildings. They may hunt and move about more often on overcast days.

The best time to encounter active owls is early morning or late evening, which during the Minnesota winter means about 7 a.m. and again at 3 p.m., or any time of day on overcast days. In years of Snowy Owl invasions, the birds are found across northern Minnesota in open or semi-open country, and may be found as far south as the extreme southern part of the state. (See the Port Terminal description on page 70.)

February

The Owl Moon

Minnesota birders know that February may be one of the state's best months for viewing owls. Great Gray Owls, a nesting species in Minnesota, are often seen on their low perches in prime habitat at this time of year. During invasion years, as many as several hundred have shown up in northern Minnesota. One birder reported seeing twenty-three different individuals in an hour during the winter of 1992-93.

Any of the areas in this book that describe Great Gray Owl locations are worth visiting at this time of year. County Road 18 northwest of McGregor, the North Shore between Grand Portage and Duluth, County Road 2 in northern Lake County, Highway 72 north of Waskish, and the bogs north of Roseau all are ideal spotting locations. Great Grays are most active early and late in the day, and on cloudy or snowy days.

Northern Hawk-Owls start showing up in Minnesota in mid-November, but their numbers should be greater in February. The birds usually stay in one location for up to a month; a call to the Birder's Hotline in Duluth will lead you to known owl locations. Hawk-Owls favor the same kinds of habitat as Great Gray Owls, but they choose the treetops—the apex, or highest point—to roost. They hunt by day, and may be active at any time. These crow-sized birds look more like a raptor than an owl, and they are very approachable.

Great Horned Owls are easier to see in the wooded southern half of the state at this time, and Barred Owls become more active and responsive to calls. Long-eared and Saw-whet Owls can be found by probing conifer shelterbelts in the west and southwest part of the state at this time of year, particularly in stands of cedar. Boreal Owls, seen only in invasion years, may be better seen in March, but they do occur in February. (Ron Brodigan, (218) 365-2126, offers cabins and trails at his Snowshoe Country Lodge in prime owl habitat near Isabella.)

March

The return of waterfowl

While Minnesota fishermen are waiting for the lake shorelines to melt, the first flood of waterfowl is winging its way into the state. Actually, the spring arrival of geese, swans, and ducks into Minnesota may be the most difficult of any bird migration to predict. The earliest migrants seem to be the most weather dependent (sometimes as early as March 1, sometimes much later), but there is an excitement in their arrival, shared by birds and birders alike.

The most dependable early waterfowl arrivals take place in March in Nobles County, in the lakes south of Worthington where the state's earliest warm temperatures are recorded. Check Lake Ocheda, Lake Bella, and Okabena Lake in Worthington.

Canada Geese are common at this time. Snow Geese, whose flight path has shifted west, may be found, and an eye should always be kept for the rare, but not impossible, Ross' Goose. Swans arrive in fair numbers, flying west at about the latitude of the Twin Cities. They often rest in fields temporarily flooded with meltwater pools.

Other first-arrivals that can be expected at this same time include Great Blue Heron, Killdeer, robins, bluebirds, Rusty and Red-winged Blackbirds, and Common Grackle.

In addition to the Worthington area, depending on weather, check lakes in the Lac Qui Parle area, including the well-known Salt Lake (see page 148).

April

Prairie Chickens booming

Minnesota's Greater Prairie-Chickens don't range over a wide part of the state, but their spring booming is worth a drive from the Twin Cities to observe. The birds range, essentially, from Crookston south to about Rothsay in the prairie region. They begin displaying on mild days in February, but it is not until mid-April that their activity peaks.

Prairie Chickens will display on any relatively flat piece of open ground they can find, and many of their dancing grounds are somewhat traditional.

Green-winged Teal may nest nearly anywhere in the state, but they are the rarest of Minnesota's breeding ducks. The best time to see them is during spring or fall migration, especially when the males wear their distinctive spring breeding plumage. BILL MARCHEL

The males choose the grounds for good visibility—they want to be seen by the hens, and they want to see anything coming that has designs for eating them.

Booming activity starts shortly before dawn, and continues for several hours. During the peak of the season, and when many prairie chickens are present, the display spectacle may go on longer. Prairie chicken watchers call these "long-playing" birds "bladder busters" for forcing birders to stay in a blind longer than planned. See the information on Moorhead and Vicinity (page 139) for blind reservations on The Nature Conservancy's Bluestem Prairie tract.

The peak for Sharp-tailed Grouse dancing on leks in Minnesota is slightly later than for prairie chickens, usually about the end of April. Sharp-tail populations are more fragmented and difficult to locate than prairie chickens. Wildlife managers in Roseau, Lake of the Woods, or Beltrami counties may be able to direct you to them, or check the Gun Lake area (page 117) near McGregor.

May

Warbler watching

Somewhere in the spring night, flocks of tiny warblers are making their way back across Minnesota. By dawn, hungry and ready to rest, they settle in the upland areas along major river valleys, searching the blooming oak trees for the tiny insects they devour.

Few Minnesota birding events are as popular, or as anticipated, as the May migration of warblers. The birds are more concentrated in spring than in fall, following river courses on their way. Their breeding plumages border on exotic, making them easier to identify than at other times of year.

A few popular warbler sites come immediately to mind: Frontenac State Park in the southern hardwood region, and Eloise Butler Wildflower Gardens and Carver Park Reserve in the Twin Cities metro region (see maps). But predicting that one place will be better than another on a given day is impossible. You may encounter large numbers in one spot, and find almost no warblers in prime habitat 10 miles away on the same morning.

A subjective list of the ten most abundant spring warblers might include (in descending order): Common Yellowthroat, Yellow-rumped, Nashville, Tennessee, Yellow, American Redstart, Palm, Orange-crowned, Chestnut-sided, and Black-and-White Warblers. The first species to show in the state (first appearing in late March to late April, depending on weather) include the Yellow-rumped, Palm, Black-and-White, Orange-crowned, Pine, Tennessee, Nashville, Ovenbird, and Northern Waterthrush.

When looking for warblers, don't begin at daylight. They seem to be lazy (or tired), and don't become active until the sun starts to warm the treetops. They are active for about a three-hour period, then difficult to find later in the day.

June

The chorus of breeding birds

"Daylight's Burning!" Jack London wrote in one of his inimitable short stories. And so it is on any June morning, when the dawn choruses of 240 bird species launch skyward from Canada to Minnesota's southern border.

June is the month of song, and you must be up and out before dawn to experience its full, marvelous effect. In the pre-dawn, some birds, like Whip-poor-will and owls, are just going to bed, while a long list of others have just begun to stir—and sing—from their overnight perches. At this time of year it is not unusual to distinguish the songs of twenty-five or thirty different birds before the sun has topped the horizon.

Of course, more birds are heard than seen at these times. While anywhere in the state is a good spot to bird, some choice options can be suggested. For singing warblers, nothing can match the forests of the northern boreal region, particularly north and east of Two Harbors. This is also the best time to learn thrush songs, when all five of the Minnesota species may be singing within a few miles of each other in Lake and Cook counties. For waterbirds, Agassiz National Wildlife Refuge is hard to match. To hear a variety of sparrows, including the likes of Savannah, Grasshopper, and Le Conte's, go to Felton Prairie.

In the southern hardwood region you can hear Acadian Flycatchers, Henslow's Sparrows, Bell's Vireos, Louisiana Waterthrush, Eastern Wood-Pewees, Eastern Screech-Owls, and Cerulean Warblers. This is also a good time to learn to distinguish the different vireos, when Yellow-throated, Warbling, and Red-eyed Vireos may be heard in deciduous woodlands and Red-eyed, Philadelphia, and Solitary Vireos sing in the northwestern boreal forests. The Twin Cities' Minnesota River valley offers such species as buntings, orioles, grosbeaks, robins, wrens, and local warblers on any given morning.

June is also a good time to learn flycatcher songs, with Yellow-bellieds singing in the boreal bogs, Willow and Alder singing in the western deciduous transition zone, and Eastern Wood-Pewees and Least Flycatchers singing all across the state. Finally, the southwestern prairies offer the chance to hear and see Bobolink, Western Meadowlark, and Upland Sandpiper in any of a number of places like the Prairie Coteau west of Chandler.

July

Western Grebes and Pelicans

July marks the time in Minnesota when temperatures rise and bird songs decline. However, a number of interesting birds become more visible at this time of year, including the large and entertaining Western Grebe and American White Pelican.

The largest of Minnesota's grebes, the Western Grebe builds floating nests in colonies on a number of lakes in the western regions of the state. Once the grebe chicks have hatched, both parents have time to be on the water, and the adults become less attached to the nest site, thus providing birders with increased viewing opportunities. It's thrilling to see parents carrying their young on their backs as they paddle across the water on a warm July morning.

Pelicans are more closely related to cormorants than grebes, but these birds also are colonial nesters. White Pelicans nest in traditional nesting sites—remote islands in Minnesota—where the entire colony is secure from predators, including man. By July, pelican chicks are large, but still flightless, and require large amounts of food. Both members of a breeding pair hunt for fish and tend to the feeding of the young, and a colony's adults will travel and feed in large flocks during this month. Flocks of nonbreeding adult pelicans also show up in widely scattered locations (mostly in western Minnesota) in July.

One doesn't have to go far from the Twin Cities to find Western Grebes. French Lake in Hennepin County now has a nesting colony, but other good viewing places include Swan Lake in Nicollet County, Big Stone National Wildlife Refuge, Mud Lake in Traverse County, Lake Osakis in Todd County, and Agassiz National Wildlife Refuge.

White Pelicans breed regularly on just two Minnesota Lakes: Marsh Lake, in Lac Qui Parle County, and Lake of the Woods. However, new colonies have been found at Minnesota Lake in Faribault County, and Lake Johanna in Pope County. Obviously, they are most frequently seen in these locations, but it is becoming increasingly common to see white pelicans in other out-of-the-way locations, including waters as large as Leech Lake and as small as potholes in the Fergus Falls area. The waters below the dam at Granite Falls have attracted large numbers of pelicans in recent summers.

August

Shorebird migration

Unfortunately, shorebirds don't make migration stopovers at traditional sites as faithfully as, for example, waterfowl seem to. That makes August a time when the birder's hotline telephone numbers listed in Chapter 1 become invaluable.

Actually, fewer shorebird species are reported in fall than in spring, but fall brings larger flocks. The first fall movement of shorebirds through Minnesota usually begins sometime in early July. Consistent early arrivals include Lesser Yellowlegs, Short-billed Dowitchers, and Least, Pectoral, and Solitary Sandpipers.

As July turns into August, more and more shorebird species begin to make birders' lists. In August, mudflats attract Semipalmated Plover, Stilt and Solitary Sandpipers, Sanderling, Baird's Sandpiper, more dowitchers, and Greater Yellowlegs. Red Knot and Buff-breasted Sandpiper can be expected in Duluth at this time, and Red-necked Phalarope show up at sewage ponds.

At the same time, sod farms seem to attract Pectoral and Baird's Sandpipers, Golden and Black-bellied Plovers, and Buff-breasted Sandpiper.

Shorebird numbers seem to be strictly tied to water levels of lakes, rivers, marshes, and sewage ponds, as they depend on exposed mudflats for feeding. In years of high water, shorebird sightings decline. Some wildlife management areas and game refuges use draw-down techniques to enhance the growth of vegetation in ponds, creating ideal shorebird habitat.

September

Hawk Ridge

With fall in the air, color on the hillsides, and the deep blue waters of Lake Superior at its feet, it's little wonder that Duluth experiences a shortage of hotel rooms during September. To add to this seasonal glory, thousands of hawks and other birds converge on the city, skirting the highlands that overlook it. Duluth's Hawk Ridge has rightfully earned its reputation nationwide as a premier birding site.

Few places in North America can match the sheer numbers of hawks that collect over Hawk Ridge in an "average" year. "The Ridge" is best known for its thousands upon thousands of migrating Broad-winged Hawks, but you may also see raptors as small as American Kestrel, or as large as Bald or Golden Eagles. Turkey Vulture, Northern Goshawk, Peregrine Falcon, and Sharp-shinned, Red-tailed, and Rough-legged Hawks also occur here. At least seventeen different raptor species have been counted at Hawk Ridge. Visitors may also see migrating owls, most commonly perched in the stands of pines along Skyline Parkway atop the ridge. In one season more than seven hundred Saw-whet Owls were banded here.

In addition to raptors, each fall large numbers of nighthawks, warblers, swallows, thrushes, waxwings, and other birds are counted from the ridge, and birding studies that require netting, banding, and releasing birds from this site are conducted each fall.

The peak of hawk movement across the ridge begins in about mid-September. By the first of November, most of the good viewing has ended. The best viewing days seem to be those when cold, clear high-pressure patterns with west or northwest winds move birds along. The text in the northern boreal region map section of this book deals specifically with Hawk Ridge (page 65), including directions to get you there.

October

Sandhill Cranes

Each fall large numbers of Sandhill Cranes gather in the open country of northwestern Minnesota during their southward migration. During this *staging* period, as many as twenty thousand of the long-legged birds may be present on various refuges and wildlife management lands in this part of the state.

Cranes begin staging at northern sites earliest, beginning about the third week of September at Agassiz National Wildlife Refuge, Thief Lake Wildlife Management Area, and Twin Lakes Wildlife Management Area. By the first or second week of October, crane concentrations have moved farther south, to the lands of Polk, Norman, and Wilkin counties. Rothsay Wildlife Management

Area, a site discussed on page 140 of this book, provides good opportunities for viewing cranes until mid-October in most years.

If you want to see cranes early (the last week of September or first week of October), one of the best viewing spots is just east of the Pembina Trail Preserve (see page 133). The cranes rest in shallow water areas by night, and fly to huge stubble fields to feed in early morning. It's an amazing sight to see thousands of Sandhill Cranes feeding and doing their characteristic jumping up and down in an open stubble field; perhaps even more impressive are the feeding flights, when hundreds of the wide-winged birds are milling and calling at the same time.

As mentioned, the Rothsay area also sees many cranes each fall, though numbers peak about two weeks later than those areas farther north. Near the Twin Cities, it is possible to see Sandhill Cranes on the north side of the Sherburne National Wildlife Refuge in October (see text page 197).

November

Tundra Swan migration

Few sounds are more thrilling than the muffled signature calls of Tundra Swans passing unseen overhead on a dark fall night. The call is so soft and abstract that it is missed by most human ears. Recognizing the sound requires some association with swans; a difficult task in a land that is only a stopover for these tundra nesters. However, there is one certain time when swans can be seen, and heard, in large numbers in Minnesota.

As you plan your Thanksgiving holiday, plan also to visit the Weaver Bottoms near Wabasha, at the foot of Lake Pepin. Each November, thousands of Tundra Swans stop to rest and feed here on their long journey toward the Atlantic seaboard and Chesapeake Bay. Swans begin arriving here in substantial numbers in early November, and their numbers peak about the second or third week of the month.

Watching the graceful flight of these great white birds is a spectacle not to be missed. Like geese, the flocks do most of their trading from feeding to resting areas at the first full light, usually about 9 a.m. They are visible in the backwaters and marshes from roadways that skirt the river, but perhaps the best place to get a close look at them is across the river at Rieck's Lake (see page 172), part of the Upper Mississippi River National Wildlife and Fish Refuge.

While you're in the area, check the waters of Lake Pepin for the large concentrations of Common Mergansers which gather here each fall during migration to gorge themselves on the lake's abundant shad. Estimates of merganser numbers have reached as high as 100,000 during one November period; the large rafts of these birds, with the males in their starkly contrasting fall plumage, create quite a spectacle.

December

Giant Canada Geese

At one time the Giant Canada Goose was considered gone from the upper Midwest, extirpated from Minnesota, and perhaps, as a subspecies, extinct. However, a graduate student studying the Canada Goose described large birds that came to winter at a lake in the center of a Minnesota town, and in the process rediscovered this "lost" race of Canada geese which breed in Manitoba and spend the early part of their winter in Minnesota.

Rochester's Silver Lake holds geese throughout the year, but at no time are these regal birds more prominent than during the month of December when as many as twenty thousand of the big birds crowd this city lake. Silver Lake has come to be almost as famous to those who enjoy watching waterfowl as the city's Mayo Clinic has become to the infirm.

Geese seem to move in and out of the lake constantly, but most flocks begin their feeding flights about 8 or 9 a.m., while other birds begin returning to the lake about 9 to 11 a.m. Afternoon feeding flights begin about an hour before dark. It's entertaining to watch the flocks approach the lake and see individual geese "tumble" as they attempt to lose altitude. The lake doesn't offer much other than the Canada Geese, although White-fronted, Snow, and Ross' Geese as well as Brant have been recorded here.

To reach the lake from the Twin Cities, take U.S. Highway 52 south to Rochester, exit at 5th Street/Civic Center Drive, and go east about 1 mile to North Broadway Avenue. Turn left (north) and proceed until you see the lake (or just follow the flocks of geese), and turn right on West Silver Lake Drive.

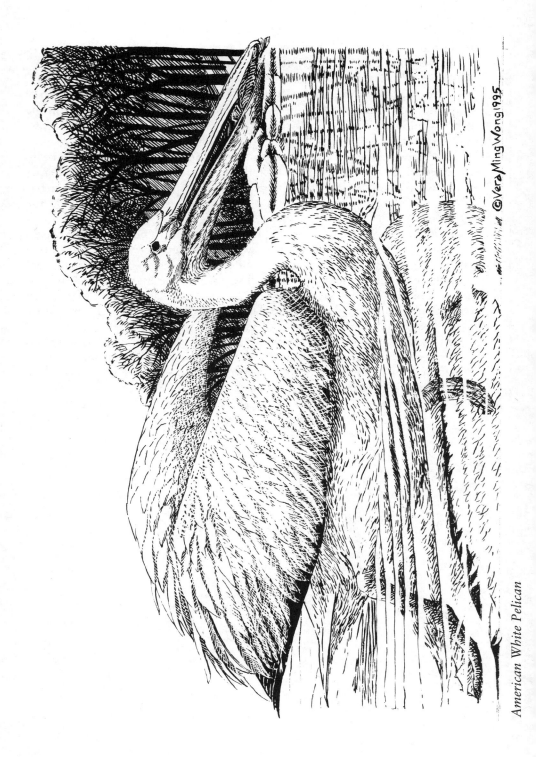

American White Pelican

CHAPTER 5

Checklist, seasonal occurrence, and abundance of Minnesota birds

To date, Minnesota retains 420 bird species on its active list.

The following checklist provides a quick reference to each of those bird species. The sequence in which species are presented in this chapter follows the checklist order established by the American Ornithologists Union and divides the birds into categories of *regular, casual,* and *accidental.* A key to the symbols used in this checklist is found at the bottom of each page.

Of Minnesota's 420 bird species, 305 are classified as *regular:* those species that occur at least somewhere in the state each year, during at least one season. Another 37 species fall into the category of *casual:* those species that occur at infrequent intervals anywhere in the state, and can be expected to occur in the future at infrequent intervals, but do not occur each year. Finally, are those 78 species which are classified as *accidental*, that have occured only once or twice in the state, and are not likely to occur again.

The information presented here is intended to represent the best knowledge available. A category for *nesting evidence* answers whether the bird breeds and nests in the state. Another category generally defines the the bird's *range*, or in which regions it is best represented. When birds are rare, or extremely limited in range, an asterisk followed by a specific locale indicates the most likely place the bird might be expected to be found. Finally, *monthly occurrence* indicates the times the bird is generally expected to be present in the state each year based on records for that bird.

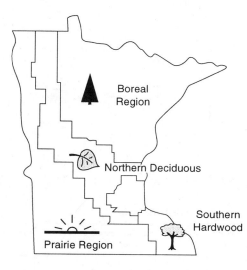

Regular species

✔ SPECIES	NESTING EVIDENCE	REGION	MONTHLY OCCURRENCE J F M A M J J A S O N D
Red-throated Loon		*Lake Superior	
†Common Loon	X	(Northern Deciduous) (Boreal)	
Pied-billed Grebe	X	(Statewide)	
Horned Grebe	X	(Prairie)	
Red-necked Grebe	X	(Northern Deciduous)	
†Eared Grebe	X	(Prairie)	
†Western Grebe	X	(Prairie) (Northern Deciduous)	
†American White Pelican	X	Local	
Double-crested Cormorant	X	(Northern Deciduous) (Prairie) (Southern Hardwood)	
†American Bittern	X	(Northern Deciduous) (Boreal)	
†Least Bittern	X	(Northern Deciduous) (Prairie)	
Great Blue Heron	X	(Northern Deciduous) (Boreal) (Southern Hardwood)	
Great Egret	X	(Northern Deciduous) (Southern Hardwood) (Prairie)	
Snowy Egret	X	Local	
Little Blue Heron	X	Local	
Cattle Egret	X	Local	
Green Heron	X	(Prairie) (Northern Deciduous) (Southern Hardwood)	
Black-crowned Night-Heron	X	(Northern Deciduous) (Prairie)	
Yellow-crowned Night-Heron	X	Local	

All locations and dates on this chart are best representations. Birds may occur outside listed range and/or average dates. Dates based on Central Minnesota; may vary up to two weeks north to south. Lack of nesting evidence indicates birds migrate through the area.

* = Most likely to occur at this place
Local = Limited numbers in widely scattered locations
† = Birds of Choice—see Chapter 6
━━━ = Birds present   ━━━ = Birds rarely present

▲ = Boreal Region
🐚 = Northern Deciduous
☀ = Prairie Region
🌳 = Southern Hardwood
(MN) = Statewide

✔	SPECIES	NESTING EVIDENCE	REGION	MONTHLY OCCURRENCE J F M A M J J A S O N D
	Tundra Swan		*Wabasha	
	Mute Swan		Local	
	Greater White-fronted Goose		(Prairie)	
	Snow Goose		(Prairie)	
	Ross' Goose		(Prairie)	
	Canada Goose	X	(Statewide)	
	Wood Duck	X	(Statewide)	
	Green-winged Teal	X	(Statewide)	
	†American Black Duck	X	(Boreal)	
	Mallard	X	(Statewide)	
	Northern Pintail	X	(Prairie, Northern Deciduous)	
	Blue-winged Teal	X	(Statewide)	
	Cinnamon Teal		(Prairie)	
	Northern Shoveler	X	(Prairie, Northern Deciduous)	
	Gadwall	X	(Prairie)	
	American Wigeon	X	(Boreal, Northern Deciduous)	
	Canvasback	X	(Prairie, Northern Deciduous)	
	Redhead	X	(Prairie, Northern Deciduous)	
	Ring-necked Duck	X	(Boreal, Northern Deciduous)	
	Greater Scaup		(Statewide)	

All locations and dates on this chart are best representations. Birds may occur outside listed range and/or average dates. Dates based on Central Minnesota; may vary up to two weeks north to south. Lack of nesting evidence indicates birds migrate through the area.

* = Most likely to occur at this place
Local = Limited numbers in widely scattered locations
† = Birds of Choice—see Chapter 6
▬▬▬ = Birds present   ▬▬▬ = Birds rarely present

🌲 = Boreal Region
🍃 = Northern Deciduous
☀ = Prairie Region
🌳 = Southern Hardwood
(MN outline) = Statewide

✔ SPECIES	NESTING EVIDENCE	REGION	MONTHLY OCCURRENCE J F M A M J J A S O N D
Lesser Scaup	X	Prairie Region	
Harlequin Duck		*Lake Superior	
Oldsquaw		*Grand Marais	
Black Scoter		*Lake Superior	
Surf Scoter		*Lake Superior	
White-winged Scoter		*Lake Superior	
Common Goldeneye	X	Boreal Region, Northern Deciduous	
Bufflehead	X	Local	
Hooded Merganser	X	Boreal Region, Northern Deciduous, Southern Hardwood	
Common Merganser	X	Boreal Region	
Red-breasted Merganser	X	Local	
†Ruddy Duck	X	Prairie Region, Northern Deciduous	
Turkey Vulture	X	Boreal Region, Southern Hardwood, Northern Deciduous	
†Osprey	X	Boreal Region, Northern Deciduous	
†Bald Eagle	X	Boreal Region, Northern Deciduous	
Northern Harrier	X	Statewide	
Sharp-shinned Hawk	X	Boreal Region	
†Cooper's Hawk	X	Northern Deciduous, Prairie Region, Southern Hardwood	
†Northern Goshawk	X	Boreal Region	
†Red-shouldered Hawk	X	Northern Deciduous, Southern Hardwood	

All locations and dates on this chart are best representations. Birds may occur outside listed range and/or average dates. Dates based on Central Minnesota; may vary up to two weeks north to south. Lack of nesting evidence indicates birds migrate through the area.

* = Most likely to occur at this place
Local = Limited numbers in widely scattered locations
† = Birds of Choice—see Chapter 6
━━━━ = Birds present   ━━━━ = Birds rarely present

▲ = Boreal Region
🍃 = Northern Deciduous
☀ = Prairie Region
🌳 = Southern Hardwood
(MN outline) = Statewide

✔	SPECIES	NESTING EVIDENCE	REGION	MONTHLY OCCURRENCE J F M A M J J A S O N D
🗺	†Broad-winged Hawk	X	🌲 🍃 🌳	
🗺	Swainson's Hawk	X	☀	
🗺	Red-tailed Hawk	X	🗺	
🗺	Ferruginous Hawk		☀	
🗺	Rough-legged Hawk		🗺	
🗺	Golden Eagle		*Whitewater WMA	
🗺	American Kestrel	X	🗺	
🗺	Merlin	X	🌲	
🗺	Peregrine Falcon	X	🗺	
🗺	Prairie Falcon		*Wilkin Co.	
🗺	Gray Partridge	X	☀	
🗺	Ring-necked Pheasant	X	☀ 🍃 🌳	
🗺	†Spruce Grouse	X	🌲	
🗺	Ruffed Grouse	X	🌲 🍃 🌳	
🗺	†Greater Prairie-Chicken	X	☀	
🗺	†Sharp-tailed Grouse	X	🌲 🍃	
🗺	†Wild Turkey	X	🌳	
🗺	Northern Bobwhite	X	🌳	
🗺	†Yellow Rail	X	🍃 🌲	
🗺	†Virginia Rail	X	🍃 🌳 ☀	

All locations and dates on this chart are best representations. Birds may occur outside listed range and/or average dates. Dates based on Central Minnesota; may vary up to two weeks north to south. Lack of nesting evidence indicates birds migrate through the area.

* = Most likely to occur at this place
Local = Limited numbers in widely scattered locations
† = Birds of Choice—see Chapter 6
━━━ = Birds present   ━━━ = Birds rarely present

🌲 = Boreal Region
🍃 = Northern Deciduous
☀ = Prairie Region
🌳 = Southern Hardwood
🗺 = Statewide

✔	SPECIES	NESTING EVIDENCE	REGION	MONTHLY OCCURRENCE J F M A M J J A S O N D
☐	Sora	X	Statewide	
☐	Common Moorhen	X	Southern Hardwood	
☐	American Coot	X	Statewide	
☐	†Sandhill Crane	X	Northern Deciduous	
☐	Black-bellied Plover		*Duluth	
☐	American Golden-Plover		Prairie Region	
☐	Semipalmated Plover		Statewide	
☐	Piping Plover	X	*Lake of the Woods	
☐	Killdeer	X	Statewide	
☐	American Avocet	X	*Lac Qui Parle Co.	
☐	Greater Yellowlegs		Statewide	
☐	Lesser Yellowlegs		Statewide	
☐	Solitary Sandpiper	X	Boreal Region	
☐	Willet	X	Prairie Region	
☐	Spotted Sandpiper	X	Statewide	
☐	†Upland Sandpiper	X	Prairie Region / Northern Deciduous	
☐	Whimbrel		*Duluth	
☐	Hudsonian Godwit		Prairie Region	
☐	†Marbled Godwit	X	Prairie Region	
☐	Ruddy Turnstone		*Duluth	

All locations and dates on this chart are best representations. Birds may occur outside listed range and/or average dates. Dates based on Central Minnesota; may vary up to two weeks north to south. Lack of nesting evidence indicates birds migrate through the area.

* = Most likely to occur at this place
Local = Limited numbers in widely scattered locations
† = Birds of Choice—see Chapter 6
━━━ = Birds present   ━━━ = Birds rarely present

▲ = Boreal Region
= Northern Deciduous
= Prairie Region
= Southern Hardwood
= Statewide

✔	SPECIES	NESTING EVIDENCE	REGION	MONTHLY OCCURRENCE J F M A M J J A S O N D
	Red Knot		*Duluth	
	Sanderling		*Duluth	
	Semipalmated Sandpiper		(Statewide)	
	Least Sandpiper		(Prairie Region)	
	White-rumped Sandpiper		*Lac Qui Parle Co.	
	Baird's Sandpiper		(Statewide)	
	Pectoral Sandpiper		(Statewide)	
	Dunlin		*Duluth	
	Stilt Sandpiper		(Prairie Region)	
	Buff-breasted Sandpiper		*Duluth	
	Short-billed Dowitcher		(Statewide)	
	Long-billed Dowitcher		(Statewide)	
	Common Snipe	X	(Northern Deciduous, Boreal Region)	
	†American Woodcock	X	(Northern Deciduous, Boreal Region, Southern Hardwood)	
	†Wilson's Phalarope	X	(Prairie Region)	
	Red-necked Phalarope		(Statewide)	
	Parasitic Jaeger		*Duluth	
	†Franklin's Gull	X	(Prairie Region)	
	Little Gull	X	*Lake Superior	
	Bonaparte's Gull		*Duluth, Mille Lacs	

All locations and dates on this chart are best representations. Birds may occur outside listed range and/or average dates. Dates based on Central Minnesota; may vary up to two weeks north to south. Lack of nesting evidence indicates birds migrate through the area.

* = Most likely to occur at this place
Local = Limited numbers in widely scattered locations
† = Birds of Choice—see Chapter 6
━━━ = Birds present   ━━━ = Birds rarely present

▲ = Boreal Region
🍁 = Northern Deciduous
☀ = Prairie Region
🌳 = Southern Hardwood
(Minnesota shape) = Statewide

✔	SPECIES	NESTING EVIDENCE	REGION	MONTHLY OCCURRENCE (J F M A M J J A S O N D)
☐	Ring-billed Gull	X	[Statewide]	present spring–fall
☐	Herring Gull	X	[Boreal Region]	present spring–fall
☐	Thayer's Gull		*Black Dog Lake	rarely present; Jan–Mar, Dec
☐	Glaucous Gull		*Lake Superior	rarely present; Jan–Mar, Dec
☐	Caspian Tern	X	Local	present Apr–May, Jul–Aug
☐	Common Tern	X	Local	present spring–summer
☐	†Forster's Tern	X	[Northern Deciduous] [Prairie Region]	present spring–summer
☐	†Black Tern	X	Local	present summer
☐	Rock Dove	X	[Statewide]	present year-round
☐	Mourning Dove	X	[Prairie Region] [Northern Deciduous] [Southern Hardwood]	present year-round
☐	†Black-billed Cuckoo	X	[Statewide]	present summer
☐	†Yellow-billed Cuckoo	X	[Southern Hardwood] [Prairie Region]	present summer
☐	†Eastern Screech-Owl	X	[Prairie Region] [Northern Deciduous] [Southern Hardwood]	present year-round
☐	Great Horned Owl	X	[Statewide]	present year-round
☐	†Snowy Owl		*Duluth Harbor	present Jan, Nov–Dec
☐	†Northern Hawk Owl	X	[Boreal Region]	present winter
☐	†Barred Owl	X	[Boreal Region] [Northern Deciduous] [Southern Hardwood]	present year-round
☐	†Great Gray Owl	X	[Boreal Region]	present year-round
☐	†Long-eared Owl	X	[Prairie Region] [Northern Deciduous] [Boreal Region]	rarely present year-round
☐	†Short-eared Owl	X	[Prairie Region]	present spring–fall

All locations and dates on this chart are best representations. Birds may occur outside listed range and/or average dates. Dates based on Central Minnesota; may vary up to two weeks north to south. Lack of nesting evidence indicates birds migrate through the area.

* = Most likely to occur at this place
Local = Limited numbers in widely scattered locations
† = Birds of Choice—see Chapter 6
▬▬▬ = Birds present   ▬▬▬ = Birds rarely present

▲ = Boreal Region
🍂 = Northern Deciduous
☀ = Prairie Region
🌳 = Southern Hardwood
[MN] = Statewide

✔	SPECIES	NESTING EVIDENCE	REGION	MONTHLY OCCURRENCE J F M A M J J A S O N D
🗒	†Boreal Owl	X	▲	▬▬▬▬▬▬▬▬▬▬▬▬
🗒	†Northern Saw-whet Owl	X	▲ 🍃 ☀	▬▬▬▬▬▬▬▬▬
🗒	Common Nighthawk	X	(MN)	▬▬▬▬
🗒	†Whip-poor-will	X	▲ 🍃 🌳	▬▬▬▬▬
🗒	Chimney Swift	X	(MN)	▬▬▬▬▬
🗒	Ruby-throated Hummingbird	X	(MN)	▬▬▬
🗒	Belted Kingfisher	X	(MN)	▬▬▬▬▬▬
🗒	†Red-headed Woodpecker	X	🍃 ☀ 🌳	▬▬▬ ▬▬
🗒	†Red-bellied Woodpecker	X	☀ 🍃 🌳	▬▬▬▬▬▬▬▬▬▬▬▬
🗒	†Yellow-bellied Sapsucker	X	(MN)	▬▬▬▬▬▬
🗒	Downy Woodpecker	X	(MN)	▬▬▬▬▬▬▬▬▬▬▬▬
🗒	Hairy Woodpecker	X	(MN)	▬▬▬▬▬▬▬▬▬▬▬▬
🗒	†Three-toed Woodpecker	X	▲ 🍃	▬▬▬▬▬▬▬▬▬▬▬▬
🗒	†Black-backed Woodpecker	X	▲	▬▬▬▬▬▬▬▬▬▬▬▬
🗒	Northern Flicker	X	(MN)	▬▬▬▬▬▬
🗒	†Pileated Woodpecker	X	🌳 🍃 ▲	▬▬▬▬▬▬▬▬▬▬▬▬
🗒	†Olive-sided Flycatcher	X	▲ 🍃	▬▬▬▬
🗒	Eastern Wood-Pewee	X	(MN)	▬▬▬▬
🗒	†Yellow-bellied Flycatcher	X	▲	▬▬▬
🗒	†Acadian Flycatcher	X	🌳	▬▬▬

All locations and dates on this chart are best representations. Birds may occur outside listed range and/or average dates. Dates based on Central Minnesota; may vary up to two weeks north to south. Lack of nesting evidence indicates birds migrate through the area.

* = Most likely to occur at this place
Local = Limited numbers in widely scattered locations
† = Birds of Choice—see Chapter 6
▬▬▬ = Birds present   ▬▬▬ = Birds rarely present

▲ = Boreal Region
🍃 = Northern Deciduous
☀ = Prairie Region
🌳 = Southern Hardwood
🗒 = Statewide

✔ SPECIES	NESTING EVIDENCE	REGION	MONTHLY OCCURRENCE
†Alder Flycatcher	X	Boreal, Northern Deciduous	▬
†Willow Flycatcher	X	Prairie, Northern Deciduous, Southern Hardwood	▬
†Least Flycatcher	X	Statewide	▬
†Eastern Phoebe	X	Statewide	▬
Great Crested Flycatcher	X	Northern Deciduous, Southern Hardwood, Prairie	▬
†Western Kingbird	X	Prairie	▬
Eastern Kingbird	X	Statewide	▬
Horned Lark	X	Northern Deciduous, Prairie, Southern Hardwood	▬▬▬
Purple Martin	X	Statewide	▬▬
Tree Swallow	X	Statewide	▬▬
Northern Rough-winged Swallow	X	Statewide	▬▬
Bank Swallow	X	Statewide	▬▬
Cliff Swallow	X	Statewide	▬▬
Barn Swallow	X	Statewide	▬▬
†Gray Jay	X	Boreal	▬▬▬
Blue Jay	X	Statewide	▬▬▬
Black-billed Magpie	X	Prairie	▬▬▬
American Crow	X	Statewide	▬▬▬
†Common Raven	X	Boreal, Northern Deciduous	▬▬▬

All locations and dates on this chart are best representations. Birds may occur outside listed range and/or average dates. Dates based on Central Minnesota; may vary up to two weeks north to south. Lack of nesting evidence indicates birds migrate through the area.

* = Most likely to occur at this place
Local = Limited numbers in widely scattered locations
† = Birds of Choice—see Chapter 6
▬▬▬ = Birds present   ▬▬▬ = Birds rarely present

▲ = Boreal Region
🍂 = Northern Deciduous
☀ = Prairie Region
🌳 = Southern Hardwood
▛ = Statewide

✔	SPECIES	NESTING EVIDENCE	REGION	MONTHLY OCCURRENCE J F M A M J J A S O N D
🗹	Black-capped Chickadee	X	(Statewide)	
🗹	†Boreal Chickadee	X	(Boreal, Northern Deciduous)	
🗹	†Tufted Titmouse	X	(Southern Hardwood)	
🗹	†Red-breasted Nuthatch	X	(Boreal, Northern Deciduous)	
🗹	White-breasted Nuthatch	X	(Statewide)	
🗹	†Brown Creeper	X	(Boreal, Northern Deciduous, Southern Hardwood)	
🗹	Carolina Wren	X	Local	
🗹	House Wren	X	(Statewide)	
🗹	†Winter Wren	X	(Boreal)	
🗹	†Sedge Wren	X	(Statewide)	
🗹	†Marsh Wren	X	(Prairie, Northern Deciduous, Southern Hardwood)	
🗹	†Golden-crowned Kinglet	X	(Boreal, Northern Deciduous)	
🗹	†Ruby-crowned Kinglet	X	(Boreal, Northern Deciduous)	
🗹	†Blue-gray Gnatcatcher	X	(Northern Deciduous, Southern Hardwood)	
🗹	Eastern Bluebird	X	(Statewide)	
🗹	Mountain Bluebird	X	(Prairie)	
🗹	Townsend's Solitaire		Local	
🗹	†Veery	X	(Boreal, Northern Deciduous, Southern Hardwood)	
🗹	Gray-cheeked Thrush		(Statewide)	
🗹	†Swainson's Thrush	X	(Boreal)	

All locations and dates on this chart are best representations. Birds may occur outside listed range and/or average dates. Dates based on Central Minnesota; may vary up to two weeks north to south. Lack of nesting evidence indicates birds migrate through the area.

* = Most likely to occur at this place
Local = Limited numbers in widely scattered locations
† = Birds of Choice—see Chapter 6
━━━━ = Birds present   ━━━━ = Birds rarely present

🌲 = Boreal Region
🍃 = Northern Deciduous
☀ = Prairie Region
🌳 = Southern Hardwood
(MN) = Statewide

✔	SPECIES	NESTING EVIDENCE	REGION	MONTHLY OCCURRENCE J F M A M J J A S O N D
🦃	Hermit Thrush	X	▲	———————
🦃	†Wood Thrush	X	▲ 🍃 🌳	———————
🦃	American Robin	X	(MN)	———————
🦃	Varied Thrush		Local	— —
🦃	Gray Catbird	X	(MN)	———————
🦃	Northern Mockingbird	X	Local	— — —
🦃	Brown Thrasher	X	(MN)	———————
🦃	American Pipit		(MN)	———————
🦃	†Bohemian Waxwing		▲	—— ——
🦃	Cedar Waxwing	X	🌳 🍃	———————
🦃	†Northern Shrike		Local	—— ——
🦃	†Loggerhead Shrike	X	☀ 🍃 🌳	———————
🦃	European Starling	X	(MN)	———————
🦃	†Bell's Vireo	X	Local	———
🦃	†Solitary Vireo	X	▲	———
🦃	†Yellow-throated Vireo	X	🍃 🌳 ▲	———
🦃	Warbling Vireo	X	(MN)	———
🦃	†Philadelphia Vireo	X	▲	———
🦃	Red-eyed Vireo	X	(MN)	———
🦃	†Blue-winged Warbler	X	🌳 🍃	———

All locations and dates on this chart are best representations. Birds may occur outside listed range and/or average dates. Dates based on Central Minnesota; may vary up to two weeks north to south. Lack of nesting evidence indicates birds migrate through the area.

* = Most likely to occur at this place
Local = Limited numbers in widely scattered locations
† = Birds of Choice—see Chapter 6
—————— = Birds present —————— = Birds rarely present

▲ = Boreal Region
🍃 = Northern Deciduous
☀ = Prairie Region
🌳 = Southern Hardwood
(MN) = Statewide

✔	SPECIES	NESTING EVIDENCE	REGION	MONTHLY OCCURRENCE (J F M A M J J A S O N D)
	†Golden-winged Warbler	X	Northern Deciduous	—
	†Tennessee Warbler	X	Boreal, Northern Deciduous	—
	Orange-crowned Warbler		Statewide	—
	†Nashville Warbler	X	Boreal, Northern Deciduous	—
	†Northern Parula	X	Boreal, Northern Deciduous	—
	Yellow Warbler	X	Statewide	—
	†Chestnut-sided Warbler	X	Boreal, Northern Deciduous	—
	†Magnolia Warbler	X	Boreal, Northern Deciduous	—
	†Cape May Warbler	X	Boreal	—
	†Black-throated Blue Warbler	X	Local	—
	†Yellow-rumped Warbler	X	Boreal, Northern Deciduous	—
	†Black-throated Green Warbler	X	Boreal, Northern Deciduous	—
	†Blackburnian Warbler	X	Boreal, Northern Deciduous	—
	†Pine Warbler	X	Boreal, Northern Deciduous	—
	†Palm Warbler	X	Boreal, Northern Deciduous	—
	† Bay-Breasted Warbler	X	Boreal, Northern Deciduous	—
	Blackpoll Warbler		Statewide	- -
	†Cerulean Warbler	X	Northern Deciduous, Southern Hardwood	—
	†Black-and-white Warbler	X	Boreal, Northern Deciduous	—

All locations and dates on this chart are best representations. Birds may occur outside listed range and/or average dates. Dates based on Central Minnesota; may vary up to two weeks north to south. Lack of nesting evidence indicates birds migrate through the area.

* = Most likely to occur at this place
Local = Limited numbers in widely scattered locations
† = Birds of Choice—see Chapter 6
▬▬ = Birds present   ▬▬ = Birds rarely present

▲ = Boreal Region
🍃 = Northern Deciduous
☀ = Prairie Region
🌳 = Southern Hardwood
(MN outline) = Statewide

✔	SPECIES	NESTING EVIDENCE	REGION	MONTHLY OCCURRENCE (J F M A M J J A S O N D)
[MN]	†American Redstart	X	[Southern Hardwood] [Northern Deciduous] [Boreal]	Birds present (summer)
[MN]	†Prothonotary Warbler	X	[Southern Hardwood]	Birds present (summer)
[MN]	Worm-eating Warbler		*Twin Cities	Birds rarely present
[MN]	Ovenbird	X	[Boreal] [Northern Deciduous] [Southern Hardwood]	Birds present (summer)
[MN]	†Northern Waterthrush	X	[Boreal]	Birds present (summer)
[MN]	†Louisiana Waterthrush	X	[Southern Hardwood]	Birds present (summer)
[MN]	Kentucky Warbler	X	[Southern Hardwood]	Birds rarely present
[MN]	†Connecticut Warbler	X	[Boreal] [Northern Deciduous]	Birds present (summer)
[MN]	†Mourning Warbler	X	[Boreal] [Northern Deciduous]	Birds present (summer)
[MN]	Common Yellowthroat	X	[Statewide]	Birds present (summer)
[MN]	Hooded Warbler	X	[Southern Hardwood]	Birds present (brief)
[MN]	Wilson's Warbler	X	Local [Boreal]	Birds present (summer)
[MN]	†Canada Warbler	X	[Boreal] [Northern Deciduous]	Birds present (summer)
[MN]	Yellow-breasted Chat	X	[Prairie]	Birds rarely present
[MN]	Summer Tanager		[Southern Hardwood] [Prairie]	Birds rarely present
[MN]	†Scarlet Tanager	X	[Southern Hardwood] [Northern Deciduous] [Boreal]	Birds present (summer)
[MN]	Northern Cardinal	X	[Prairie] [Northern Deciduous] [Southern Hardwood]	Birds present (year-round)
[MN]	Rose-breasted Grosbeak	X	[Statewide]	Birds present (summer)
[MN]	†Blue Grosbeak	X	[Prairie]	Birds present (summer)
[MN]	†Indigo Bunting	X	[Statewide]	Birds present (summer)

All locations and dates on this chart are best representations. Birds may occur outside listed range and/or average dates. Dates based on Central Minnesota; may vary up to two weeks north to south. Lack of nesting evidence indicates birds migrate through the area.

* = Most likely to occur at this place
Local = Limited numbers in widely scattered locations
† = Birds of Choice—see Chapter 6
▬▬▬ = Birds present   ▬▬▬ = Birds rarely present

▲ = Boreal Region
🍂 = Northern Deciduous
☀ = Prairie Region
🌳 = Southern Hardwood
[MN] = Statewide

✔	SPECIES	NESTING EVIDENCE	REGION	MONTHLY OCCURRENCE J F M A M J J A S O N D
☐	†Dickcissel	X	Prairie, Northern Deciduous, Southern Hardwood	
☐	†Eastern Towhee	X	Northern Deciduous, Southern Hardwood	
☐	American Tree Sparrow		Statewide	
☐	Chipping Sparrow	X	Statewide	
☐	Clay-colored Sparrow	X	Northern Deciduous, Prairie, Boreal	
☐	Field Sparrow	X	Prairie, Northern Deciduous, Southern Hardwood	
☐	Vesper Sparrow	X	Prairie, Northern Deciduous, Southern Hardwood	
☐	†Lark Sparrow	X	Local	
☐	Lark Bunting	X	Local	
☐	Savannah Sparrow	X	Statewide	
☐	†Grasshopper Sparrow	X	Prairie, Southern Hardwood	
☐	Henslow's Sparrow	X	Local	
☐	†Le Conte's Sparrow	X	Prairie, Northern Deciduous, Boreal	
☐	†Nelson's Sharp-tailed Sparrow	X	Local	
☐	Fox Sparrow		Northern Deciduous	
☐	Song Sparrow	X	Statewide	
☐	†Lincoln's Sparrow	X	Boreal	
☐	Swamp Sparrow	X	Statewide	
☐	†White-throated Sparrow	X	Boreal, Northern Deciduous	

All locations and dates on this chart are best representations. Birds may occur outside listed range and/or average dates. Dates based on Central Minnesota; may vary up to two weeks north to south. Lack of nesting evidence indicates birds migrate through the area.

* = Most likely to occur at this place
Local = Limited numbers in widely scattered locations
† = Birds of Choice—see Chapter 6
▬▬▬ = Birds present   ▬▬▬ = Birds rarely present

▲ = Boreal Region
🍂 = Northern Deciduous
☀ = Prairie Region
🌳 = Southern Hardwood
⬙ = Statewide

✔	SPECIES	NESTING EVIDENCE	REGION	MONTHLY OCCURRENCE J F M A M J J A S O N D
☐	White-crowned Sparrow		Statewide	
☐	Harris' Sparrow		Statewide	
☐	†Dark-eyed Junco	X	Boreal	
☐	Lapland Longspur		Statewide	
☐	Smith's Longspur		Prairie	
☐	†Chestnut-collared Longspur	X	Prairie	
☐	Snow Bunting		Statewide	
☐	†Bobolink	X	Prairie, Northern Deciduous, Southern Hardwood	
☐	Red-winged Blackbird	X	Statewide	
☐	Eastern Meadowlark	X	Southern Hardwood, Northern Deciduous, Boreal	
☐	†Western Meadowlark	X	Prairie, Northern Deciduous, Southern Hardwood	
☐	†Yellow-headed Blackbird	X	Prairie, Northern Deciduous, Southern Hardwood	
☐	Rusty Blackbird	X	Boreal	
☐	Brewer's Blackbird	X	Northern Deciduous, Boreal	
☐	Common Grackle	X	Statewide	
☐	Brown-headed Cowbird	X	Statewide	
☐	†Orchard Oriole	X	Prairie, Southern Hardwood	
☐	Baltimore Oriole	X	Statewide	
☐	†Pine Grosbeak		Boreal, Northern Deciduous	
☐	†Purple Finch	X	Boreal, Northern Deciduous	

All locations and dates on this chart are best representations. Birds may occur outside listed range and/or average dates. Dates based on Central Minnesota; may vary up to two weeks north to south. Lack of nesting evidence indicates birds migrate through the area.

* = Most likely to occur at this place
Local = Limited numbers in widely scattered locations
† = Birds of Choice—see Chapter 6
━━━ = Birds present   ▬▬▬ = Birds rarely present

▲ = Boreal Region
🍂 = Northern Deciduous
☀ = Prairie Region
🌳 = Southern Hardwood
⬙ = Statewide

✔	SPECIES	NESTING EVIDENCE	REGION	MONTHLY OCCURRENCE J F M A M J J A S O N D
🗺	House Finch	X	🗺	
🗺	†Red Crossbill	X	Local	
🗺	White-winged Crossbill		▲	
🗺	Common Redpoll		🗺	
🗺	Hoary Redpoll		▲	
🗺	Pine Siskin	X	▲ 🍂 ☀	
🗺	American Goldfinch	X	🗺	
🗺	†Evening Grosbeak	X	▲ 🍂	
🗺	House Sparrow	X	🗺	

All locations and dates on this chart are best representations. Birds may occur outside listed range and/or average dates. Dates based on Central Minnesota; may vary up to two weeks north to south. Lack of nesting evidence indicates birds migrate through the area.

* = Most likely to occur at this place
Local = Limited numbers in widely scattered locations
† = Birds of Choice—see Chapter 6
━━━ = Birds present   ▬▬▬ = Birds rarely present

▲ = Boreal Region
🍂 = Northern Deciduous
☀ = Prairie Region
🌳 = Southern Hardwood
🗺 = Statewide

Casual species

✔	SPECIES	NESTING EVIDENCE	REGION	MONTHLY OCCURRENCE J F M A M J J A S O N D
[MN]	Pacific Loon		*Lake Superior	
[MN]	Clark's Grebe		*Western MN	
[MN]	Tricolored Heron			
[MN]	White-faced Ibis		*Western/Southern MN	
[MN]	Brant			
[MN]	Eurasian Wigeon			
[MN]	Barrow's Goldeneye		*Twin Cities Rivers/ Lake Superior	
[MN]	Mississippi Kite			
[MN]	Gyrfalcon		*Duluth	
[MN]	King Rail	X	*Southern MN	
[MN]	Long-billed Curlew		*West Central MN	
[MN]	Western Sandpiper			
[MN]	Ruff			
[MN]	Laughing Gull		*Duluth/Mississippi River Southeast	
[MN]	California Gull			
[MN]	Iceland Gull		*Lake Superior, Twin Cities	
[MN]	Lesser Black-backed Gull		*Twin Cities	
[MN]	Great Black-backed Gull		*Duluth	
[MN]	Black-legged Kittiwake		*Lake Superior	

All locations and dates on this chart are best representations. Birds may occur outside listed range and/or average dates. Dates based on Central Minnesota; may vary up to two weeks north to south. Lack of nesting evidence indicates birds migrate through the area.

* = Most likely to occur at this place
Local = Limited numbers in widely scattered locations
† = Birds of Choice—see Chapter 6
▬▬▬ = Birds present   ▬▬▬ = Birds rarely present

▲ = Boreal Region
🍂 = Northern Deciduous
☀ = Prairie Region
🌳 = Southern Hardwood
[MN] = Statewide

238

✔	SPECIES	NESTING EVIDENCE	REGION	MONTHLY OCCURRENCE J F M A M J J A S O N D
🦅	Sabine's Gull			
🦅	Least Tern		*Southwest MN/ Twin Cities	
🦅	Barn Owl	X	*Southern MN	
🦅	Burrowing Owl	X	*Western MN	
🦅	Rufous Hummingbird		*Northern MN	
🦅	Western Wood-Pewee	X	*Northwest MN	
🦅	Say's Phoebe		*Western MN	
🦅	Scissor-tailed Flycatcher		*Northeast MN/ Lake Superior	
🦅	Rock Wren			
🦅	Sage Thrasher			
🦅	Sprague's Pipit		*Western MN	
🦅	White-eyed Vireo		*Twin Cities/ Southeast MN	
🦅	Yellow-throated Warbler		*Twin Cities/ Southeast MN	
🦅	Western Tanager			
🦅	Black-headed Grosbeak		*Twin Cities/ Southwest MN	
🦅	Lazuli Bunting		*Western MN	
🦅	Spotted Towhee		*Western MN	
🦅	Baird's Sparrow		*Western MN	

All locations and dates on this chart are best representations. Birds may occur outside listed range and/or average dates. Dates based on Central Minnesota; may vary up to two weeks north to south. Lack of nesting evidence indicates birds migrate through the area.

* = Most likely to occur at this place
Local = Limited numbers in widely scattered locations
† = Birds of Choice—see Chapter 6
■■■ = Birds present   ▬▬▬ = Birds rarely present

▲ = Boreal Region
🌲 = Northern Deciduous
🌾 = Prairie Region
🌳 = Southern Hardwood
🗺 = Statewide

Accidental species

☐ Yellow-billed Loon

☐ Neotropic Cormorant

☐ Magnificent Frigatebird

☐ White-faced Ibis

☐ Glossy Ibis

☐ Fulvous Whistling-Duck

☐ Black-bellied Whistling-Duck

☐ Trumpeter Swan

☐ Garganey

☐ Common Eider

☐ King Eider

☐ Swallow-tailed Kite

☐ Crested Caracara

☐ Willow Ptarmigan

☐ Black Rail

☐ Purple Gallinule

☐ Whooping Crane

☐ Snowy Plover

☐ Wilson's Plover

☐ Black-necked Stilt

☐ Eskimo Curlew (Extirpated)

☐ Purple Sandpiper

☐ Curlew Sandpiper

☐ Red Phalarope

☐ Pomarine Jaeger

☐ Long-tailed Jaeger

☐ Black-headed Gull

☐ Mew Gull

☐ Glaucous-winged Gull

☐ Ross' Gull

☐ Ivory Gull

☐ Sandwich Tern

☐ Arctic Tern

☐ Dovekie

☐ Ancient Murrelet

☐ Band-tailed Pigeon

☐ White-winged Dove

☐ Passenger Pigeon (Extinct)

☐ Common Ground-Dove

☐ Groove-billed Ani

☐ Common Poorwill

☐ Chuck-will's-widow

☐ Magnificent Hummingbird

☐ Anna's Hummingbird

☐ Calliope Hummingbird

☐ Lewis' Woodpecker

- ☑ Williamson's Sapsucker
- ☑ Black Phoebe
- ☑ Vermilion Flycatcher
- ☑ Ash-throated Flycatcher
- ☑ Fork-tailed Flycatcher
- ☑ Violet-green Swallow
- ☑ Clark's Nutcracker
- ☑ Bewick's Wren
- ☑ American Dipper
- ☑ Northern Wheatear
- ☑ Fieldfare
- ☑ Curve-billed Thrasher
- ☑ Black-throated Gray Warbler
- ☑ Townsend's Warbler
- ☑ Hermit Warbler
- ☑ Kirtland's Warbler
- ☑ Prairie Warbler
- ☑ MacGillivray's Warbler
- ☑ Painted Redstart
- ☑ Painted Bunting
- ☑ Green-tailed Towhee
- ☑ Brewer's Sparrow
- ☑ Black-throated Sparrow

- ☑ Golden-crowned Sparrow
- ☑ McCown's Longspur
- ☑ Great-tailed Grackle
- ☑ Bullock's Oriole
- ☑ Scott's Oriole
- ☑ Brambling
- ☑ Gray-crowned Rosy Finch
- ☑ Cassin's Finch
- ☑ Eurasian Tree Sparrow

242

CHAPTER 6

Minnesota's choice species

Mention "Minnesota" to a birder and the word quickly brings to mind visions of a dozen different birds, each characteristic of a specific region or type of habitat: Common Loon, Northern Goshawk, Spruce Grouse, Greater Prairie-Chicken, Great Gray Owl, Upland Sandpiper, Franklin's Gull, Alder Flycatcher, Gray Jay, Boreal Chickadee, Winter Wren, Swainson's Thrush, Palm Warbler, Bay-breasted Warbler, White-throated Sparrow, Bobolink, and Evening Grosbeak. More than one-hundred birds can be classified as Minnesota's "choice" species, birds that are unique or representative of Minnesota habitats, and that remain eagerly sought by North American birders who visit the state.

This chapter presents information on the seasonal distribution of 122 Minnesota birds of choice. Included for each species are maps showing general bird distribution across the state, comments about the bird, your chances of seeing or hearing the bird, and a list of key sites (described in Chapter 3) where the bird is known to occur.

Maps are representative only, and indicate generally distinct areas to expect the birds. Consult the key at the bottom of each page for an explanation to shading. Accompanying text should be consulted for a more specific understanding of the bird's known range.

√ = not seen, as of 6/97
+ = see again

Common Loon

COMMENTS: Common in summer on lakes in north-central and northern parts of state. Larger lakes statewide in migration, but especially in the eastern portion. Minnesota's State Bird.

CHANCES: Excellent

KEY SITES: Gunflint Trail lakes, Leech Lake. Migration: Mille Lacs Lake and lakes in and around Twin Cities area

Eared Grebe

COMMENTS: Uncommon in summer on shallow potholes and marshes of prairie region, primarily west-central. Uncommon spring and fall migrant in western portion. May occur in concentrations during fall migration.

CHANCES: Moderate

KEY SITES: Salt Lake, Agassiz National Wildlife Refuge, Swan Lake and sewage ponds in western Minnesota

Western Grebe +

COMMENTS: Locally common in summer on large marshes or lakes with associated marshes, bullrushes in central and prairie region. Concentrations may be seen during fall migration primarily west.

CHANCES: Excellent

KEY SITES: French Lake (Twin Cities, summer), Lac Qui Parle Lake, Lake Osakis, Swan Lake, Lake Traverse, Minnesota Lake

American White Pelican

COMMENTS: Locally common in west during summer. Increasing numbers, expanding range. Common migrant in west-central and south-central with concentrations in fall.

CHANCES: Excellent

KEY SITES: Marsh Lake, Lake of the Woods, Minnesota Lake, Lake Johanna

American Bittern

COMMENTS: Range shrinking northeastward. Common in summer only in northwest. Uncommon in marshes in north-central, northeast, rare elsewhere. More easily heard than seen. Statewide in migration.

CHANCES: Moderate (in north)

KEY SITES: Agassiz National Wildlife Refuge, Bemidji area

 = Migrating ▢ = Breeding ■ = Migrating and Breeding ○ = Breeding (localized) ▦ = Winter

Least Bittern ✓

COMMENTS: Summer resident, uncommon and local in marshes primarily in central portions of state and southeast. More often heard than seen. Southern portion of state during migration.

CHANCES: Poor

KEY SITES: Wood Lake Nature Center, Big Stone National Wildlife Refuge

American Black Duck

COMMENTS: Local and uncommon in summer in forested lakes, marshes and slow creeks of the northeast. Concentrations may be found in central rice paddies during migration, otherwise scattered individuals and pairs.

CHANCES: Poor

KEY SITES: Rice Lake National Wildlife Refuge, Agassiz National Wildlife Refuge, BWCA

Ruddy Duck

COMMENTS: Common in summer in shallow lakes of western, east-central, and south-central portions. Common during migration statewide, except northeast and north-central, frequently in concentrations.

CHANCES: Excellent

KEY SITES: Agassiz National Wildlife Refuge, Heron Lake, Swan Lake

Osprey

COMMENTS: Summer resident, uncommon and local in northeast, north-central and east-central portions along lakeshores. Recent nesting records in Twin Cities' Hennepin County. Uncommon spring and fall migrant statewide. Dependable migrant at Hawk Ridge.

CHANCES: Moderate

KEY SITES: Chippewa National Forest, Superior National Forest, Carver Park Reserve

Bald Eagle

COMMENTS: Uncommon and local summer resident in northeast, north-central, and east-central portions in extensive mature forests of lake country. Spring and fall migrant, common locally, especially Hawk Ridge and Mississippi River southeast. Winter resident near open water of wildlife refuges statewide, but especially dependable along lower Mississippi River.

CHANCES: Moderate

KEY SITES: Read's Landing (winter), Chippewa National Forest (summer)

■ = Migrating   □ = Breeding   ■ = Migrating and Breeding   ◐ = Breeding (localized)   ▦ = Winter

Cooper's Hawk

COMMENTS: Uncommon summer resident statewide, absent from northeast. Uncommon, even in migration, throughout the state. Best chance for viewing during fall migration. Recently becoming more common.

CHANCES: Poor

KEY SITES: Hawk Ridge, Whitewater Wildlife Management Area, Reno Trail

Northern Goshawk √

COMMENTS: Local summer resident in northeast, absent elsewhere. Shy. Best chances for viewing along forest edges, road cuts and power line clearings. Statewide during fall migration.

CHANCES: Poor

KEY SITES: Hawk Ridge, Highway 53 between Virginia and International Falls

Red-shouldered Hawk

COMMENTS: May have disappeared as a summer resident of the southeast, expanding northwestward, Uncommon resident of central portion. Primarily central and southeast regions during migration, even into winter.

CHANCES: Poor

KEY SITES: Carver Park Reserve (summer), Whitewater Wildlife Management Area (fall), Camp Ripley, (summer)

Broad-winged Hawk

COMMENTS: Common summer resident in forest areas of north. Uncommon in central and rare in west-central. Common spring and fall migrant statewide. Large concentrations may be seen traveling in fall.

CHANCES: Excellent

KEY SITES: Hawk Ridge in fall, especially mid-September. Itasca State Park, summer, Twin Cities' woodlands

Spruce Grouse

COMMENTS: Uncommon permanent resident of conifer forests of extreme northern portion, excluding the extreme northwest. Best chance to see: July through September when broods are traveling and breaking up. Early morning on little-used dirt roads, primarily in association with jack pine or balsam stands.

CHANCES: Poor

KEY SITES: Beltrami Island State Forest roads, north end Lake County 2, Echo Trail, Gunflint Trail

■ = Migrating   □ = Breeding   ■ = Migrating and Breeding   ○ = Breeding (localized)   ▦ = Winter

Greater Prairie-Chicken

COMMENTS: Uncommon permanent resident of local areas in northwest and north-central. Best seen on dancing grounds, March through May. Rare migrant. Sometimes appears in counties of west-central and southwest.

CHANCES: Moderate

KEY SITES: Felton Prairie area, Rothsay Wildlife Management Area. Polk Co. wildlife management areas near Crookston

Sharp-tailed Grouse

COMMENTS: Numbers continue to decline, but still uncommon permanent resident of northwest and north-central portions. Once common statewide, now associated with mixed forest openings and bog lands.

CHANCES: Moderate

KEY SITES: Aitkin Co. Rd. 18, Sax-Zim Bog, Gun Lake Rd., Twin Lakes Wildlife Management Area

Wild Turkey ✓

COMMENTS: Range expanding due to releases of wild, trapped birds. Common permanent resident of southeast, uncommon permanent resident recently in Minnesota River valley. Easiest to locate during spring breeding season (April/May) when males are most vocal (respond readily to owl call).

CHANCES: Poor

KEY SITES: Whitewater Wildlife Management Area and Houston and Fillmore counties

Yellow Rail ✓

COMMENTS: Local and uncommon summer resident, formerly in north-central, but may occur across north today. Prefers shallow marshes with short emergent vegetation. Best discovered by call in early summer.

CHANCES: Moderate

KEY SITES: Agassiz National Wildlife Refuge, McGregor Marsh, Sax-Zim Bog

Virginia Rail

COMMENTS: Summer resident in marshlands statewide, except northeast. Most common in southern one-half. Uncommon migrant in spring and fall. Best viewed dawn or dusk. May respond to a loud hand clap or call recording.

CHANCES: Moderate

KEY SITES: Wood Lake Nature Center, Agassiz National Wildlife Refuge

■ = Migrating   ☐ = Breeding   ■ = Migrating and Breeding   ◐ = Breeding (localized)   ▤ = Winter

Sandhill Crane

COMMENTS: Local summer resident in northwest, less common but present in east-central portions. Large numbers stage in migration in northwest. Uncommon to rare elsewhere in the state. Best seen in October.

CHANCES: Moderate

KEY SITES: Rothsay Wildlife Management Area and Agassiz National Wildlife Refuge, Twin Lakes Wildlife Management Area, Carlos Avery

Upland Sandpiper ✝

COMMENTS: Summer resident throughout most of the state, but populations tend to be local. Often associated with hayfields. Most common in western portions. Uncommon migrant, spring and fall, primarily west.

CHANCES: Moderate

KEY SITES: Felton Prairie, hayfields of Sax-Zim Bog area, Pembina Trail Preserve

Marbled Godwit ✓

COMMENTS: Summer resident, uncommon in western and northwestern portions. Spring migrant in western regions, but uncommon to rare in fall. Most individuals have begun southward migration by August.

CHANCES: Poor

KEY SITES: Pembina Trail Preserve, Rothsay Wildlife Management Area, Agassiz National Wildlife Refuge.

American Woodcock

COMMENTS: Summer resident, common especially in areas of mixed deciduous forest and lowlands. Best seen in spring during dusk courtship flights, and in fall at dusk flying over roadways that separate wooded lowlands.

CHANCES: Moderate

KEY SITES: Sax-Zim Bog, McGregor Marsh, Rice Lake National Wildlife Refuge, Itasca State Park

Wilson's Phalarope ✓

COMMENTS: Summer resident, uncommon in local wetlands. Once more widespread, now reduced primarily to northwestern portions. Found in central and western portions during spring and fall migrations. Numbers declining.

CHANCES: Poor

KEY SITES: Twin Lakes Wildlife Management Area, Agassiz National Wildlife Refuge, Felton Prairie

---

■ = Migrating ▢ = Breeding ■ = Migrating and Breeding ◯ = Breeding (localized) ▦ = Winter

Franklin's Gull

COMMENTS: Summer resident, generally nesting in colonies which fluctuate in size from year to year. Now primarily reduced to northwest. Common in migration in western and central portions.

CHANCES: Excellent

KEY SITES: Agassiz National Wildlife Refuge, Heron Lake

Forster's Tern

COMMENTS: Summer resident, common in west and south-central. Common spring migrant in southeast, central, and west. Uncommon fall migrant in same areas.

CHANCES: Excellent

KEY SITES: Agassiz National Wildlife Refuge, Heron Lake, Minnesota Lake, Swan Lake

Black Tern

COMMENTS: Summer resident, common but local in lakes and marshes. Declining as a nesting species along Mississippi River valley. Common migrant in flocks, especially in fall.

CHANCES: Excellent

KEY SITES: Lake of the Woods, Leech Lake, Rice Lake National Wildlife Refuge, Sherburne National Wildlife Refuge, Twin Cities metro marshes

Black-billed Cuckoo

COMMENTS: Summer resident statewide. Uncommon most years, but may be common in others. Best numbers north. Populations seem to follow invasions of tent caterpillars. Best located by its call. Spring and fall migrant, but uncommon and normally seen as single birds.

CHANCES: Moderate

KEY SITES: Minnesota Valley NWR, Beaver Creek Valley State Park

Yellow-billed Cuckoo

COMMENTS: Summer resident, uncommon in most areas but may be common in some portions of south some years. Prefers thicker forest than Black-billed. Uncommon spring and fall migrant, mostly south.

CHANCES: Poor

KEY SITES: Beaver Creek Valley State Park, Whitewater State Park

---

■ = Migrating   ▢ = Breeding   ■ = Migrating and Breeding   ◯ = Breeding (localized)   ▦ = Winter

Eastern Screech-Owl

COMMENTS: Permanent resident, mostly south half, but may be encountered northwest. Best located by call—normally much closer than it sounds. Responds to recordings.

CHANCES: Moderate

KEY SITES: Twin Cities park reserves

Snowy Owl ┬

COMMENTS: Winter visitant, rare to locally common north half, with infrequent invasions south half. Dependable in winter in Duluth Harbor area. Uncommon in large, open bog areas of north most winters.

CHANCES: Moderate

KEY SITES: Duluth Harbor, Waskish bogs

Northern Hawk Owl √

COMMENTS: Local and rare summer resident, with a few breeding records in the north. Winter visitant in open habitat of north, usually uncommon, but invasions infrequently occur.

CHANCES: Poor

KEY SITES: Winter: Big Bog near Waskish, Sax-Zim Bog, North Shore

Barred Owl

COMMENTS: Permanent resident, common in woodlands, especially mature hardwoods. Easily heard, especially early spring through summer. May be somewhat migratory, with invasions sometimes occurring in north.

CHANCES: Excellent

KEY SITES: Minnesota Valley National Wildlife Refuge, Twin Cities Park Reserves

Great Gray Owl √

COMMENTS: Permanent resident, locally common in northeast and north-central. Winter invasions may occur and may be seen in central and east-central portions. Best spotted when trees are bare of leaves —low perches along roadsides.

CHANCES: Moderate

KEY SITES: Aitkin Co. Rd. 18, Big Bog near Waskish, Sax-Zim Bog, Highway 310 north of Roseau

▇ = Migrating ☐ = Breeding ■ = Migrating and Breeding ◯ = Breeding (localized) ▥ = Winter

Long-eared Owl ✓

COMMENTS: Rare migrant and summer resident. Little known about this secretive owl. Widespread nesting in mixed woodlands. Regular migration in spring and fall. Strictly nocturnal but may be found perched close to tree trunk in roosting (evergreen) trees on wildlife management areas. Listen for calls in March and April. Check Birder's Hotline.

CHANCES: Poor

KEY SITES: Central Lake County, conifer shelterbelts southwest Jan.—early to mid-April

Short-eared Owl

COMMENTS: Rare migrant and summer resident, declining recently. Best represented in north-central and northwest. Prefers open country, particularly grasslands and marshes. Active in evenings before dark. Best seen in grasslands, (wildlife management and set-aside lands) of west during April.

CHANCES: Poor

KEY SITES: Agassiz National Wildlife Refuge, Rothsay Wildlife Management Area, Tympanuchus Wildlife Management Area

Boreal Owl ✓

COMMENTS: A regular, though rare winter visitor beginning in late December and extremely rare and elusive summer resident in the extreme north. Most winter visitors have exited northward by March. Calls on spring territory in April and May.

CHANCES: Poor

KEY SITES: Gunflint Trail, Lake County Forest Road 104, Hwy 1-Co. 2 Junction (check Duluth birder's hotline for spring locales)

Northern Saw-whet Owl ✓

COMMENTS: Summer resident throughout wooded portions, but rare south. Rare migrant, spring and fall statewide. Rare and elusive in winter, but present locally. Responds well to calls.

CHANCES: Poor

KEY SITES: Spring: Roadsides throughout Boreal Region. October: Hawk Ridge, Itasca State Park

Whip-poor-will

COMMENTS: Very local. Summer resident of wooded portions of state, except North Shore inland. Well represented in northern Twin Cities suburbs and northward, and along the Mississippi River. Elusive but widespread in migration, spring and fall.

CHANCES: Poor

KEY SITES: Whitewater State Park, Bunker Hills Regional Park, Manomin Park in Fridley

■ = Migrating   ▢ = Breeding   ■ = Migrating and Breeding   ◯ = Breeding (localized)   ▦ = Winter

Red-headed Woodpecker

COMMENTS: Summer resident, common locally statewide except northeast. Most common in southeast and east-central. Common migrant spring and fall, especially south.

CHANCES: Moderate

KEY SITES: Nerstrand State Park, Reno Unit - Houston County, Carver Park Reserve, Cedar Creek Natural History Area, Sherburne National Wildlife Refuge

Red-bellied Woodpecker

COMMENTS: Permanent resident, common in south half, especially southeast portion. Range has expanded into central, east-central, and northwest portions in recent years.

CHANCES: Excellent

KEY SITES: Carver Park Reserve, Flandrau State Park, Frontenac State Park, Whitewater Wildlife Management Area

Yellow-bellied Sapsucker

COMMENTS: Summer resident statewide except extreme southwest. Common, especially north of Minnesota River. Common spring and fall migrant statewide.

CHANCES: Excellent

KEY SITES: Carver Park Reserve, Hyland Lake Park Reserve

Three-toed Woodpecker ✓

COMMENTS: Rare permanent resident in forests of northeast portion. Most commonly seen in winter around recent logging sites and areas of recent burns. Often associated with mature spruce trees.

CHANCES: Poor

KEY SITES: Gunflint Trail, Zippel Bay State Park, Lima Mountain Road, Spruce Road

Black-backed Woodpecker ✓

COMMENTS: Permanent resident, rare to locally uncommon in forests of northeast. Winter migrant, may be more numerous (and obvious), especially in October. Rare in winter south of boreal portion.

CHANCES: Poor

KEY SITES: Gunflint Trail, Spruce Road—northwestern Lake County, pine groves at Hawk Ridge Sept.-Oct.

■ = Migrating   ☐ = Breeding   ■ = Migrating and Breeding   ◯ = Breeding (localized)   ▦ = Winter

Pileated Woodpecker

COMMENTS: Permanent resident, common to uncommon locally in wooded portions, particularly south-central in Big Woods and along wooded river valleys. Loud "laughing" cry often reveals presence.

CHANCES: Moderate

KEY SITES: Carver Park Reserve, Flandrau State Park, Wolsfeld Woods, Rice Lake National Wildlife Refuge, Tettegouche State Park

Olive-sided Flycatcher ┼

COMMENTS: Summer resident, uncommon in coniferous forests of northeast and north-central portions. Uncommon migrant, spring and fall statewide.

CHANCES: Moderate

KEY SITES: Aitkin Co. Rd. 18, Itasca State Park, Big Bog, Chippewa National Forest, Echo Trail

Yellow-bellied Flycatcher

COMMENTS: Summer resident, uncommon in coniferous forests of northeast and north-central portions. Common migrant statewide, common in small groups during peaks in May and September.

CHANCES: Moderate

KEY SITES: Sax-Zim Bog, Hwy. 310 north of Roseau, spruce bogs along Gunflint Trail, Aitkin Co. Rd. 18

Acadian Flycatcher

COMMENTS: Summer resident, rare and local southeast north to Hennepin County. Regular only at Beaver Creek Valley State Park. Rare migrant, quiet except on breeding sites in spring.

CHANCES: Poor

KEY SITES: Beaver Creek Valley State Park, Murphy-Hanrehan Park Reserve

Alder Flycatcher

COMMENTS: Summer resident, common in forest edge shrubs of swamp areas north half of state. Migrant spring and fall, but hard to track. Gone from breeding areas by late August.

CHANCES: Excellent

KEY SITES: Carlos Avery Wildlife Management Area, McGregor Marsh, Sax-Zim Bog

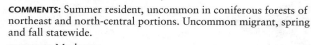

= Migrating   = Breeding   = Migrating and Breeding   ◯ = Breeding (localized)   ▦ = Winter

Willow Flycatcher

COMMENTS: Summer resident, uncommon in south, extreme west and northwest prairies in brushy (willow) wetlands. Most easily found southeast during spring and early summer. Migrant, uncommon spring and fall south half.

CHANCES: Moderate

KEY SITES: Whitewater Wildlife Management Area, Black Dog Lake, La Crescent Brush Dump, Heron Lake, Swan Lake

Least Flycatcher

COMMENTS: Summer resident, common in wooded areas statewide. Uncommon southwest portion. Common spring and fall migrant, especially May and September.

CHANCES: Excellent

KEY SITES: Carver Park Reserve, Carlos Avery, William O'Brien State Park, Frontenac State Park, Beaver Creek Valley State Park

Eastern Phoebe

COMMENTS: Summer resident, common in most of state, but less abundant in much of southwest. Common spring and fall migrant, arrives mid-March, earlier than other flycatchers and departs as late as November in south. Last flycatcher to leave.

CHANCES: Excellent

KEY SITES: Hyland Lake Park Reserve, Manomin Park

Western Kingbird

COMMENTS: Summer resident, common in extreme west in towns and around farmsteads with groves. Has disappeared from former breeding range in central and southwest portions. Uncommon migrant, spring and fall in western regions.

CHANCES: Poor

KEY SITES: Agassiz National Wildlife Refuge, Felton Prairie

Gray Jay

COMMENTS: Permanent resident, uncommon in northeast and north-central portions, usually associated with conifer or mixed conifer. Occasionally wanders south in winter as far as northern Twin Cities.

CHANCES: Moderate

KEY SITES: Gunflint Trail, Zippel Bay State Park, Sax-Zim Bog

■ = Migrating ▢ = Breeding ■ = Migrating and Breeding ◯ = Breeding (localized) ▦ = Winter

Common Raven

COMMENTS: Permanent resident, common northeast and north-central portions. Common fall migrant along North Shore, Lake Superior. Easily seen at rural garbage dumps, particularly in winter.

CHANCES: Excellent

KEY SITES: Itasca State Park, Lake County Road 2, Agassiz National Wildlife Refuge, Rice Lake National Wildlife Refuge

Boreal Chickadee

COMMENTS: Permanent Resident, uncommon in northern sections of northeast and north-central. Range has declined slightly northward. Casual migration southward in fall along North Shore. Infrequently winters south to Twin Cities.

CHANCES: Moderate

KEY SITES: Gunflint Trail, Environmental Learning Center, Sax-Zim Bog

Tufted Titmouse

COMMENTS: Permanent resident, rare and local in southeast and extremely reduced in range and numbers in recent years. Most easily found at winter feeders in extreme southeast.

CHANCES: Poor

KEY SITES: Beaver Creek Valley State Park, Frontenac State Park

Red-breasted Nuthatch

COMMENTS: Permanent resident, common in northeast and east-central portions. Uncommon migrant statewide, common in breeding range and least common in western portions. Migrates into northeast and north-central portions in winter, but abundance varies year to year.

CHANCES: Excellent

KEY SITES: Sax-Zim Bog, Aitkin Co. Rd. 18, North Shore State Parks

Brown Creeper

COMMENTS: Summer resident, uncommon in contiguous heavily wooded areas. Fall migrant statewide, but least common northwest. Rare winter visitor in southern portions.

CHANCES: Moderate

KEY SITES: Lowry Nature Center, Wood Lake Nature Center, North Shore State Parks

■ = Migrating   ▢ = Breeding   ■ = Migrating and Breeding   ◐ = Breeding (localized)   ▦ = Winter

Winter Wren

COMMENTS: Summer resident, common in conifer forests of northeast and north-central portions. Migrates spring and fall in eastern and central regions, less numerous west. Accidental winter visitor in southeast.

CHANCES: Excellent

KEY SITES: Aitkin Co. Rd. 18, Gunflint Trail, North Shore State Parks

Sedge Wren +

COMMENTS: Summer resident statewide, common in grassy marshes and short-grass fields, especially central and west, least common northeast. Migrates spring and fall but continues to be found in breeding habitat, same locales.

CHANCES: Excellent

KEY SITES: Sax-Zim Bog, wet pastures—Blue Mounds State Park, McGregor Marsh

Marsh Wren +

COMMENTS: A common resident wherever cattail marshes exist, except absent northeast. Most common west-central. Migrates spring and fall, but secretive and nocturnal in movement.

CHANCES: Excellent

KEY SITES: Swan Lake, Heron Lake, Agassiz National Wildlife Refuge

Golden-crowned Kinglet

COMMENTS: Summer resident, common in conifer forests, northeast and north-central portions. Migrant spring and fall throughout, common in April and September. Uncommon in winter in southeast.

CHANCES: Excellent

KEY SITES: Sawbill Trail, Gunflint Trail

Ruby-crowned Kinglet

COMMENTS: Summer resident, uncommon in northeast, rare north-central. Common statewide in migration, often seen in small, loose flocks.

CHANCES: Moderate

KEY SITES: Sax-Zim Bog, Gunflint Trail

= Migrating   = Breeding   = Migrating and Breeding   ○ = Breeding (localized)   = Winter

Blue-gray Gnatcatcher

COMMENTS: Summer resident, common in mature woodlands east central, southeast and along Minnesota River valley. Expanding northward. Uncommon spring and fall migrant, most often seen in breeding habitat.

CHANCES: Moderate

KEY SITES: Eloise Butler Wildflower Gardens, Carver Park Reserve, Whitewater State Park

Veery

COMMENTS: Summer resident, common in woodlands and forests, primarily in northern half, but represented southeast, easily heard on quiet evenings. Uncommon spring and fall migrant statewide, but rare in west-central and southwest.

CHANCES: Excellent

KEY SITES: Itasca State Park, William O'Brien State Park

Swainson's Thrush

COMMENTS: Summer resident, common in conifer forests northeast and north-central portions. Common spring and fall migrant statewide, often locally abundant but seen singly.

CHANCES: Moderate

KEY SITES: Echo Trail, Itasca State Park

Wood Thrush

COMMENTS: Summer resident, uncommon in deciduous woodlands, most likely to be seen in southeast and east-central portions. Expanding westward along Minnesota River valley. Seldom seen in migration. Rare statewide by early fall.

CHANCES: Moderate

KEY SITES: Beaver Creek Valley State Park, Whitewater State Park, deciduous woods in Cook Co.

Bohemian Waxwing ✓

COMMENTS: Fall and winter visitant, common but local north and east-central portions. Often occurs in flocks, occasionally numbering hundreds of birds. Most dependable along North Shore and in Duluth. Attracted to urban mountain ash trees.

CHANCES: Excellent

KEY SITES: November through February City of Duluth, City of Two Harbors, City of Grand Marais

■ = Migrating   ▢ = Breeding   ■ = Migrating and Breeding   ◔ = Breeding (localized)   ▦ = Winter

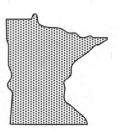

Northern Shrike √

COMMENTS: Winter visitant statewide, but more often seen north half. Uncommon in open areas with mixed brush. Winter shrike almost always a Northern Shrike.

CHANCES: Poor

KEY SITES: (winter) Sax-Zim Bog, Carlos Avery Wildlife Management Area, wildlife management areas throughout the state

Loggerhead Shrike ┼

COMMENTS: Summer resident, rare in most of range. Rare migrant, spring and fall. Almost never lingers into winter. Numbers continue to decline in the state.

CHANCES: Poor

KEY SITES: Felton Prairie, Dakota County—Vermillion Township

Bell's Vireo ┼

COMMENTS: Summer resident, rare locally in raised wet areas with woody shrubs along the Mississippi River valley as far north as Twin Cities. Rare migrant, spring and fall in southeast portion of state.

CHANCES: Poor

KEY SITES: Black Dog Prairie, McCarthy Lake Wildlife Management Area, Mud Lake Hike and Bike Trail

Solitary Vireo

COMMENTS: Summer resident, common in northeast and north-central portions. Spring and fall migrant statewide, common during peak periods of early May and late August.

CHANCES: Excellent

KEY SITES: Judge Magney State Park, Spruce Road, Itasca State Park, Echo Trail

Yellow-throated Vireo

COMMENTS: Summer resident, common in deciduous woodlands. Uncommon spring and fall migrant in most of the state. Absent in northeast and less numerous in southwest and west-central portions.

CHANCES: Excellent

KEY SITES: Carver Park Reserve, Carlos Avery, Maplewood State Park, Whitewater State Park

---

■ = Migrating   ■ = Breeding   ■ = Migrating and Breeding   ◉ = Breeding (localized)   ▦ = Winter

Philadelphia Vireo

COMMENTS: Summer resident, uncommon and local in the extreme northeast. Song may be confused with red-eyed vireo. Uncommon to common locally during spring and fall migration.

CHANCES: Poor

KEY SITES: Kramer Site, Gunflint Trail

Blue-winged Warbler

COMMENTS: Summer resident, uncommon Twin Cities and southeast, expanding northwestward recently. Rare spring and fall migrant from Twin Cities southeast.

CHANCES: Moderate

KEY SITES: O.L. Kipp State Park, Murphy-Hanrehan Park Reserve, Beaver Creek Valley State Park

Golden-winged Warbler

COMMENTS: Summer resident, uncommon north-central portion. Uncommon spring and fall migrant eastern half, though seldom identified in fall. Best located by song on breeding territory.

CHANCES: Moderate

KEY SITES: Outer marshes—Sax-Zim Bog, Agassiz National Wildlife Refuge, Cedar Creek Natural History Area

Tennessee Warbler

COMMENTS: Summer resident, extremely rare in the extreme north and north-central. Populations vary from year to year. Common migrant statewide.

CHANCES: Poor

KEY SITES: Gunflint Trail

Nashville Warbler

COMMENTS: Summer resident, common and widespread northeast and north-central as far south as northern metro counties. Common migrant statewide in spring and fall. Often confused with Connecticut Warbler.

CHANCES: Excellent

KEY SITES: Gunflint Trail, Sawbill Trail, Sax-Zim Bog

■ = Migrating ▫ = Breeding ■ = Migrating and Breeding ◉ = Breeding (localized) ▦ = Winter

Northern Parula

COMMENTS: Summer resident, common but scattered in northeast and north-central portions. Uncommon migrant east half, rare west half. Smallest of the state's regular warblers.

CHANCES: Excellent

KEY SITES: Gunflint Trail, Itasca State Park

Chesnut-sided Warbler

COMMENTS: Summer resident, common in woody brush north half, rare and local west-central and extreme northwest. Common spring and fall migrant in east half. Song resembles yellow warbler.

CHANCES: Excellent

KEY SITES: Gunflint Trail, Sax-Zim Bog, Sawbill Trail

Magnolia Warbler

COMMENTS: Summer resident, common in conifer forests of northeast and north-central portions. Uncommon to common spring and fall migrant statewide, but most numerous eastern half.

CHANCES: Excellent

KEY SITES: Gunflint Trail, Sax-Zim Bog, Sawbill Trail

Cape May Warbler

COMMENTS: Summer resident, uncommon in conifer forests of northeast and north-central. Typically nests in balsam fir and spruce, and primarily seen in association with these trees. Spring and fall migrant, uncommon east half, rare west half.

CHANCES: Moderate

KEY SITES: Gunflint Trail

Black-throated Blue Warbler

COMMENTS: Summer resident, rare in extreme northeast corner. Most often associated with stands of deciduous hardwoods within conifer forest. Rare spring migrant mostly seen along North Shore.

CHANCES: Poor

KEY SITES: Remote areas of Tettegouche State Park, Oberg Mountain

■ = Migrating   ▢ = Breeding   ■ = Migrating and Breeding   ◐ = Breeding (localized)   ▦ = Winter

Yellow-rumped Warbler

COMMENTS: Summer resident, common in northeast and north-central. Spring and fall migrant statewide. The most abundant migrant among wood warblers, often in large, loose flocks. Stragglers may be seen in winter months.

CHANCES: Excellent

KEY SITES: Gunflint Trail, Sax-Zim Bog, Sawbill Trail

Black-throated Green Warbler

COMMENTS: Summer resident, common in northeast and north-central in mixed forests. Uncommon migrant, spring and fall, encountered singly northeast and east-central portions and less common southeast.

CHANCES: Excellent

KEY SITES: Gunflint Trail, Sax-Zim Bog, Sawbill Trail

Blackburnian Warbler

COMMENTS: Summer resident, common northeast and north-central portion. Often associated with spruce in mixed forests. Regular spring and fall migrant statewide.

CHANCES: Excellent

KEY SITES: Gunflint Trail, Sax-Zim Bog

Pine Warbler

COMMENTS: Summer resident, uncommon north-central and east-central portions, rare and local northeast. Prefers mature white pine stands, especially around cemeteries in the north portion of the state. Rare in spring migration and difficult to identify in fall.

CHANCES: Moderate

KEY SITES: Itasca State Park, Beltrami Island State Forest

Palm Warbler

COMMENTS: Summer resident, uncommon and local in north-central portions in bogs. Common spring and fall migrant in eastern half, best seen along North Shore in fall. May be mistaken for yellow-rumped.

CHANCES: Poor

KEY SITES: Sax-Zim Bog

■ = Migrating   ▨ = Breeding   ■ = Migrating and Breeding   ○ = Breeding (localized)   ▦ = Winter

Bay-breasted Warbler

COMMENTS: Summer resident, uncommon in conifer forests of northern, northeast, and north-central. Rare spring and fall migrant, east half, better seen in fall than spring.

CHANCES: Moderate

KEY SITES: Gunflint Trail, Spruce Road

Cerulean Warbler

COMMENTS: Summer resident, uncommon in tall deciduous trees of river bottoms and hollows southeast and southern east-central and recently along Minnesota River Valley. Rare in same region in spring and fall migration.

CHANCES: Poor

KEY SITES: Beaver Creek Valley State Park, Murphy-Hanrehan Park Reserve

Black-and-white Warbler

COMMENTS: Summer resident, common in deciduous forest stands in northeast, north-central, and east-central portions. Common spring and fall migrant statewide.

CHANCES: Excellent

KEY SITES: Gunflint Trail, Sax-Zim Bog, Sawbill Trail

American Redstart

COMMENTS: Summer resident, common, but less abundant west-central and absent southwest. Common migrant spring and fall statewide, but less common in southwest.

CHANCES: Excellent

KEY SITES: Eloise Butler Wildflower Gardens, Duluth City Parks, Gunflint Trail, Flandrau State Park, Maplewood State Park

Prothonotary Warbler

COMMENTS: Summer resident, uncommon along Minnesota River valley in Twin Cities and along the Mississippi River in the southeast. Cavity nester, best found in dead standing timber along river bottoms. Rare in migration in spring.

CHANCES: Poor

KEY SITES: Millstone Landing—Houston County, La Crescent Brush Dump

---

■ = Migrating   □ = Breeding   ■ = Migrating and Breeding   ○ = Breeding (localized)   ▦ = Winter

Northern Waterthrush

COMMENTS: Summer resident, uncommon, whose breeding range has recently receded to northern, north-central, and northeast. Check small, brushy, running creeks. Noted breeding at Cedar Creek Natural History Area, east central. Uncommon migrant locally, spring and fall statewide.

CHANCES: Poor

KEY SITES: Gunflint Trail

Louisiana Waterthrush

COMMENTS: Summer resident along heavily wooded creeks, uncommon and local in southeast and rare in Minnesota River valley. Spring and fall migrant, rarely seen in spring and seldom seen in fall.

CHANCES: Poor

KEY SITES: Beaver Creek Valley State Park, Lawrence Creek

Connecticut Warbler +

COMMENTS: Summer resident, uncommon and local in north-central and northeast portions. Rare migrant, spring and fall in eastern half.

CHANCES: Excellent

KEY SITES: Sax-Zim Bog, Hwy. 310 north of Roseau, Hayes Lake State Park

Mourning Warbler +

COMMENTS: Summer resident, common in forested northern half reaching northern fringes of metro counties. Uncommon to common in spring and fall migration statewide.

CHANCES: Excellent

KEY SITES: Sax-Zim Bog, Gunflint Trail, Hwy. 310 north of Roseau, Echo Trail

Canada Warbler

COMMENTS: Summer resident, uncommon in dense mixed forests north-central and somewhat more common in northeast portion. Uncommon migrant, spring and fall statewide, but less common west.

CHANCES: Moderate

KEY SITES: Gunflint Trail

■ = Migrating   □ = Breeding   ■ = Migrating and Breeding   ◉ = Breeding (localized)   ▦ = Winter

Scarlet Tanager

COMMENTS: Summer resident, common in forested portion of state, especially east. Nests along Minnesota Valley to western border. Uncommon migrant east half, rare west half.

CHANCES: Excellent

KEY SITES: Carver Park Reserve, Carlos Avery, Whitewater State Park, Itasca State Park.

Blue Grosbeak

COMMENTS: Summer resident, uncommon in extreme southwest corner, best seen during three months of summer. Rare migrant, spring and fall in southwest portion. May be extending its range northward.

CHANCES: Poor

KEY SITES: Blue Mounds State Park

Indigo Bunting

COMMENTS: Summer resident statewide, most common in southeast, south-central, and east, less common north. Common migrant, spring and fall in east half, excluding north-central and northeast portion.

CHANCES: Excellent

KEY SITES: Carver Park Reserve, Carlos Avery, Whitewater State Park, Maplewood State Park

Dickcissel +

COMMENTS: Summer resident, common south half in roadsides and alfalfa fields. Common to uncommon migrant spring and fall south half of state. Numbers fluctuate from year to year. Absent many years in northern portions of its range.

CHANCES: Excellent

KEY SITES: Open alfalfa fields of southern counties

Eastern Towhee

COMMENTS: Summer resident, common locally throughout northern deciduous region. Uncommon migrant, spring and fall within breeding range, rare elsewhere. Prefers burned-over or cut-over lands.

CHANCES: Poor

KEY SITES: Beaver Valley Creek State Park, Whitewater State Park, Tamarac National Wildlife Refuge

■ = Migrating   ▢ = Breeding   ■ = Migrating and Breeding   ○ = Breeding (localized)   ▦ = Winter

Lark Sparrow ✓

COMMENTS: Summer resident, uncommon and local in savannah-type grasslands in widely separated locales. Rare migrant in spring in same areas. Extremely rare after August.

CHANCES: Moderate

KEY SITES: Cedar Creek Natural History Area, McCarthy Lake Wildlife Management Area, Sherburne National Wildlife Refuge

Grasshopper Sparrow

COMMENTS: Summer resident, common statewide in hay fields and pastures but rare or absent north-central and northeast. Uncommon migrant, spring and fall in breeding areas. Numbers declining.

CHANCES: Moderate

KEY SITES: Felton Prairie, Rothsay Wildlife Management Area, McCarthy Lake Wildlife Management Area

Le Conte's Sparrow

COMMENTS: Summer resident, uncommon on marsh edges and in brushy wet meadows north half but absent extreme northeast. Locally common migrant west half, rare east half.

CHANCES: Poor

KEY SITES: Agassiz National Wildlife Refuge, Felton Prairie, Rice Lake National Wildlife Refuge

Nelson's Sharp-tailed Sparrow ✓

COMMENTS: Summer resident, local and uncommon in north-central and northwest portions. Little is known of its migration patterns in the state.

CHANCES: Poor

KEY SITES: Agassiz National Wildlife Refuge, McGregor Marsh, Federal Dam Road (Leech Lake)

Lincoln's Sparrow

COMMENTS: Summer resident, locally common in the northeast and extreme north-central in bog lands. Uncommon to locally common migrant spring and fall statewide, primarily in east half.

CHANCES: Poor

KEY SITES: Sax-Zim Bog, Beltrami Island State Forest

■ = Migrating   ▢ = Breeding   ■ = Migrating and Breeding   ◐ = Breeding (localized)   ▦ = Winter

White-Throated Sparrow

COMMENTS: Summer resident, common in northeast and north central portions in forest underbrush. Common migrant spring and fall statewide, especially east half, often in large flocks. May linger in winter south-central and southeast.

CHANCES: Excellent

KEY SITES: Sawbill Trail, Itasca State Park

Dark-eyed Junco

COMMENTS: Summer resident, common in northeast and north-central in conifer forests. Common migrant spring and fall statewide, often in large flocks. Flocks with American Tree Sparrows.

CHANCES: Excellent

KEY SITES: Sax-Zim Bog, Sawbill Trail, Gunflint Trail

Bobolink

COMMENTS: Summer resident, common in south half and northwest where suitable grassland habitat is available. Common migrant spring and fall, west and south portions, often in large flocks. Seldom seen after mid-September.

CHANCES: Excellent

KEY SITES: Felton Prairie, Agassiz National Wildlife Refuge, O. L. Kipp State Park, Tympanuchus Wildlife Management Area

Chestnut-collared Longspur

COMMENTS: Summer resident, rare and local in prairie tracts in Clay County only. Rare migrant spring and fall in western portions.

CHANCES: Poor

KEY SITES: Felton Prairie

Western Meadowlark

COMMENTS: Summer resident, common statewide in grass fields, except uncommon north-central and rare northeast. Common migrant, spring and fall statewide except north-central and northeast.

CHANCES: Excellent

KEY SITES: Carver Park Reserve, Felton Prairie

■ = Migrating   ▢ = Breeding   ■ = Migrating and Breeding   ○ = Breeding (localized)   ▦ = Winter

Yellow-headed Blackbird

COMMENTS: Summer resident, common statewide in cattail marshes, except northeast. Common migrant statewide spring and fall, except north-central and northeast.

CHANCES: Excellent

KEY SITES: Carlos Avery, Big Stone National Wildlife Refuge, Agassiz National Wildlife Refuge, Swan Lake, Heron Lake

Orchard Oriole

COMMENTS: Summer resident, uncommon in wood edges and groves in southern part of state. Most easily seen during early summer while singing on nesting territory.

CHANCES: Moderate

KEY SITES: Beaver Valley Creek State Park, Blue Mounds State Park, Big Stone National Wildlife Refuge

Pine Grosbeak √

COMMENTS: Fall migrant, uncommon to occasionally common in northeast and north-central portions. Winter visitant, may occur statewide during invasion years. Absent by late winter or early spring. Occurs in loose flocks in conifers or mixed conifer forests. May frequent bird feeders.

CHANCES: Moderate

KEY SITES: (Late fall, winter) North Shore State Parks, City of Duluth

Purple Finch ✝

COMMENTS: Summer resident, common in open woods in northeast, north-central, and east-central portions. Common migrant, spring and fall eastern two-thirds in small groups. Uncommon to locally common in winter east-central and southeast.

CHANCES: Excellent

KEY SITES: Sawbill Trail, Gunflint Trail. Common at winter feeders in Duluth area and Twin Cities in some years.

White-winged Crossbill

COMMENTS: Erratic fall and winter migrant; locally common in northeast and north-central in years of major invasions. Check birder's hotline.

CHANCES: Poor

KEY SITES: County Road 2—Lake County in winter

■ = Migrating   ▫ = Breeding   ■ = Migrating and Breeding   ◉ = Breeding (localized)   ▦ = Winter

Red Crossbill +

COMMENTS: Erratic fall and winter migrant, locally common in northeast and north-central portions in years of major invasions. A rare summer visitor in northeast and north-central areas. Check Birder's' Hotline

CHANCES: Poor

KEY SITES: County Road 2—Lake County, in winter

Evening Grosbeak +

COMMENTS: Summer resident, uncommon in northeast and north-central portions. Common winter visitant north half, especially in areas with stands of conifers and feeders. Erratic winter visitor in other portions of state.

CHANCES: Moderate

KEY SITES: Northwoods Audubon Center (winter), summer along Sawbill Trail and Gunflint Trail, city of Grand Marais

■ = Migrating   ☐ = Breeding   ■ = Migrating and Breeding   ◉ = Breeding (localized)   ▦ = Winter

Minnesota's endangered, threatened, and special concern birds

The latest listing of birds endangered, threatened, and of special concern in Minnesota includes 28 species. Such classifications aim to alert us to the need for protection not only of the birds themselves, but of the habitats that allow them to survive and breed successfully. It is worth noting that most of these birds are directly dependent on two sensitive and often diminished habitat types in the state: wetlands and prairie grassland. These habitats should be protected wherever possible and care should be taken to avoid disturbing these birds where they are known to breed.

A number of positive changes have recently been made to these lists. Among them, the Trumpeter Swan, now present through captive breeding programs and resultant free-flying offspring, has been removed from the list of extirpated birds. The Peregrine Falcon, recovering from disastrous declines of the past, has been removed from the state's endangered list. Increasing numbers of breeding Bald Eagles have resulted in this bird being removed from the state's threatened list. Other birds that have seen improved status are the American Bittern, Osprey, Sandhill Crane, and Upland Sandpiper, all removed from the state's special concern list.

Unfortunately, a number of Minnesota birds have faced declines in recent years, and their status has become more critical than ever before. King Rail and Henslow's Sparrow have been added to the state's endangered list. Horned Grebe, Wilson's Phalarope, and Common Tern have been reclassified from special concern to threatened. And a number of formerly unclassified species have been added to the list of special concern, including Franklin's Gull, Acadian Flycatcher, Cerulean Warbler, and Hooded Warbler. Following are the state listings for these sensitive species.

Endangered

King Rail
Piping Plover
Burrowing Owl
Sprague's Pipit
Baird's Sparrow
Henslow's Sparrow
Chestnut-collared Longspur

Threatened

Horned Grebe
Trumpeter Swan
Peregrine Falcon
Wilson's Phalarope
Common Tern
Loggerhead Shrike

Special concern

American White Pelican
Bald Eagle
Red-shouldered Hawk
Greater Prairie-Chicken
Yellow Rail
Common Moorhen
Marbled Godwit
Franklin's Gull
Forster's Tern
Short-eared Owl
Acadian Flycatcher
Louisiana Waterthrush
Cerulean Warbler
Hooded Warbler
Nelson's Sharp-tailed Sparrow

Suggested readings

Minnesota Underfoot: A Field Guide to the state's outstanding geologic features. Constance Jefferson Sansome; Voyageur Press, 1983.

Minnesota Atlas and Gazetteer. DeLorne Mapping, 1990.

Minnesota's Endangered Flora and Fauna. Barbara Coffin and Lee Pfannmuller, Editors; University of Minnesota Press, 1988.

Minnesota Geographic Names: Their Origin and Historic Significance; Warren Upham, Minnesota Historical Society, 1969.

The Birder's Handbook: A Field Guide to the Natural History of North American Birds. Paul R. Ehrlich, David S. Dobkin, and Darryl Wheye. Simon & Schuster/Fireside, 1988.

Birds in Minnesota: A field guide to the distribution of 400 species of birds in Minnesota. Robert B. Janssen; University of Minnesota Press, 1987.

A Birder's Guide To Minnesota. Kim R. Eckert; Williams Publications, 1994.

Families of Birds. Oliver L. Austin, Jr.; Western Publishing Company, 1971.

A World of Watchers. Joseph Kastner; Alfred A. Knopf, Inc., 1986.

Travels and Traditions of Waterfowl. H. Albert Hochbaum; The University of Minnesota Press, 1955.

Western Birds. Roger Tory Peterson, Editor; Houghton Mifflin Company, 1990.

The Lives of Birds: Birds of the World and Their Behavior. Lester L. Short; Henry Holt and Company, 1993.

Life Histories of North American Birds (Series). Arthur Cleveland Bent; Dover Publications, Inc., 1963.

Ornithology in Laboratory and Field. Olin Sewall Pettingill, Jr.; Burgess Pulishing Company, 1970

The Practical Ornithologist. John Gooders; Simon & Schuster/Fireside, 1990.

Bird Migration. Donald R. Griffin; Dover Publications, Inc., 1974.

A Guide to Field Identification: Birds of North America. Chandler S. Robbins, Bertel Bruun, and Herbert S. Zim; Golden Press, 1966.

Secrets of The Nest: The Family Life of North American Birds. Joan Dunning; Houghton Mifflin Company, 1994.

Parks & Wildlands: A Guide to 170 Special Places in and Around The Twin Cities. Kai Hagen; Nodin Press, 1989.

The Life of Birds. Joel Carl Welty; Sunders College Publishing, 1982.

The Streams and Rivers of Minnesota. Thomas F. Waters; University of Minnesota Press, 1977.

Minnesota Production Guide (Annual). Kelly J. Pratt, Editor; Planet Publications.

Minnesota Weatherguide Calendar (Annual). Bruce F. Watson and James R. Gilbert; Freshwater Foundation and WCCO Weather Center.

About the author and illustrator

AUTHOR JAY MICHAEL STRANGIS possesses a unique familiarity with Minnesota's lakes, fields, and forests. Born in the Twin Cities, Jay has spent a lifetime in the Minnesota outdoors, encouraged by relatives and friends from across the state. He has combined his interest in nature with a degree in journalism and minor degree in wildlife management from the University of Minnesota to produce compelling outdoor writing for the past 15 years. Jay's career has produced hundreds of published articles and photographs and he has served as researcher, writer, and editor on a number of published books on outdoor topics. During his studies at the University of Minnesota, Jay worked in the ornithology lab at the James Ford Bell Museum of Natural History, where he also conducted tours for the public education department. He also participated in summer field work censusing birds in the Minnesota River Valley. Recently he accepted an editor's position for Petersen Publishing's Outdoor Group in Los Angeles, California.

ILLUSTRATOR VERA MING WONG combines her interests and degrees in biology (B.A. from Swarthmore College, Swarthmore, PA) and art (B.F.A. from the University of Minnesota, College of Liberal Arts) in her work as a natural science illustrator, artist, and interdisciplinary arts-and-environmental educator. A member of the Guild of Natural Sciences Illustrators, her drawings, watercolors, and cut paper collages of plants, animals, and habitats illustrate several books and magazines, including: *Minnesota's Endangered Flora and Fauna, Northwoods Wildlife, A Watcher's Guide To Habitats,* and *Orchids of Minnesota*. Her work has also been exhibited nationally and internationally.

Index

BIRDER'S GUIDES

Birding Arizona
Birding Minnesota
Birder's Guide to Montana

THE WATCHABLE WILDLIFE SERIES

Alaska Wildlife Viewing Guide
Arizona Wildlife Viewing Guide
California Wildlife Viewing Guide
Colorado Wildlife Viewing Guide
Florida Wildlife Viewing Guide
Idaho Wildlife Viewing Guide
Indiana Wildlife Viewing Guide
Iowa Wildlife Viewing Guide
Kentucky Wildlife Viewing Guide
Montana Wildlife Viewing Guide
Nevada Wildlife Viewing Guide
New Mexico Wildlife Viewing Guide
North Carolina Wildlife Viewing Guide
North Dakota Wildlife Viewing Guide
Oregon Wildlife Viewing Guide
Tennessee Wildlife Viewing Guide
Texas Wildlife Viewing Guide
Utah Wildlife Viewing Guide
Vermont Wildlife Viewing Guide

SCENIC DRIVING GUIDES

Scenic Byways
Scenic Byways II
Back Country Byways
Scenic Driving Arizona
Scenic Driving California
Scenic Driving Colorado
Scenic Driving Georgia
Scenic Driving Montana
Scenic Driving New Mexico
Oregon Scenic Drives
Scenic Driving Texas
Traveler's Guide to the Lewis & Clark Trail
Traveler's Guide to the Oregon Trail
Traveler's Guide to the Pony Express Trail

ROCKHOUND'S GUIDES

Rockhounding Arizona
Rockhound's Guide to California
Rockhound's Guide to Colorado
Rockhounding Montana
Rockhound's Guide to New Mexico
Rockhounding to Texas

■ *To order any of these books, or to request an expanded list of available titles,*
*please call **1-800-582-2665**, or write to Falcon, P.O. Box 1718, Helena, MT 59624.*

FALCON™